HOT ROD
MILESTONES

America's Coolest Coupes, Roadsters, & Racers

Ken Gross & Robert Genat

CarTech®

Edited by Travis Thompson
Layout by Josh Limbaugh

ISBN 1-884089-80-1
Item No. CT980

Printed in China

CarTech®

CarTech®, Inc.
39966 Grand Avenue
North Branch, MN 55056
Telephone: (651) 277-1200 or (800) 551-4754
Fax: (651) 277-1203
www.cartechbooks.com

Library of Congress Cataloging-in-Publication Data

Gross, Ken, 1941-
  Hot rod milestones : America's coolest coupes, roadsters, and racers / by
Ken Gross and Robert Genat ; forward by Pete Chapouris.
    p. cm.
  Includes index.
  ISBN 1-884089-80-1
  1. Hot rods--United States. I. Genat, Robert, 1945- II. Title.

  TL236.3.G76 2004
  629.228'6'0973--dc22

                          2004021952

On the Front Cover: *McGee did not want to imitate the radically raked appearance of many contemporary roadsters. He installed one of Ed Stewart's dropped and stretched front axles, reversed the front spring eyes, and put fashionable 5.00 x 16-inch ribbed Firestones on V-8/60 wheels for an additional drop. Next, he Z-ed the rear section of the frame, added a Model A crossmember, and reversed the rear spring eyes to get the car down fashionably in back. While not as low as a typical channeled '32, the McGee car sits well down, with its rear 7.00 x 16s (on wide-base Lincoln Zephyr rims) neatly filling the wheel wells.*

On the Back Cover, Top: *Compare Dick Flint's channeled, belly-panned '29 Model A roadster to its early upright 1950s contemporaries, and you'll realize the effect extraordinary low-boy had. Its proportions are perfect; the racecar nose, that some have compared to that of a Ferrari or Maserati Grand Prix, was very contemporary. The '39 teardrop taillights, plated Auburn dash panel, big and little, ribbed/grooved rubber combo, and fashionably protective nerf bars are hot rod iconic.*

On the Back Cover, Bottom: *Leaping off the cover of the February 1954 issue of Hot Rod magazine was a car the editors called, "The Most Fantastic Coupe!" Chosen as Hot Rod of the Month, the copper Chrisman Model A was featured in a Rex Burnett cutaway pen-and-ink drawing that peeked beneath the car's bodywork and showed HRM readers how it was built. Back in its day, this cool coupe was cutting edge in conception.*

On the Front Flap: *Here's a rare photo of two hot rod veterans under restoration – the McGee roadster on the right, and the Doane Spencer car on the left (with the slick steel hardtop installed) at the So-Cal shop. It's interesting to note how different these cars are, despite the obvious similarities. (Steve Coonan photo, courtesy Bruce Meyer)*

On the Back Flap: *Ray Brown (second from left) with his '32 Ford roadster. Ray's best time at El Mirage for this car was 123.62 mph on alcohol, very good considering this was a dual-purpose highboy that he drove to work daily at Eddie Meyer's shop. The unique louver pattern helped to identify Ray's roadster in old dry lakes photographs. (Tom Sparks/Ray Brown)*

On the Title Page: *Here's the shot of Joe Nitti's roadster you didn't see in Hot Rod in 1950. Crack lensman Tom Medley was restricted to black and white in those days. The June 1950 Hot Rod magazine article was called "Deep Purple '32." Now you can see why.*

OVERSEAS DISTRIBUTION BY:

Brooklands Books Ltd.
P.O. Box 146, Cobham, Surrey, KT11 1LG, England
Telephone 01932 865051 • Fax 01932 868803
www.brooklands-books.com

Brooklands Books Aus.
3/37-39 Green Street, Banksmeadow, NSW 2109, Australia
Telephone 2 9695 7055 • Fax 2 9695 7355

Contents

Ken's Acknowledgements

No author truly works alone. Books like this one simply can't be completed without the assistance of many people. I'd first like to thank Robert Genat and Steve Hendrickson. Without their encouragement and hard work, not to mention their infinite patience and support as the work dragged on (my fault, not theirs), this book would still be simply a good idea, waiting for an editor, a photographer, and a writer.

You know, the best part of writing about this wonderful pastime is that along the way, your heroes can become your friends. I've had the privilege of meeting the guys who made the history and first built the cars we respect and honor here, and it's been fun to share that through my writing and Robert's photography. I'd like to thank my personal hot rod heroes: Wally Parks, Ray Brown, Alex Xydias, Tom Sparks, Dean Jeffries, Barney Navarro, Jim Khougaz, Bud Meyer, Ed Iskenderian, Blackie Gejeian, Lynn Yakel, Neal East, Don Montgomery (whose books have been an inspiration for so many of us), Bobby Meeks, Bill Burke, Roy Brizio, Art Chrisman, Don Prieto (who helped with several chapters), Norm Lean, Pete Chapouris, Jim "Jake" Jacobs, Pete Eastwood, Bob Petersen, Bob D'Olivo, Jim Cherry, and A. B. Shuman.

I'd also like to thank six departed, very knowledgeable hot rod friends: the late Dean Batchelor, Mark Dees, Gray Baskerville, Ray Brock, Tony Nancy, and Tom McMullen, all of whom encouraged my interest. I'll never forget them.

This book could not have been completed without help from Dave Simard, Steve Coonan, David Zivot, Bill Couch, Brian Brennan, Eric Geisert, Bruce Meyer, Don Orosco, Bob Larivee (Sr. and Jr.), Mark Morton, Vern Tardell, Greg Sharp, Kirk White, Bob and Dick Pierson, Dick Flint, Jim Palmer, Dave Crouse, Curt Catallo, Pat Ganahl, Mike Bishop, Richard Munz, Bob Everts, Fred Steele, Chuck Vranas, Bill Moeller, Tony Thacker, Bill Andresen, Ross Myers, Tom Glatch, and Tom Shaw.

If I've left anyone out, I am truly sorry.

One note of caution: The earliest hot rodding dates back to the 1920s, which means nearly 80 years of history have passed. Inevitably, there's still controversy about who ran what heads and which manifold, who did this or that first, and even who set a particular record. So, if any errors have crept into this book, I'll take full responsibility for them. And if you find one, I hope you'll write and tell me so we can try to set the record straight.

Finally, sincere thanks go to my wife Trish and my children, Kayla, Jake, Jeremy, and Chris. They've cheerfully let me drag them to hot rod shows, the Donut Derelicts, the Long Beach Swap Meet, out to Pomona, and even just out to the garage to look at something I thought was cool. And they never let on if it wasn't. They've let me tow them through flea markets and allowed me to indulge my passion for collecting everything remotely automotive, especially if it's for a Ford flathead. Best of all, they never made me feel that this hot rod obsession I've had since I was a kid was anything less than terrific — and perhaps even normal!

Ken Gross

Robert's Acknowledgements

As soon as I heard that Ken Gross had left the Petersen Museum, I contacted him to let him know that if the right book project came along, I'd love to work with him. A few months later, CarTech editor Steve Hendrickson and I were kicking around book ideas and this book is what we came up with. At the time, I was swamped with other projects and could not see myself doing both the photography and writing, but I didn't want to let the project get away either. I suggested to Steve that Ken write it. Ken agreed and we were off and running.

I knew this would be a great project because we all own '32 Fords; Ken has one of the most beautiful traditional roadsters ever built, Steve owns a Buick nailhead-powered three-window that was rescued from a chicken coop, and I own a 327-powered five-window highboy. We're a hot rod "Dream Team" if there ever was one.

I deferred to both Ken and Steve's deeper sense of hot rod history to select the cars. The cars they chose certainly reflect the history of hot rodding and most would have been on my list. Some are well known and others are a little more obscure, but they're all great. I was the lucky one who got to see, touch, smell, hear, and capture these beautiful cars on film. I even had a chance to drive the Nitti roadster, ride in Chili Catallo's deuce coupe, a car that I first saw when I was 10 years old, and sit in many of the other cars — it was almost a religious experience. The best part was meeting the owners of these historic hot rods. They were all gracious and gave me the time I needed to capture these images.

Thanks to Bill Couch, Don Orosco, Blackie Gejeian, Mark Mountanos, Bruce Meyer, Dr. Mark Van Buskirk, Jim Palmer, and Jim Busby, for keeping, restoring, and loving these beautiful old machines. A special thanks to Curt Catallo for giving me a ride in his dad's famous coupe and for the late dinner of his famous "Mac" at his restaurant, *The Union*.

Thanks must also go out to Don Prieto, Greg Sharp, Gordie Craig, David Zivot, Pete Eastwood, the staff at the Petersen Museum, the staff at the Wally Parks NHRA Museum, Dain ingerelli, Don Cox, and to Tom Shaw and Thomas Glatch for their outstanding photographic skills.

Robert Genat

Dedication

A wonderful aspect of hot rodding is that your heroes can become your friends. We respectfully dedicate this book to two hot rod pioneers: our friends, Alex Xydias and Ray Brown.

Foreword

My earliest recollection in life is standing between my parents on the front seat of my dad's semi-custom '39 Ford convertible. I think what makes that moment so memorable is that he was getting one of two traffic violations that day for loud exhausts. Mom said I was four or five years old at the time, and I've been entrenched in the hot rod world ever since.

My dad had great taste in cars and certainly impressed me early on. We spent most Saturday mornings checking out the progress of his projects at establishments such as Drasco's Body Shop, D'Arcy Coach Works, and Ayala's Chop Shop. I think that at an early age I was seeing and recognizing what I call "turning point cars;" cars I think of with the same affection that Ken and Robert have when they refer to "milestones." These are the hot rods that you would see or read about, and you just couldn't get them out of your mind.

When I was a kid on the West Coast, you built a '32 highboy one of two ways: McGee or Spencer style. The same was true of Model Ts: either Ivo or Blackie. Track roadsters: Flint or Niekamp. These are the cars that set the styles we still follow today. Even today, the mere mention of the cars featured in this book stirs my imagination as much as they did when I was a kid, visiting shops with my Dad. The incredible part of my life with these cars is that I've not only been influenced by the original builders' insights, I've been involved in the restorations of a few of these cars as well. I never would have dreamed that Bruce Meyer would give me the responsibility of restoring the Pierson Brothers' coupe, Doane Spencer's highboy, and Bob McGee's roadster – much less the So-Cal belly tank. You can't imagine what it's like to have admired these cars from such a youthful distance, then to actually be commissioned to head the restoration team. It's a rare privilege for a hot rodder.

Speaking of the Bill Niekamp track/lakes roadster, my friend Jim "Jake" Jacobs was way ahead of the curve on restoring the right early hot rod. He acquired Bill's roadster in the mid 1960s as his friends scoffed; today that car is the cornerstone of the Petersen collection. What Jake started 35 years ago has continued – hot rods have even earned a spot on the grass at the Pebble Beach Concours d'Elegance. Why, 10 years ago, no one in his or her right mind could have ever conjured-up such a notion.

Every car described and pictured in these pages has, in some way, seduced three generations of hot rodders, including me. As a hot rod fan, the direction of my teenage years was deeply changed by men like Art Chrisman, Alex Xydias, Wally Parks, "Isky," Tommy Ivo, Ray Brown, Dick Flint, and "Blackie" Gejeian. What's ironic is that I am involved in a phenomenon that now allows me to count these guys, my heroes, as friends. For me, hot rods are a vocation and a passion. If you share that passion, you're in for a rare treat, as Ken Gross and Robert Genat take you on an extremely insightful adventure into the timeless world of *Hot Rod Milestones*.

Pete Chapouris

Introduction

You've probably seen these cars before. They're some of the best-known, coolest hot rods ever built. Each represents a clear vision, usually from one talented person. Virtually every builder here took an old car, stripped it down, souped it up, and in most cases, took it to the dry lakes or to a drag strip to see what she'd do.

Remarkably, several of these old hot rods, like Blackie Gejeian's lakes modified, and Ed Iskenderian's crusty old T, are still with their original builders. And most of them are known by the names of the men who first put them together, like Dick Flint's '29, or the Doane Spencer roadster. That's a rodding tradition – a historic hot rod nearly always retains the name of the guy who built it. The Pacific Gunsight Special and the So-Cal coupe are exceptions, because their builders – Leo Juri and Alex Xydias – respectfully, named their cars after their sponsors or businesses.

I love old hot rods, and the 1940s and 1950s are my favorite eras, because that's when I was growing up. These timeless coupes and roadsters appeared each month in *Hot Rod*, *Hop Up*, and *Speed Age*, and later in *R&C*, *Car Craft*, and *Rodding and Restyling*, showcasing a never-ending parade of creativity, color, chrome, and speed. Most of these hot rods were nationally known, having achieved fame virtually overnight when they were built and/or raced, and featured in those and other long-forgotten rodding magazines.

These hot rods set the standards – they were imitated – and when they made show appearances, they were coveted and revered. Guys clipped their pictures out of the "little books" and tacked them on the wall like pin-ups. They were our reference points. If you didn't have a hot rod, you selected your speed equipment and modification choices, mentally built your own car, and you vowed, someday... I know I did, and I'll bet you did too.

There was a subtly indefinable, rebellious, "outlaw" element about hot rodding that appealed to me, and to many hot rodders. While there was plenty of Yankee ingenuity involved in taking a car apart and rebuilding it to go faster, the notion that you, a kid from wherever, could make your car better than Detroit could, was certainly rebellious. And the truth was, you probably could, given the restrictions the factories were locked into.

As hot rodding became more clearly defined, the hobby evolved from a backyard effort of cars built mostly with junkyard parts, to a more professional approach using increasingly improved speed equipment available from dozens of manufacturers and local speed shops. If you lived in the Los Angeles area, you could buy parts from speed emporiums like Bell Auto Parts, Ansen Automotive, So-Cal Speed Shop, Don Blair, and Ray Brown Automotive. If you lived anywhere else across the country, you perused the Honest Charlie, Ed Almquist, F. E. Zimmer, and Newhouse catalogs (or a score of others), sent off a money order, and the postman or Railway Express delivered the goods. Or you could write directly to Iskenderian, Lewie Shell, Edelbrock, Navarro, or Harman & Collins, and they'd send the parts right out.

Even 50 years ago, hot rodding was beginning to evolve away from its earlier era when many guys could do it all, from metal work, to engine building and machining, even paint and upholstery. Ray Brown built his '32 roadster week by week while he worked at Eddie Meyer's shop in West Hollywood. It was his daily driver and his dry lakes racer. Check out the photo of Ray's roadster on page 58

with a top and chains, taken at Big Bear ski resort during a snowstorm. The early guys used their cars. Doane Spencer drove his roadster to the Indy 500. So did Tom Sparks. Fran Bannister drove his roadster to Bonneville from Massachusetts. That took balls, but these guys had 'em.

This was also the start of the period when, if you street drove *and* raced your roadster at the lakes or the drags, it probably wasn't going to be that competitive. Full-on racers took home the big trophies, so a few legendary competition cars are represented here, like the Pierson Brothers, So-Cal, and Chrisman coupes. The Piersons conclusively proved that coupes could be made as aerodynamic as modifieds and lakesters, and chopped tops and track noses increasingly found their way onto street machines.

Every car in this book has elements that are unique about it. They were – and are still – memorable examples of the hot-rodder's art. The late Dean Batchelor (a roadster racer who later helped develop the first internationally known hot rod streamliner) wrote that hot rodding exemplified American ingenuity at its best. Hot rodding also contributed many top race drivers (not to mention the speed equipment) who drove early Champ cars and midgets: Dan Gurney, Jack McAfee, Skip Hudson, Manny Ayulo, and many more.

And that leads us to the purpose behind this book. Robert Genat and I wanted to present some timeless cars that have long influenced rodders, from the start of the sport up though the present day. But when you try to select just 25 cars from literally hundreds that were built in the 1940s and 1950s, you're bound to leave some out. Time and space considerations dictate that you may not see all of your (and our) favorites here – the Wentworth-Sidebotham '32 roadster, Fred Steele's wicked channeled deuce, Dr. Henry Wetzel's Barris-built '32, Walker Morrison's '32 roadster, or the ex-Ralph Cooper '32 highboy, to name a few. Due to time and location constraints, we simply couldn't fit them all in. But if you enjoy this volume, write and tell us the cars you liked best, and perhaps we will do another book some day.

Ace lensman Robert Genat went to great efforts to shoot these cars, aided by Tom Shaw, Tom Glatch, Bill Andreson, and our editor, Steve Hendrickson. Where nearly every car is concerned, I've tried to find new material and to correct some old mistakes. Writers were fast and loose with facts in the early days of hot rodding, and many of the pioneers still with us are in their eighties, and their memories have faded. For this book, we've tried to dig a little deeper, double-check the details, and take some time with the elder rodding statesmen who were all-too-willing to speak with us, to produce the definitive, up-to-date story on each of these great cars. They – and you – deserve no less.

Over just the last few years, interest in restoring and preserving historic hot rods has grown exponentially. From Jim Jacobs' initial efforts with the Niekamp roadster over 25 years ago, to Kirk White's and Ron San Giovanni's forays against the stodgy Antique Automobile Club of America concerning the ex-Ray Brown '32 and the *Cam Carriers'* '23 T competition roadster, the fascination with vintage rods has mushroomed. Bruce Meyer, with help from Bob Bauder, Pete Chapouris, Pete Eastwood, and Jim Jacobs, restored the Pierson Brothers' '34, the So-Cal belly tank, and several other milestone cars. Don Orosco's shop resurrected the Flint and La Masa roadsters and the So-Cal coupe. Roy Brizio did the Mooneyham & Sharp coupe, and as this is written, his shop just completed Tom McMullen's first roadster and started on Jack Calori's '36 coupe. Dave Simard restored the ex-Jim Khougaz '32 roadster; Dave and Rob Crouse brought back the Joe Nitti '32; Chuck Longley and his son Mike did the Pete Henderson '32, and still more restorations are under way.

The Petersen Automotive Museum maintains a first-class replica of the old Bell Auto Parts Speed Shop, and its Bruce Meyer Gallery showcases great rods on a full-time basis. Historic hot rod exhibits have also appeared at the Oakland Museum, the Saratoga Automobile Museum in Saratoga Springs, New York, and the National Automotive Museum in Reno, Nevada. And there will undoubtedly be more.

In 1997, I helped curate the first class of historic hot rods at the prestigious Pebble Beach Concours d'Elegance. We've had three successive hot rod classes since, in 1999, 2001, and 2003, and there's an early custom car class slated for 2005. Several of the historic roadsters and coupes that have appeared at Pebble Beach are included in this book. Boyd Coddington, himself a legend, calls them, "our ancestor cars," and he's right. Years ago, the patterns for hot rodding were laid down by many of these cool rides, and we're still looking at them in our rear-view mirrors.

The times are certainly changing. The Antique Automobile Club of America has permitted historic hot rods with racing provenance to compete in Class 24-A, and while they've resisted a "real" vintage hot rod class, I think it's inevitable. The Pebble Beach Concours d'Elegance delayed the entry of hot rods for many years; now the bi-annual Hot Rod Class and the accompanying Dean Batchelor Memorial Trophy, sponsored by Ford Motor Company, is hotly contested. J. Heumann, Chairman Emeritus at Pebble Beach, has said, "if we can't recognize the importance of hot rods in American automotive racing history, there's something wrong."

I couldn't agree more. Jump in, and enjoy the ride.

Sassy, slinky, sexy? All of the above. Isky captured the hot rod image some 65 years ago with this car, and then froze it in time. It would be a crime to restore this remarkable car.

Hot Rodding's "Camfather," Ed Iskenderian, still owns his high-school roadster. Ed Iskenderian is a short, stubby fireplug of a man with a broad, perpetual grin. His camshaft expertise is the stuff of legends. So is his grizzled old '23 T, as much for its preservation, as it is for its condition. Cam grinding pioneers like Ed Winfield, Pierre "Pete" Bertrand, and Clay Smith all achieved notoriety, but the doughty Iskenderian outlasted them all, making a commercial success out of a black art that still baffles most rodders, even in the age of computers.

Unrestored, minimally preserved, its patina unquestioned, the down-and-out, authentic pre-war look of Isky's roadster is frequently and shamelessly duplicated by the so-called "rat rod" crowd. In an era where show 'n' shine is the rule rather than the exception, Isky's rod looks as though it stopped time in its tracks some 60 years ago – a hallowed era that every rodder respects, but few today can remember.

Iskenderian is a veteran of it all. He was born in Tulare County, California, in 1921. His parents lost their vineyard after a severe frost, and they moved to Los Angeles when Ed was just one year old. A born mechanic, he began tinkering with engines when he was 14, and built his first hot rod, a Frontenac-head Model T, when he was 16. An engine with an eight-plug, "twin-spark" Riley head followed the Fronty. Isky was soon discouraged with four-cylinders, because the T crankshafts broke so easily when subjected to higher outputs.

Isky built his first V-8-powered T in 1939, turning 97 mph at an SCTA meet at El Mirage. Primed for more speed, Ed bought a second T roadster, a car he drove, raced, and never, ever sold. Ed recently contradicted the oft-told tale that he entered the cam business because the "Old Master," Ed Winfield, told young Isky he'd just have to wait for a cam.

"Ed was actually very nice to me," Isky recalls today. "We were all fascinated by [Ed] Winfield and [George] Riley. We lived by what we heard. But I really didn't have to wait for a Winfield cam."

Ed Iskenderian's '24 T Roadster

"But," Isky recalls, "some time later, when I wanted a camshaft for my Maxi F-head-equipped flathead V-8, I went to Clay Smith. I needed a special cam with a soft profile for the overhead exhaust and a faster profile for the intake. Even Smith said it would take a month."

That's when Iskenderian realized there was quite a demand for racing cams and decided he'd found his niche. He bought a second-hand, cylindrical cam grinder, which he still owns, and which eventually formed the basis for what became a million-dollar business.

Today, Ed's venerable T (often referred to as a '24, but actually a 1923 model) resembles a time warp, with its tarnished chrome, faded black paint, and weary whitewalls. Indeed it is, for the build began in 1939, and with a few small exceptions, the roadster has remained preserved since 1940.

It was originally built and owned by pioneer hot rodder John Athan, whose '29 highboy was used in the Elvis Presley movie, *Lovin' You*. Athan sold the T to Iskenderian because he was disillusioned with the unreliability of its hopped-up, Rajo-equipped, four-cylinder engine.

Ed Iskenderian's '23 T, completed in 1940 (!) looks like it came through a time warp. Unrestored, with tarnished chrome, faded paint, weary whitewalls, and cracked leather, it still runs, and on the few occasions where it shows up for muster, it's unmistakable.

ED ISKENDERIAN'S FIRST HOT ROD
This T-body car was a real eye-stopper when Isky built it in the early days of Hot Rodding in 1938-39 . . . and he still has it to this day!

Best wishes from one Hot Rodder to another

Ed Iskenderian

When I was a kid, you could send away for Isky decals and/or one of these souvenir photos. They were (I believe) just 25 cents. I still have mine, and here it is. (Ken Gross Archives)

Isky acquired the roadster while at Polytechnical High School in Los Angeles. Fed up with feeble fours, Ed dropped a 1932 Ford 21-stud V-8 between the T's low-slung Essex rails, and commissioned ace Hollywood bodyman and customizer, Jimmy Summers, to do some panel freshening. "Jimmy was over on Melrose Avenue: he was the best guy around," remembers Ed. "We gave him 10 bucks and he pounded out a few dents and dings."

Isky's roadster turned 120 mph at a Western Timing Association meet in 1942, and here's the timing tag to prove it. Adjacent is one of Isky's clever cam tags. They were given out to camshaft purchasers with every new bumpstick. Occasionally, guys could buy them even if they didn't have a coveted Isky cam. Everybody wanted one. You could stamp the cam specs on it and, whether you were a lakes guy or not, you had instant credibility.

Ed drove the completed car on trips as far away as Mexico, where supposedly a local sheriff gave it the nickname, "La Cucaracha." An apprentice machinist, Isky extensively modified the flathead, which was ported and relieved, "bored to Merc," (meaning it was bored out to 3-1/16th inch), and at first was fitted with a Winfield racing cam.

Soon afterward, Ed stepped up to those then-and-now very rare Maxi overhead valve F-heads. The Maxi cylinder heads, originally intended to prevent overheating in Ford trucks, retained the stock intake valve setup in the block, while the exhaust valves were overheads. Better valve separation and improved cooling were supposedly the result, but the Maxi (like the postwar Ardun full-OHV conversion), was never a commercial success, and only a handful were ever made.

Two '33 Pontiac grilles joined top to bottom comprise this car's unique frontal aspect. Before you wonder why more guys didn't do this, ask yourself where you would find even one '33 Pontiac.

"I liked 'em 'cause they looked like racing overheads," Ed confesses today, "and not many guys were running overhead valves. I got them from a guy, believe it or not, whose name was Rex A. Head; I paid $65 for them. Dixon and Alexander made similar F-heads."

Ed modified the Maxi heads to his own specs, filled the combustion chambers for higher compression, and hand cut the complex, solid copper head gaskets. "John [Athan] made the pattern. A student at Santa Monica Trade School cast the handsome polished, full-length aluminum rocker covers (the Maxi heads came with shorter covers), and chiseled my name in script on both," says Ed. His is arguably the only car running (occasionally) today with Maxi heads. Ed made those full-length chromed headers too.

Although the roadster had a Navarro dual intake and a converted Lincoln Zephyr distributor when it appeared in *Hot Rod* in June 1948, Ed says that he ran an Edelbrock "slingshot" dual. I've seen a period picture that shows the slingshot under a makeshift tin hood top, required so Ed could race the car. He says he also tried four Chandler-Grove twin-throat carburetors on a handmade "flat plate" intake because he wanted to see what one barrel per cylinder would do. The over-carbureted car only went 96 mph in tests, and Ed quickly returned to the proven V'd Edelbrock unit. Some time later, the roadster acquired an Edelbrock triple manifold and a Vertex magneto. Isky clocked 120.0 mph at a May 8, 1942, Western Timing Association meet in the car, a very impressive speed for a 239-ci flatty.

He plated the rear crossmember, so the frame horns end in a box and a single stop/tail/license light warns close followers. The rear red Kelsey wires (purchased a half century ago for two bucks apiece) were shod with 6.00 x 16 US Royal DeLuxe whitewalls, purchased back in 1941; the fronts are 5.50 x 16 Dayton Aristocrats that Ed says he bought just after the war. (Makes you wonder when the oil was last changed.)

The T body was cut down about three inches in the rear, at John Athan's suggestion, for a lower silhouette. That one-of-a-kind grille is actually a pair of 1933 Pontiac grille shell top halves welded together with new grille bars. Ed cast the unique flying skull radiator ornament in high school shop class – eat your hearts out, all you rat rodders! He also engine-turned the firewall like many racers of the period did. Those cool chromed headlights perch on aircraft wing struts.

Maxi heads, red-painted block, and triple carb Edelbrock manifold – it may be dusty, but this engine's definitely got the look. Originally, Maxi's came with two separate small valve covers on each side. Ed has the "signature" one-piece valve covers cast, giving his engine a unique look for all time.

At John Athans' suggestion, Isky cut the T body down by three inches. Although the car's appearance is somewhat neglected, the workmanship is top drawer, and worlds ahead of contemporary retro rods.

This roadster's drivetrain, like so many hot rods of the period, used what was available cheaply in wrecking yards, so the brakes are Plymouth hydraulics. Remember Ford didn't go that way until 1939, and it would very likely have been impossible to find new Ford juicers in a boneyard. A '37 Ford banjo wheel operates Franklin steering. In front, there's a '32 Ford axle with split '37 wishbones. To lower the car, the Ford transverse leaf spring hangs in front of the axle; friction shocks keep things snubbed. Ed mounted the 3.78:1 ratio Ford banjo rear behind the spring to lengthen the wheelbase six inches, and the rear end housings were swapped side to side to lower the car a few inches more, and were suspended with tubular hydraulic shocks.

Although the car's appearance is a bit neglected, the workmanship is top drawer, and arguably better than most then-contemporary rods. Inside, there's a much-coveted dash from an 8-cylinder Auburn with a 100-mph speedo (the V-12 Auburns read to 120 mph), and the angular aluminum column drop incorporates an aircraft electric tach. Ed cleverly fashioned an upholstery trim strip from half round steel; it's plated and secured with countersunk screws. Laddie Jerbeck did the oxblood leather upholstery. Ed told *Hot Rod*'s Steve Alexander that the leather cost $60 and the upholstery work cost $40.

In an interview done 20 years ago, Isky said, "it wasn't so much money in those days. You couldn't go out and buy the stuff you needed, even if you had the dough. A little welding and a lot of work, that's what it took. Actually, this car cost me about $1,000 to build."

The T led an active life at first, running as Isky's street transportation, taking a turn at the lakes, and it was even used as an advertising icon. But by the 1950s, Ed no longer drove the roadster and it has since spent most of its life in limbo. The air in the tires is probably more than half a century old. There was no desire on Ed's part to update it. Fast for the 1940s, it was obsolete a decade later, and by then, Ed was too busy with his remarkably successful camshaft business to spend time on it. Although it was last officially registered

Isky extensively modified the flathead, which was ported and relieved, "bored to Merc," i.e., punched out to 3-1/16 inches. At first, it was fitted with a Winfield racing cam. Later, Ed bought a set of Maxi overhead-valve F-heads. Originally intended to prevent overheating in Ford trucks, the Maxi conversion retained the stock intake valve setup in the block, while the exhaust valves were overheads. Better valve separation and improved cooling were the result, but the short-lived Maxi (like the postwar Ardun full OHV conversion), was never a commercial success. Only a handful were ever made.

A custom column drop that contains the tachometer – a nice touch, then and now – supports the steering wheel. "We didn't have any magazines then to tell us what to do," Ed once told Pat Ganahl. Obviously Ed didn't need any help in that department.

in 1951, from time to time over the years, Ed would take it out and run it for kicks. He took it to the LA Roadster Show twice and was refused entrance both times because of the car's scruffy appearance.

Ed Iskenderian typifies the "rags to riches" story of many of the great hot rodders we'll celebrate in this book. In 1944, he became an Army Air Corps cadet. He'd hoped to fly as a pilot, but competition was stiff, they had plenty of candidates, and "…I washed out of flying school. They wanted guys who were taller and better looking," he quips. Some references state that he was a tail gunner on a B-24 Liberator bomber in the South Pacific. Today, Isky laughs at that reference. "I flew in transports," he said, "and we went to Australia, New Guinea, and eventually Japan. I used to tell those Australian girls I was a tail gunner on a C-54…if you know aircraft, you know that's a transport plane. It went over pretty good."

When the war ended, he and his first employee, Norris Baronian, began turning out camshafts, using the same second-hand cam grinder Isky had picked up before the war. Ed Almquist, in his terrific book, *Hot Rod Pioneers*, recalls

Kelsey-Hayes wires in red; black body. Ed really nailed it with this car. With all the people who updated their street rods, you have to wonder why Ed never changed his. Of course, we're all glad he didn't.

There's room for two in that snug cockpit. The '37 Ford flat banjo wheel is a classic. Considering this car came from an era when most rods were made of junkyard parts, this ride is the antithesis of junk.

"Norris began part time by rough grinding five camshafts per day while Ed would finish them by night." They worked in a two-car garage behind Ed's father's house. Fifty years ago, Ed was advertising his camshafts in *Hot Rod* and *Speed Age* virtually every month, and the ads grew bigger and bigger. From the beginning, up against tough competitors like Harry Weber, Chet Herbert, and (Kenny) Harman and (Cliff) Collins, Isky's flamboyant print ads caught hot rodders' attentions, and his fine products set speed and drag racing records. "Vic Edelbrock, Sr. helped me a lot. His building was across the street from ours, and when he had an engine on a dyno and wanted a cam change or modification, we'd do it right away. He really helped us get known fast."

In *Speed Age*, July 1953, under a rendering of Confucius, China's legendary philosopher, Isky's ad read: "Confucius says, 'he who copies shows great respect and admiration for that which he copies.'" The text went on to warn readers that there were many imitators, but that Iskenderian cams were the real deal. Isky, for years, would send free decals to anyone who asked, and every cam purchaser received a brass cam lift and duration settings plate (about the size of a timing tag) that could be screwed to the firewall or dash, announcing that the car had a "genuine" Isky cam.

Ed says he loved giving his camshafts catchy designations, like the famed "404 Eliminator" for flatheads, so that people would talk about them and ask for them by name. When the overheads came in, Isky was one of the first to make the switch and provide hot cams for Chevys, Chrysler Hemis, and nearly everything else. Soon his roller-tappet cams were setting records in the hands of hot shoes like Mickey Thompson,

Chris Karamesines, Tommy Ivo, and Don Garlits, to name just a few. And, of course, the irrepressible, stogie-chomping, publicity-conscious Ed Iskenderian made sure everybody knew it.

Isky's monthly ads railed against the dreaded "cam bootleggers," and for a time, he even leased camshafts to selected racers so they couldn't be copied. His flamboyant promotions earned him the title, "The PT Barnum of the camshaft business," but racers and enthusiasts remembered red-hot cam names like Polydyne Profile, Five-Cycle, 550 Magnum, and Ultra Super Magnum. Isky's business prospered, despite the efforts of new firms like Crane and Crower.

Isky was always an innovator, and although his ad budget must have been huge, his aggressive tactics worked. Ed's logo T-shirts, early sponsorship deals, full-page, prominent ads in *HRM*, his direct phone line to the dyno room, Top Tuner Tips, and effective on-track promotions set precedents that still exist today. During the notorious fuel wars, the NHRA temporarily banned nitro, and *HRM* didn't report the fuel meets and their high speeds. But Ed's big advertisements, usually on the first pages or inside back covers, prominently highlighted new records. They reminded *HRM*'s readers what was *really* happening, and whose cams were powering the winning racers.

Meanwhile, the old "T" languished in the back of Ed's shop. Writing in *Rod & Custom*, in April 1993, his last issue after once again rescuing the magazine, then-Editor Pat Ganahl wrote, "When I saw Isky come tooling around the corner of the grandstands in his black T roadster at the Bakersfield reunion, I just about dropped my camera on the track. I remembered a couple of times – once in the mid-'50s and again about 20 to 25 years ago – that some magazine guys talked him into getting it out, cleaning it up, and taking it for a spin for a story. I had seen it several times over the past 20 years, sitting in a storage area behind the dyno room at Iskenderian Cams, covered with cardboard, collecting dust, and rusting. I never thought I'd see – and hear – it running again."

After closer inspection, Ganahl commented: "Although it's beyond being cleaned up now, the car is still completely intact, just the way Ed built it in the late 1930s. As I looked closer at the details…I realized that the car was not only beautifully proportioned, innovative, and fast – but that the craftsmanship on this car far outdistanced any typical rods of the '30s or '40s. Using junkyard parts ('We didn't have any magazines then to tell us what to do,' he told Pat), Ed built it all himself, with the help of his longtime friend John Athan."

And that's really the point about Isky's T. It's one of the oldest surviving hot rods; it's very close to the way it was built, and most of the parts are exactly as Ed assembled them. Even better, it still runs. Proportionally, the roadster is nicely done; the flowing exhaust headers lend the sensation that this car is moving while it's standing still. It's a classic, just like Ed, and if some of the rat rod guys want to bootleg its best features, I suspect Ed Iskenderian would take that as a compliment.

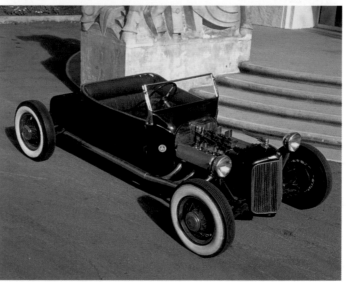

Gennie Auburn panels like this one are hard to find. Hot rodders loved them because they contained four large instruments and a speedometer, originally supplied by Stewart-Warner to Auburn. Alternatively, if the original Auburn dials were trashed, you could substitute convex-lensed 2-5/8-inch hot rod or nautical Stewart-Warners. Ed's panel has the gauges as Auburn supplied them. The key slot takes the place of the Columbia overdrive switch.

The winged skull hood ornament captures the insouciance of this wonderful old car. Ed says he cast the ornament in shop class – I bet he could sell a lot of them today.

With its V'd twin '33 Pontiac grilles, raked windscreen, and flowing three-into-one headers, Isky's roadster looked fast standing still, and it still does. Ace Hollywood bodyman Jimmy Summers pounded out a few dents in 1940 for ten bucks. The car hasn't been touched since.

(2)

Bill Niekamp's '29 street and lakes car won the inaugural America's Most Beautiful Roadster trophy at the first Oakland Roadster Show in 1950. Long before most hot rodders began reshaping their cars and finishing them to unheard-of levels, Bill Niekamp's roadster set a precedent. Its track-nosed, altered, and channeled Model A body, full belly pan, and soon-to-be-proven dry lakes prowess helped make it the first Oakland winner. It set high standards and inspired many significant early rods, like the Eddie Dye and Dick Flint roadsters.

At age 44, Bill Niekamp built this Oakland-winning '29 to show younger guys how to do a roadster **right.** Jim "Jake" Jacobs rescued the car and owned it for 30 years. We're still learning things from it. Think of a historic hot rod icon and it's likely you'll picture the low-slung, track-nosed '29 of Bill Niekamp, winner of the first America's Most Beautiful Roadster trophy at Oakland in 1950. Niekamp reportedly built this car because he wanted to "...show up the neighborhood younger guys." He was 44 at the time – somewhat old for a hot rodder back then.

A professional auto painter by trade, Bill trailered his freshly completed car some 500 miles from his Long Beach home to Oakland. Although indoor hot rod shows with well established rules weren't common, Niekamp's car had them shaking their heads. Out of more than 100 cars, he won the right to have his name placed first on the nine-foot-tall America's Most Beautiful Roadster (AMBR) gold statue, and took a smaller replica home.

The Oakland judges were discerning; this was and is no ordinary '29. It boasts a considerable amount of artistically reworked sheetmetal. The result is a stunningly well-proportioned roadster that looks great from any angle. If you park it alongside a typical '29 on '32 rails, one of rodding's classic marriages, you'll note the Niekamp roadster's body had been shortened 2-1/2 inches in the door area, and the driver's side door was welded shut and finished smoothly. This car was unusual for its time, and it's still stylish.

Reportedly, and as was the case in that era, Niekamp did much of the mechanical work on the roadster himself. Years ago (he passed away in the late 1970s), Bill admitted to subsequent owner, Jim "Jake" Jacobs, that he didn't even own a torch. "Torch cutting and arc welding speeds up oxidation in the metals, so I patiently cut everything by handsaw," insisted Niekamp proudly. He craftily aligned all the crossmembers and key brackets, and then bolted the parts together. Welding was done only when it was absolutely essential.

Bill Niekamp's '29 Roadster

Besides its discretely altered proportions, the Niekamp '29 is noted for its stunning track nose, smoothed hood with lunch box latches, and full belly pan. A very complete car visually, with no protruding or errant edges, it's one man's vision of a shape that would look great on the street and still be aerodynamic enough to perform acceptably at the lakes. And perform it did, after its show-winning days were over. There's an SCTA timing tag affixed to the flat dash that states that the Niekamp '29 turned 142.40 mph at El Mirage dry lake on July 13, 1952, a very impressive speed for a flathead-powered car.

Although some reports say Niekamp built the car himself, that's not the case. Though he barely got a line of credit in the first feature on this car in the March 1950 *Hot Rod*, metal magician Dwight "Whitey" Clayton handcrafted the nose, grille, hood, and belly pan. Whitey probably did the aluminum floorboards, as well. It's unclear as to whether Whitey performed the vertical section that shortened the original steel body, but since Niekamp eschewed torch craft, it's likely Clayton or another talented bodyman was involved here as well.

Hot Rod devoted three pages of text and photos, plus a Rex Burnett cutaway drawing, to its first Niekamp car feature. They say the "devil is in the details." This milestone rod is no exception. The roadster body was fabricated from four separate 1929 Model A bodies, one of which was actually a coupe, and channeled over narrow frame rails from a 1927 Essex, chosen for their abrupt rear kick up. Bill salvaged two Model A crossmembers; one was fitted in the rear, with a '31 Model A spring, and the other was inverted to form the rear engine support. The front-most crossmember was formed

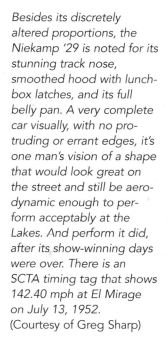

Besides its discretely altered proportions, the Niekamp '29 is noted for its stunning track nose, smoothed hood with lunch-box latches, and its full belly pan. A very complete car visually, with no protruding or errant edges, it's one man's vision of a shape that would look great on the street and still be aerodynamic enough to perform acceptably at the Lakes. And perform it did, after its show-winning days were over. There is an SCTA timing tag that shows 142.40 mph at El Mirage on July 13, 1952. (Courtesy of Greg Sharp)

Forever a historic hot rod icon, the low-slung, track-nosed '29 of Bill Niekamp won the first America's Most Beautiful Roadster trophy at Oakland in 1950. Niekamp, who was 44 (old for a hot rodder, even then), reportedly built this car because he wanted to "…show up the neighborhood younger guys." Niekamp reportedly spent $1,888.52 and took 13 months to build his dream rod, working in a one-car garage behind his Long Beach home. (Courtesy of Greg Sharp)

Jim Jacobs and his dad returned the roadster to flathead power. This engine was a Jerry Kugel-built 260-ci 59A, mildly overbored with a Merc crank, Edelbrock dual intake and heads, and a Weber cam, mated to a '39 Ford three-speed floor shift with a Zephyr cluster. Jake installed the flathead rearward four inches. Earlier, the driveshaft had to be shortened to accommodate a '38 Buick transmission. The space gained facilitated the installation of a much larger Babb radiator (Jake says Niekamp's original installation ended above the tie rods), as well as a sorely needed cooling fan.

Niekamp's '29 looks great from any angle. Park it alongside a typical '29 on '32 rails, and you'll realize the body has been shortened 2-1/2 inches in the door area. The driver's side door was welded shut and finished smoothly. The roadster was fabricated from four separate 1929 Model A bodies, one of which was a coupe. It was channeled over narrow frame rails from a 1927 Essex, chosen for their abrupt rear kick up. Bill salvaged two Model A crossmembers; one was fitted in the rear, with a '31 Model A spring, and the other was inverted to form the rear engine support.

from stout chrome-moly tubing. A gusseted spring mount bracket clamped a transverse leaf spring with reversed spring eyes. A 1937 Ford V-8/60 contributed the tubular front axle, the spring perches are from an earlier model Ford, and the front spindles and hydraulic brakes are 1940 Ford. The tubular shock absorbers in front were supplemented with two sets of rear shocks: a set of Ford Houdaille, needle-adjusted, lever-action friction units handled rebounds, and twin tubular Gabriels controlled body sway.

The 3.54:1 rear end was adapted from a 1937 Ford, necessitating that the torque tube be shortened some 18-1/8 inches. The resulting wheelbase was 110 inches, (later sources say 113 inches), 10 inches longer than a stock Model A. The driveshaft was a shortened and re-splined Model A unit. To reduce turbulence, unique tear-drop-shaped fairings were built to surround the rear axle and the rear spring assembly. Unusual for that early period, the wheels were 15-inchers all around. The fronts are 15 x 5-inch '48 Mercurys, mounting 5.50 x 15-inch tires; the rears are special 15 x 6-inch units by Riggs, sporting 7.00 x 15-inch rubber.

Typical of hot rods from the 1940s, the steering is a clever compendium of modified stock pieces. Bill used a cross-steering unit from a 1935 Ford, but rotated the box one-quarter turn on its side to facilitate an upright pitman arm. That allowed the side-mounted drag link to be installed level, with no bending required. Hand-formed and chrome-plated hairpin wishbones round out the package.

The engine was a stock bore and stroke, 239.4-ci '42 Mercury (Fords for 1942 were 221.0 ci) with Thompson three-ring pistons, Evans heads, a Weiand dual manifold, Kurten ignition, and a Winfield cam. The Electronic Balancing Company of Long Beach balanced the moving assembly. Bill didn't bother with adjustable tappets; he built up the valve

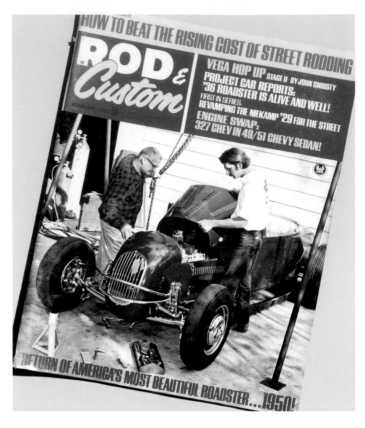

ends with Stellite. Niekamp also ported and relieved the block. W-shaped headers round out the engine's exterior, but there's virtually no chrome; just a clean, painted, and raw engine with a firewall-mounted accessory oil filter.

Cars with full belly pans usually suffer from excessive cockpit and under hood heat, especially with a narrow grille opening and no hood louvers, like this one. The firewall and belly pan were reportedly designed so that the air exits from

According to Griffith Borgeson, who wrote the show coverage in *Hot Rod* (and would later write for *Sports Cars Illustrated* and *Car and Driver*), some 27,624 visitors attended the first Oakland Show. Borgeson was most impressed with the Niekamp car, although he spelled Bill's name incorrectly. "First prize," he wrote, "a handy nine foot golden cup – was carried off by William NieKamp [sic] of Long Beach, for a car that is neither flashy, spectacular, or even tested for speed. What is remarkable about the car, and the feature that enabled it to take seven other major awards, is the perfect purity of its layout and workmanship. Everything about the job is subdued and – there's that word again – perfect."

Borgeson went on to comment that the roadster's trunk area, "usually neglected...is finished as immaculately as the rest of the car." Even the frame channels "...had been worked down with emery and finished with baked enamel." From the outset, Niekamp had one-upped the competition, with a level of fit and finish that might have qualified for today's Ridler Award. An *SCTA Road Runners* member, Niekamp announced plans to race the car at the earliest opportunity. Subsequently the car earned 12 timing tags, with the best speed being the aforementioned 142.40-mph mark at El Mirage. Niekamp won the Pasadena Reliability Run's "Best Appearing" car award in 1950 and 1951, an honor later earned but once by the great Doane Spencer '32.

Although Bill Niekamp was reportedly offered $2,800 for the '29 in 1952, he demurred, electing instead to donate the car as first prize in a raffle to benefit a friend who was injured in a Bonneville crash. Sources say just $700 was raised, and the winner was a young soldier home on leave named Dick Russell. Russell used the roadster as a daily driver, ran it at the Santa Ana drags, installed a '55 Chevy V-8, painted the car red, and then sold it in 1956 to Delmer Brink. Brink repainted the car several more times, drove it for a few years, and then began an engine swap with a '57 Buick nailhead. The car was never finished, and it languished in Brink's Bellflower, California, garage until 1969.

Whitey Clayton fabricated the Niekamp roadster's aluminum hood, side panels, and belly pan. Working out of his small one-person shop in Whittier, California, Clayton hand-hammered beautiful shapes like this one out of sheet aluminum.

under the hood. Did it work? Niekamp told Jim Jacobs, "It'd start to boil before we'd get out of the driveway." In an attempt to keep occupants from slowly roasting, Bill wrapped the M&M mufflers with asbestos. Two plugs were fitted on either side of the belly pan so that short lakes stacks could be inserted to bypass the mufflers.

Niekamp reportedly spent $1,888.52 and took 13 months of long days and nights to build his dream rod, working in a one-car garage behind his Long Beach home. That expense seems a pittance today, but it was a lot of money in 1949-50, and partially the result of high postwar prices for scrap steel and aluminum.

Since Bill intended to race the car as well as drive it on the street, he fitted a readily removable Model A windshield, and a full tonneau cover enclosed the cockpit for racing. Inside, there was a white 1940 Ford two-spoke steering wheel and a column shift (a frequent practice in the postwar hot rodding era). Those three round instrument dials came from a nearly new 1949 Plymouth, and everything inside is neatly finished in blue to match the body. The trunk features a remote latch and contains a 1928 Chevrolet cylindrical fuel tank with a central filler. Chromed nerf bars, resembling the hand-formed units preferred by oval track racers, protected that lovely nose and the rolled pan in the rear. The exhausts exited with chrome stacks through the rear pan.

The original engine in the Niekamp roadster was a stock bore and stroke, 239.4-ci '42 Mercury (Fords for '42 were 221 ci) with Thompson three-ring pistons, Evans heads, a Weiand dual manifold, Kurten ignition, and a Winfield cam. Bill didn't bother with adjustable tappets; he built up the valve ends with Stellite. Niekamp also ported and relieved the block. W-shaped headers round out the exterior. There's virtually no chrome, just a clean, painted, raw casting engine with a firewall-mounted oil filter. This later engine has a Weiand intake and Offy heads.

Simple art-deco '40 Ford steering wheel, and plain but functional '49 Plymouth instruments are a model of understatement – compare this car with today's AMBR winners and their elaborate, often hand-made gauges. The overall effect, right down to that Chrysler medium blue hue and Anniversary Silver finish, is Oakland, 1950. Because Bill intended to race the car as well as drive it on the street, he fitted a readily removable Model A windshield. A full tonneau cover enclosed the cockpit for racing. Everything inside is neatly finished in blue to match the body.

Carrying the simple theme forward, Niekamp used black tuck-and-roll Naugahyde and dark gray carpets. Column shift conversions were a popular update in the late 1940s and early 1950s. You didn't have to speed-shift at the dry lakes, and a column shifter allowed occasional front seat room for three – or an arm around your best girl.

Enter Jim Jacobs, the "Jake" of Pete and Jake's fame. Jake heard the car was for sale and bought it for just $1,800. In two weeks he had it finished and running, but the now-Buick-powered '29, with swing pedals, a shortened driveshaft, etc., was living way out of character. A torsion bar snapped; the big mill overheated and Jake took the advice of Bud Bryan and Tom Medley, and soon returned the roadster to flathead power. This time, the engine was a Jerry Kugel-built 260-ci 59A, mildly over bored with a Merc crank, Edelbrock dual intake and heads, and a Weber cam, mated to a '39 Ford 3-speed floor shift with a Zephyr cluster. Jake installed the flathead rearward four inches since the driveshaft had been shortened that much to accommodate a '38 Buick transmission. That facilitated the installation of a much larger Babb radiator (Jake says Niekamp's original installation ended above the tie rods), as well as a sorely needed fan.

Jake says today that he wasn't particularly prescient in buying the roadster. "I thought it'd be a neat car, and I was thinking at the time that nobody was going that way. Actually, most of my friends tried to discourage me from buying it." Writing in *Rod & Custom* in February 1971, in a piece entitled "Old Roadsters Never Die," he defended the Niekamp's restoration saying, "Inevitably it had to happen, and a better time we couldn't think of…what with trends as they are now: 'glass bodies, 4-corner independent ride, (Art) Himsl-type artistry. What better time could there be for this *most* traditional hot rod to reappear?"

Even then, Jim Jacobs wisely insisted that "…in the case of this or any classic, careful consideration should be given to original identity (and) the value it gives…. Yes, it was a grand ol' roadster those many years ago," he insisted, "and there's only one way those fond remembrances can be brought to full impact, to see the car once again in all its original splendor." A '40 Ford wheel replaced the '41, and the dash received Stewart-Warner instruments, but the overall effect, right down to that Chrysler medium blue hue and Anniversary Silver, was Oakland, 1950, all over again. Beneath the skin, Jake had done a lot of work. For a time, he installed three cross-connected gasoline tanks, bringing fuel

Bill used a cross-steering unit from a 1935 Ford, but he rotated the box one-quarter turn on its side to facilitate an upright pitman arm. That allowed the side-mounted drag link to be installed on a level with no bending required. Hand-formed and plated hairpin wishbones round out the package.

capacity up to 18 gallons. A previous owner had torched the rear frame. "I couldn't find an Essex," Jake says, "so I used part of an old Willys frame to make the repairs and partially boxed the frame to better mount the rear shocks." The auxiliary Gabriels were gone by that time. Jake had some great moments in the roadster, including a monumental 5,000-mile trip to the Street Rod Nationals with the late Tom Senter.

When I curated the first Pebble Beach hot rod class in 1997, I asked Jake to bring the Niekamp car and he graciously did. The second flathead engine had given up the ghost during a previous trip home from the 25th Anniversary Oakland Roadster Show, and Jake had installed a Chevy small-block. Somewhere in its lifetime (possibly with Niekamp), the car acquired a Cyclone quick-change rear, and that was retained. For the Concours d'Elegance, Jake "backdated" the Niekamp, installing the car's third flathead, this time with a Weiand dual intake and Offenhauser heads, and he showed the car in lakes guise with a tonneau and sans windshield. While the old roadster didn't win an award, it impressed everyone with its classic good looks and fine workmanship.

Not long afterward, while I was the director of the Petersen Automotive Museum in Los Angeles, Jake made it known that the car could be purchased. On behalf of Robert E. Petersen, I was able to negotiate the deal that saw the reconstituted, artfully restored Niekamp, complete with its original Oakland trophy and many other awards, become part of Bob Petersen's

Simple but clever front shock mounts support tubular accessory units. Unusual for this early period, the wheels were 15-inch steel units all around; most rodders were still using 16s. The fronts are 15 x 5-inch '48 Mercurys, with 5.50 x 15-inch tires; the rears are special 15 x 6-inch units by Riggs, sporting 7.00 x 15-inch rubber. The front spindles and hydraulic brakes are 1940 Ford.

A professional auto painter, Niekamp brought his freshly completed car on a trailer from Long Beach 500 miles north to Oakland. Indoor hot rod shows weren't yet common, and Niekamp's lovely '29 had the crowds shaking their heads. Out of over 100 cars, he won the right to have his name placed first on the nine-foot-tall gold AMBR statue, and took a replica home. (Courtesy of Robert Genat)

The clean, uncluttered flathead can still deliver the goods. From the outset, Niekamp had one-upped the competition, with a level of fit and finish that might have qualified for today's Ridler Award. An SCTA Road Runners club member, Niekamp announced plans to race the car at the earliest opportunity and subsequently earned 12 timing tags, with the best speed of 142.40 mph at El Mirage. Niekamp won the Pasadena Reliability Run's Best Appearing Car award in 1950 and 1951, an honor later earned just once by the great Doane Spencer '32.

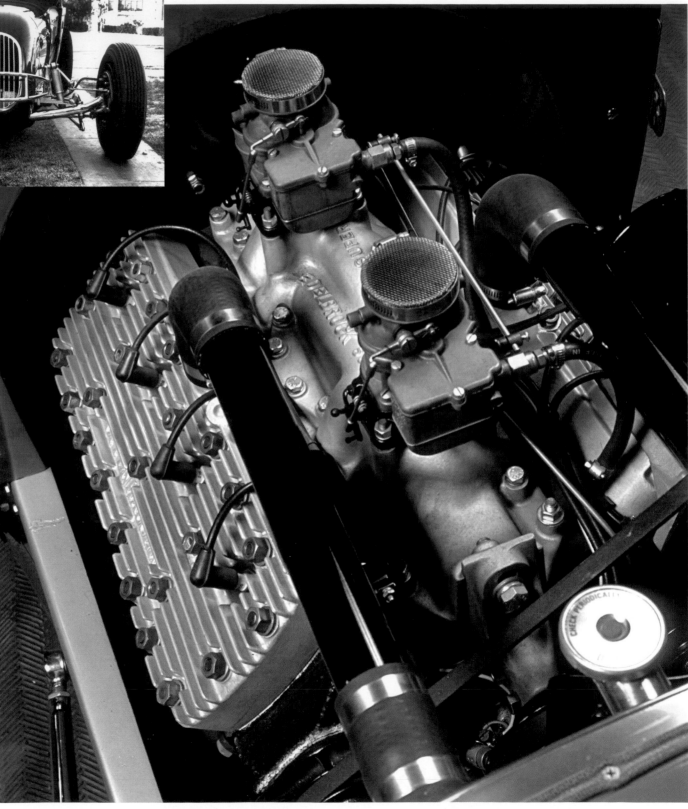

personal collection. It's usually on display in the Bruce Meyer Gallery for all to admire. "I had owned it for 30 years," Jake says, "I didn't drive it anymore, so it was time for me to move on, and for the car to become a museum piece for others to admire. I didn't want it to be some rich guy's trophy."

Long before most hot rodders began seriously reshaping their cars and finishing them to unheard-of levels, Bill Niekamp's lovely roadster set a precedent. Its track-nosed, altered and channeled Model A body, full belly pan and soon-to-be-proven dry lakes prowess helped make it the first Oakland winner, set high standards, and provided the inspiration for many significant early rods, in particular the Eddie Dye and Dick Flint roadsters. Elegance, simplicity, clean design, and functionality, with a minimum of plating, were its hallmarks –– and they still are.

Former owner, Jim Jacobs, described driving the Niekamp '29 in *Street Rod Quarterly*, in the Winter 1971 issue.

"The Niekamp car is like no other I have ever had the pleasure to ride in… It is a street machine, an all-out racecar, and a go-kart all in one. With its smooth nose cutting through the wind like a hot knife, the 'panned roadster body accelerates from 65 to 90 mph and above in a matter of seconds…hang it in the sharpest curve at any speed with total control…like a sprint car, you can throw its weight into a corner, then ride the throttle to the very limit of traction…

"Driving the Niekamp is an experience I relish quite frequently and mostly late at night… Rolling this low-slung machine from the garage, I find myself hurtling down the empty Long Beach freeway before the flathead's water has time to warm. One mile down, you exit to the right, then make a hard left as the roadster streaks up and across a high-banked two-lane overpass…controlled with steering and throttle, the car whirls you through the tight curve like it's on rails. Then it starts to drift; the body remains flat giving you no warning, but the tires make a ripping sound as they slide sideways across the asphalt. You correct, only for a moment though, getting a fresh bite on the road…you're in the front seat of a roller coaster doing 75 mph off the ramp as you swing right and down onto the Artesia freeway, taking three of its four lanes to pull out.

"By this time, the water temp is up and my head is taching 5,000 rpm. Every part of the car has become a nerve. I feel the road's very surface. The churning quick-change rings in my ears sending harmonic vibration through my entire soul. I am united with the machine as the dark sleeping world passes by. It's a trip, that's what it is…an honest-to-goodness trip."

No one could say it better. Jake owned the Niekamp car for nearly 30 years. He had the foresight to seek it out, restore it accurately, and preserve it for posterity. Those of us who love historic hot rods owe Jim Jacobs a great deal of gratitude.

Horizontal Plymouth tail-lights, pipes through the rear panel, and beautifully formed nerf bars are distinctive elements that contributed to the Niekamp '29's first Oakland win.

With its louvered hood, smooth track nose, and tubular front axle, this car would look right at home at a show today – particularly with the return to nostalgia.

(3)

The McGee '32 featured hidden door hinges, a filled cowl vent, a three-piece hood, with a clever latching system that eschewed external "lunch box" latches. Its neat internal latching system anticipated the kits sold by suppliers like Dan Fink today. Other notable items included a custom-fabricated dash, a complete folding top, an unusual deck lid treatment (that was, to my knowledge, never imitated), and (we believe) this was probably the first use of round '46 Pontiac taillights on a '32 roadster.

Red and righteous, this roadster really set the style. Bob McGee's stunning '32 Ford roadster graced the cover of the tenth issue of *Hot Rod* magazine way back in October 1948. Bob Petersen himself (aka Photos by Pete) took the action cover shot of the roadster tooling around the USC campus, where McGee was a student and a member of the vaunted football squad. The two-page story debuted talented Rex Burnett's first cutaway drawing for the magazine. Somewhat prophetically, it began: "with the growing demand for smart street roadsters, Bob McGee's car should serve as a model to hot rod builders."

It was certainly true. McGee's car set a very high standard for the period, thanks to its raked stance, contemporary body and frame modifications, as well as its high degree of fit and finish. This deuce was already 16 years old in 1948, but McGee's "improvements" made it a more contemporary vehicle, despite a few unusual exceptions that we'll discuss.

Remember, this was the era when functionality was the norm

for most roadsters, especially in California. A guy wanted his rod to look cool, but performance at the lakes on weekends was the key criterion. Paint was often the last thing considered. Except for a few engine accessories, and in rare cases, a plated front axle or suspension, most cars were pretty basic.

McGee took a different tack, one that would soon be repeated by many car owners who sought coverage in the emerging rodding magazines. He carefully planned all the elements of his roadster's presentation, and employed two of the best metal craftsmen of his day, Jimmy Summers (Hollywood) and Whitey Clayton (Bellflower), to execute his ideas. McGee's roadster was one of the first cars to feature a filled and peaked front spreader bar, and the frame horns were shortened for a neater appearance. To be fair, the late Hank Negley may have beaten Bob to the punch on this feature, but Negley's lakes-racing '32 never received the acclaim Bob's roadster did.

The McGee '32 also featured hidden door hinges, a filled cowl vent, and a three-piece hood with a clever latching system that

Bob McGee's '32 Roadster

eschewed external "lunch box" latches, which anticipated the latch kits sold by suppliers like Dan Fink today. Other notable items included a custom-fabricated dash, a complete folding top, an unusual deck lid treatment (which was, to my knowledge, never imitated), and (we believe) this was probably the first use of round, '46 Pontiac taillights on a '32 roadster.

The story of how this car came to be is an interesting one. *Hot Rod* reported that Bob built his first '32 roadster in 1940, as a member of the *Gear Grinders* car club. He apparently ran at the lakes in this car in 1941. Then, like so many young men of his generation, Bob McGee was off to war. He served three years in the Pacific theater, winding up his military service as an M.P. in the Philippines. While he was away, he entrusted the roadster to his friend, Bob Binyon. Unfortunately, while driving home one night from a *Gear Grinders* beach party, Binyon fell asleep, went off the road, and wrecked McGee's '32 in an orange grove.

Good friend that he was, and probably as much out of guilt as obligation, Bob Binyon began gathering the necessary parts so that McGee could build another '32 roadster. He apparently bought a roadster body from Pico Auto salvage for just $10. By the time McGee was discharged in 1946, Bob Binyon had collected many of the pieces needed for his friend's "new" car.

McGee was well entrenched in the growing hot rod culture. He was pals with rodders/racers Jack McGrath and Manuel Ayulo, two talented stalwarts in the CRA (California Racing Association). He was soon back on the road in a '32 cabriolet that was a loaner from a buddy named Harry Ringer, but he was anxious to have his own wheels once again. He began in earnest in May 1947, with a number of modifications that crossed the line between customs and hot rods. By doing so, he set precedents that we're all still following. When you look at his completed roadster, it's evident that McGee evaluated every area of the car and made decisions to change things if he felt the Ford's stock elements could be simplified or improved.

Fortunately, Bob compiled a detailed record, complete with

Hot rod clubs from all over Los Angeles gathered in September 1948 at the Maywood Lincoln-Mercury plant for the famous National Safety Council "Green Cross for Safety" NSC/SCTA oath-taking. Bob McGee's picture-perfect, bright red '32 became the poster child, and it received the first green cross windshield decal. Bob was also a member of the Gear Grinders club. Note Doane Spencer's '32 in the background.
(Don Cox)

Although he didn't run a generator originally (the Federal-Mogul heads didn't require water pumps so there was no fan or fan belt either), McGee drove his car extensively. Reportedly, he kept a spare battery fully charged at all times, and swapped batteries as needed. This snug top was also a model for others. In the era when these were street cars as well as lakes racers, many roadster jockeys had top and side windows – and they were used on chilly LA nights.
(Bruce Meyer Collection)

photographs, of the work done on his car. I had a chance to see that book when the restorers, Pete Chapouris and his associates from the So-Cal Speed Shop, presented the completed car in 1999 at the Oakland Grand National Roadster Show. McGee began by filling extraneous frame holes, boxing the front section of the frame, bobbing the front frame horns, and completing the smooth look with a filled and peaked spreader bar.

He decided he did not want to imitate the raked appearance of many contemporary roadsters. He installed one of Ed Stewart's dropped and stretched front axles, reversed the front spring eyes, and put then-fashionable 5.00 x 16-inch ribbed Firestones on '40 Ford V-8/60 wheels for an additional drop. Next, he Z-ed the rear section of the frame, added a Model A crossmember, and reversed the rear spring eyes to get the car down fashionably in back. While not as low as a typical channeled '32, the McGee car sits well down, with its rear 7.00 x 16s (on wide-base Lincoln-Zephyr rims) neatly filling the wheel wells.

The front shocks were modern chromed Gabriel tubular units; in the rear, McGee retained Ford 50/50 Houdaille lever arm shocks. The '40 Ford hydraulic brakes were installed in place of the original "push-and-pray" mechanicals favored by Henry Ford. The hubcaps (some sources say Mercury, but I believe they're '46-'48-style Ford) had the logos hammered out for a clean appearance, and were re-polished. The tie rod and pitman arm were chrome plated, the brake drums were cadmium plated, and the axle and other running gear was painted Ford black.

The '32 roadster body was modified by shaving the stock external hinges and replacing them with hidden hinges using reworked units from a '40 Studebaker Champion. McGee, who unfortunately died in 1998, before the car's restoration was completed, talked with So-Cal's Tony Thacker who wrote that, "...to Bob's knowledge, this was the first roadster to ever have the hidden hinge treatment."

McGee also told Thacker, "One inherent problem with the '32 roadster body is the cracking out of the lower rear panel's (the panel just above the gas tank) vertical seams." He elected to eliminate that panel and have California Metal Shaping hammer up a full-length deck lid that ended at the roadster's lower rear body reveal. The deck is opened via a cable release, with the knob behind the seat. The resulting deck has a neat, very functional look, especially with the license plate centered between round Pontiac lights. I'm surprised no one ever imitated this feature.

Next, McGee turned his attention to the grille and hood. The stock radiator cap was removed and the grille was filled and peaked. A new three-piece hood was fabricated from aluminum, probably by Whitey Clayton (although there's no record of who did it), whose talents in aluminum were

exhibited on cars like the Eddie Dye and Harold Osgood roadsters, to name a few. The hood received three rows of louvers on the top section, and two rows on each side panel. Sans the obligatory stock latches, or "lunch box" units that were popular in the early years, the hood area is clean, with an all-of-a-piece look that echoes the theme of the car.

Jimmy Summers filled the cowl and hammered out miscellaneous dings and dents. Then the car was painted with a custom red lacquer mix sprayed by Bill Colvig. The wheels were also painted red for a unified appearance. The original headlight bar was cut apart to make individual headlight stands. The windshield was chopped (some sources say 1-1/2 inches, but it looks closer to 2 inches to me), and Glenn Houser's famed Carson Top Shop, at 4910 South Vermont Ave., in Los Angeles, fabricated a beautiful light tan canvas top for the car, along with side curtains and a zippered tonneau cover. Complementary brown leather upholstery was created and installed by McGee's friend, George Fabry.

Apparently, Bob McGee was enamored with the fabulous Miller-Ford front-drive racing cars of 1935. He commissioned Whitey Clayton to fabricate a dash panel that was similar to the ones done for the Miller racers. It flows down to enclose the steering column, then sweeps gracefully to the right. The lower edge of the panel incorporates what has been referred to as an "Auburn roll," but I've been unable to substantiate that reference. Possibly, it refers to a lower reveal, but the McGee/Clayton panel is straight on the bottom. The panel incorporates a hand pump that could pressurize the stock fuel tank and/or an auxiliary fuel tank (for alcohol or other fuel) mounted in the trunk.

McGee cleverly hid a radio on the reverse side of the dash and mounted the antenna on a panel behind the cockpit. That unique instrument panel was painted a medium shade of maroon, possibly Ford Dynamic Maroon, a popular postwar hue. In it, there are four instruments: three of them period 2-5/8-inch, flat-bezel, curved-glass Stewart-Warners, along with a large tachometer. No speedometer appears to have been fitted. The art-deco '40 Ford steering wheel, steering column, and column shifter are all painted red. This car pleases the eye with its cool understatement – unlike so many rods that try to overwhelm the viewer with flames, plating, and busy external details.

The really remarkable thing about Bob McGee's car is that it was started in January 1947 and completed in September of that year. Like many returning vets, Bob took advantage of the GI Bill to attend USC, and the car had to be done so he could drive it to school. To save time, McGee elected to use the engine from his wrecked roadster while he built up another engine. According to the *Hot Rod* article, it was a 21-stud '34 flathead block, bored (probably about .060 inch), taking it from 221 ci to 237 ci. The camshaft was originally a Winfield, but McGee, who liked to be different,

In the early 1960s, Dick Scritchfield updated the car with an early metal flake paint job, pearl white leatherette interior, chrome slot wheels, and some pinstriping by Andy Southard, shown here laying down a beltline stripe. Visible here is one of the roadster's most distinctive features – the extended deck lid that replaced the stock rear panel. (Bruce Meyer Collection)

In the early 1970s, Scritchfield took the roadster Bonneville racing with a Chevy 350 for power. Its best performance came in 1971, where it set a C/Street Roadster record of 167.212 mph – a record that stood until 1979. (Bruce Meyer Collection)

In the late 1990s, Bruce Meyer bought the now-black roadster and took it to the So-Cal Speed Shop for restoration. Despite its many years in Scritchfield's hands, it was decided to restore the car to its early 1950s McGee status. Here, Bob McGee (behind the wheel, of course) checks out the restoration work. That's Wally Parks in the passenger seat, and Alex Xydias and Bruce Meyer standing. Sadly, McGee passed away before the car was finished. (Bruce Meyer Collection)

Here's a rare photo of two hot rod veterans under restoration – the McGee roadster on the right, and the Doane Spencer car on the left (with the slick steel hardtop installed) at the So-Cal shop. It's interesting to note how different these cars are, despite the obvious similarities. (Steve Coonan photo, courtesy Bruce Meyer)

This was the era when functionality was the norm for most roadsters, especially in California. A guy wanted his rod to look cool, but its performance at the lakes on weekends was the key criterion. Paint was often the last thing considered. Although a few engine accessories and, in rare cases, a front axle and some suspension parts, might have been plated, most cars were pretty basic.

installed a Pierre "Pete" Bertrand grind with a nasty lope. Bertrand, who ground cams for Karl Orr and many others, was one of hot rodding's early camshaft geniuses, ranked right along with Ed Winfield. Reportedly, Clay Smith, a legendary cam grinder in his own right, told Bob McGee that Pete Bertrand had taught him a great deal.

The engine itself was a study in "dare to be different." Those unusual, finned, solid copper heads were rare Federal-Mogul items. They did not incorporate water jackets, but instead worked on the thermosyphon principle (like a Model T!), so atmospheric pressure moved the coolant (there were no water pumps!). The water was nominally cooled in the radiator; the copper heads supposedly dissipated some heat (they turn almost purple when the engine has been running), but how well this all worked is conjecture. It was probably fine at the lakes for short periods. Fortunately in the late 1940s, traffic as we know it today in Los Angeles was not yet a problem. McGee did not fit a generator either, since there was no fan belt. He reportedly

brought along a spare battery, so that when the battery in the car ran down, he could swap a freshly charged unit.

When Pete Chapouris was preparing this roadster for the Pebble Beach Concours d'Elegance in 1999, we had a conversation about the rules. As a result, Pete decided to use a more practical '37 Ford block, fitted with water pumps, a fan belt, and a generator. The Concours regulations clearly specify that selected mechanical updates, if they were possible in the period that the car was built, and if they are done with period pieces, may be fitted at the judges' discretion. This engine and its accessories made the roadster far more practical to drive.

The original engine benefited from a Filcoolator finned oil filter, popularly known as a "Beehive," on the firewall. The ignition system was a converted dual-point distributor, topped with an integral dual coil. It originated in a Lincoln-Zephyr V-12 and had been modified by the Spaulding brothers for a Ford V-8 application. Induction was handled by a Burns dual manifold, topped with twin Stromberg 97s, and "baloney-sliced" racing stacks. Flowing exhaust headers (closely resembling Clark catalog items) led to capped lakes pipes under the car, then split off through mufflers to twin shortened tailpipes.

Bob completed his car with a Lincoln-Zephyr 26-tooth close-ratio gear set. Tony Thacker stated that Bob learned about the Zephyr units from racers Vern Houle and Jack Henry, and that McGee believed he was the first to install the Zephyrs, which permitted longer runs in first and second, in a street roadster. We can't confirm whether it's true he was first, but there are so many trend-setting facets of this fine roadster, it's almost as though McGee had a glimpse into the future.

Like many of his fellow hot rodders, McGee ran the occasional street race, but he also resumed lakes racing. As his roadster's dash-mounted SCTA timing tag states, McGee ran a respectable (for a small-displacement flathead) 112.21 mph at Harpers dry lake in July 1947. As mentioned above, McGee planned to build a new engine for the car, but this doesn't seem to have happened during his ownership.

Perhaps the roadster's finest hour (besides the *Hot Rod* cover) came earlier in September 1948. It's well documented that 30 SCTA associate clubs met at the Lincoln Mercury plant in Maywood, California, to take the National Safety Council's Safety Pledge. McGee's '32 was chosen from the assembled cars as the NSC's symbolic hot rod, and Ak Miller (looking a lot like Humphrey Bogart in old photographs of the event), placed a "Green Cross for Safety" NSC sticker on Bob's windshield. Thanks to its neat appearance, and no doubt helped by its bright red finish, the McGee car was chosen for this honor over some very impressive iron assembled that day, including Doane Spencer's '32.

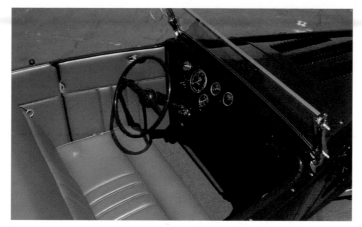

Jimmy Summers filled the cowl and hammered out odd dings and dents. Bill Colvig painted the car with a custom red lacquer mix. The wheels were also painted red, for a more unified appearance. The original headlight bar was cut apart to make individual headlight stands. The windshield was chopped – some sources say 1.5 inches, but it looks closer to 2 inches to me. Glenn Houser's famed Carson Top Shop, at 4910 South Vermont Ave., in Los Angeles, fabricated a beautiful light tan canvas top for the car, along with side curtains and a zippered tonneau cover. Complimentary brown leather upholstery was originally created and installed by McGee's friend, George Fabry.

Bob McGee's roadster was his daily driver until 1952. It was driven occasionally for two more years, and then stored at his parents' home in Huntington Park, California. He sold the car in 1955 to Dick Hirschberg of Hollywood. The new owner installed a Corvette engine the following year, built external lakes-type headers for it that were fashioned from '36 Ford driveshafts, and painted the roadster a bright yellow. But he wasn't destined to have the car for very long….

Dick Scritchfield was one of the founders of the Los Angeles Roadster Club, along with Tony La Masa and Leroi "Tex" Smith, and he was one of the first NHRA regional advisors. He spotted the '32 in a service station, and soon traded his OHV Cadillac-powered '48 Lincoln Continental for it, straight up.

Scritchfield drove the roadster extensively. At first he didn't make many changes, and of all things, the car was paying for itself. Sensational "B" movies with a hot rod or custom car theme had become popular, and Scritchfield made his roadster available to the movie studios. It appeared in films like *Hot Rod Gang* in 1957, as well as in TV shows like *Dobie Gillis*, *Dragnet*, *77 Sunset Strip*, *The Lawrence Welk Show*, and then in *Happy Days* and *Fantasy Island*. Later film appearances included *Love in a Goldfish Bowl* in 1960, *The Hollywood Knights*, and *Hometown USA*, to name just a few.

Scritchfield's roadster subtly achieved quite a bit of notoriety. It was the subject of a *Car Craft* magazine feature after Dean Jeffries applied one of the first metal flake paint jobs. Eddie Martinez redid the interior in pearl white leatherette. The *LA Roadsters* used its classic silhouette, complete with lakes pipes, for their club logo, and it still appears on the dash plaques they distribute each year at Father's Day.

Scritchfield, by now, was working for Petersen Publishing, starting at *Car Craft* as an associate editor, then moving to *Rod & Custom* as ad manager. Since he was an R&C staffer, more power was in order for the '32. A stout 1969 350-ci small-block, built by Dave Carpenter, was installed. The intake was a then-fashionable Weiand tunnel ram with twin

The front shocks were modern chromed Gabriel tubular units; in the rear, McGee retained Ford 50/50 Houdaille lever arm shocks. The original "push-and-pray" mechanical brakes favored by Henry Ford were replaced by some '40 Ford hydraulics for better braking. The hubcaps (some sources say Mercury, but I believe they are '46-48-style Ford) had the logo hammered out for a clean appearance and were re-plated. The tie rod and pitman arm were chrome plated, the brake drums were cadmium plated, and the axle and other running gear was painted Ford black.

4-bbl Holleys, and Mallory supplied the ignition system. The lake pipes ran through the louvered hood sides, and then split off to run through mufflers under the car. Twin tailpipes paralleled the frame horns. A new Warner T-10 transmission was fitted, and a Halibrand quick-change rear end replaced the old Ford banjo. The roadster was repainted black with white pinstriped accents, and alloy wheels with non-functional knock-offs replaced the venerable steelies.

Scritchfield brought the '32 to Bonneville in 1970 and topped 165 mph in the C/Street Roadster Class; a remarkable speed for what was basically a street-driven roadster with "barn-door" aerodynamics. Scritchfield returned to the salt the following year with Greg Sharp, made a best one-way run of 168.067 mph, and backed it up with an impressive 167.212-mph average, a record that remained until 1979. A quarter-mile run at Orange County International Raceway resulted in a 13.9-second e.t. The '32 now had the punch to underscore its traditional good looks. A tubular Bell axle and Airheart disc brakes replaced the older equipment, as did updated Stewart-Warner gauges, and a Grant steering wheel hooked to a '56 Ford pickup steering box. Like many hot rods, this car was steadily upgraded over time, but its original guise was largely preserved.

After owning it for over 33 years, Dick Scritchfield moved to Hawaii in 1989, and the car was sold to Brian LaBonge, a nephew of rodding legends Ray Brock and Don Francisco. LaBonge made very few changes in the car before selling it to Arizona collector, Bob Everts, who in turn sold the car to Bruce Meyer. Meyer kept the roadster as he had acquired it for several years, and then decided to have it restored in time for the second hot rod class at the Pebble Beach Concours d'Elegance in 1999.

"It was always my idea to return the car to its original form," says Bruce, "but it wasn't an easy decision. Scritchfield had that car a long time; it was the fastest street roadster for a long while." Recalling the fine work they had done with the So-Cal Belly Tank, the Doane Spencer '32 roadster, and the Pierson Brothers' '34 coupe, Bruce entrusted the roadster to Pete Chapouris and his talented crew. The decision was made to restore the car to match its appearance on the cover of *Hot Rod* in 1948, thus erasing all traces of the '32 in its various Dick Scritchfield iterations. Scritchfield was understandably not pleased, but as a historian, I can only applaud the decision.

The So-Cal Speed Shop completely disassembled the car. I visited while it was apart and noted that the welds on the

"Flathead Mike" Gilbert built the new engine after a priceless set of Federal-Mogul heads and a correct Burns dual manifold were located. He also rebuilt the early Ford transmission. Tim Beard is credited with the lustrous red finish. Baker Paint in El Monte, California, carefully matched the PPG paint to the original color. Expert trimmer, Tom Sewell, recreated the brown leather upholstery and the padded top, again drawing on Bob McGee's meticulous records to ensure accuracy.

The So-Cal crew was very careful not to over-restore this car, which was originally done to a high standard. They brought it back to that level, but they avoided any temptation to add plating or other geegaws that weren't original. Bruce debuted the freshly redone '32 at the 50th Anniversary Grand National Roadster Show at the Cow Palace in San Francisco in January 1999. It received a great deal of respect and acclaim. In August of that year, Pebble Beach had nine restored hot rods competing for three awards. It all came down to two cars, Meyer's ex-McGee roadster and the former Dick Flint '29 on '32 rails, owned and restored by Don Orosco. The Flint car won first place, as well as the Dean Batchelor Memorial Trophy, by the narrowest of margins. Both cars were exceptionally well restored, but the judges felt the channeled Flint '29 held a minute edge in styling, technical achievement, and historical significance. Still, it was very, very close.

The McGee roadster remains a tribute to the collective abilities of Bruce Meyer and Pete Chapouris to locate, research, and restore a vintage hot rod to the highest standard, yet preserve it as it was first built. Bruce Meyer has an extensive collection of hot rod "drivers," so the McGee roadster spends most of its time on display at the Petersen Automotive Museum in Los Angeles. It's well worth studying. Over 55 years ago, Bob McGee showed us the definitive deuce roadster. Owners of the best "retro" rods today owe his memory a sincere tip of the cap.

The original engine was a study in "dare to be different." Those unusual, finned, solid copper heads were rare Federal-Mogul items. They did not incorporate water jackets, but instead worked on the thermosyphon principle (like a Model T). Since atmospheric pressure moved the coolant, there were no water pumps fitted while McGee ran the car. The water was nominally cooled in the radiator, and the copper heads supposedly dissipated some heat (they turn almost purple when the engine has been running). How well this all worked is conjecture; it was probably fine at the lakes for short periods. Fortunately in the late 1940s, traffic as we know it today in Los Angeles was not yet a problem. Note the polished Filcoolater A-4 finned accessory oil cooler mounted on the firewall.

Z-ed section of the frame seemed pretty crude. I asked Jim "Jake" Jacobs, who was working there at the time, if they were going to redo the frame. "Nope," he said, "It was good enough to run Bonneville at 168 miles per hour, so it'll stay the way it is." Pete Eastwood, Bill "Birdman" Stewart, and Rick LeFever are just a few of the many talented guys who brought the McGee car back.

"I wanted to find Bob McGee," Bruce commented, "but I thought he'd passed away. After letting people know we were going to restore the car, I was able to get his son on the phone, and I was surprised when he said, 'Do you want to talk to my Dad?' We had a great conversation. Bob was surprised to learn that the car had survived. It was like he was born again. His records, his old pictures – he even had the original pink slip – and his sharp memory were a big help, and he visited So-Cal's shop several times to watch the restoration. He couldn't thank all of us enough." Sadly, McGee died before the work was completed. "It would have been so great to have had him at Pebble Beach with the car," Bruce commented.

Bob McGee was enamored with the fabulous Miller-Ford front-drive racing cars of 1935. He commissioned Whitey Clayton to fabricate a dash panel that was similar to the ones in the Miller racers. It flows down to enclose the steering column, then sweeps gracefully to the right. The lower edge of the panel incorporates what has been referred to as an "Auburn roll," but I've been unable to substantiate that reference. The panel incorporates a pressure pump for the stock fuel tank and/or an auxiliary fuel tank (for alcohol or other fuel) mounted in the trunk.

Here's the shot of Joe Nitti's roadster you didn't see in Hot Rod *in 1950. Crack lensman Tom Medley was restricted to black and white in those days. The June 1950* Hot Rod *magazine article was called "Deep Purple '32." Now you can see why.*

This is one very cool ride from East LA. If you know vintage hot rods, you'll recall a special picture taken by Tom Medley in the June 1950 issue of *Hot Rod*. Over half a century ago, this feature shot of a '32 highboy roadster, with its owner behind the wheel, is an enduring classic. Medley's photos were black and white, so you can only imagine this deuce's nearly iridescent purple paint, glowing brightly above its wide whitewall tires, reflecting the chromed lakes header that runs under the frame to the midpoint of the driver's door.

There's a racing tarp over the passenger compartment, and the windshield and headlights are removed. But you can clearly make out the driver, a dark-haired kid with pursed lips and wraparound hair with a hint of a curl in front. He was copping an attitude decades before the expression became popular. His name was Joe Nitti, and he was a member of the *Vultures* of East Los Angeles, an active dry lakes racing hot rod club that was affiliated with the Russetta Timing Association.

Standing alongside the roadster, wearing cuffed jeans and a World War II-style leather "bomber" jacket with a fur collar, holding a Cromwell type cork racing helmet, is another young man, who we now know is Dave Gillette. The main photograph has been neatly outlined, so it looks as though it could have been shot up at the dry lakes. In point of fact, and all credit here to Pat Ganahl's research, he believes it was taken in a driveway at 420 South Lorraine, in LA's fashionable Hancock Park section. The article headline reads, "Deep Purple '32," and it should have been a color cover, but *Hot Rod* wouldn't have those until April 1951.

Nitti's roadster epitomized the best street and lakes practice of its era. Although the "dry lakes" photo was faked a bit in terms of its location, this car was the real deal. It was the quintessential deuce highboy — with a super straight roadster body. A dropped axle (that appears to be a Mor-Drop) and big-and-little whitewalls gave it an insolent tilt. In a concession to the relentless cops of that era, the yellow 1949-50 California license tag was affixed to the grille bars,

Joe Nitti's '32 Roadster

which were left painted in stock '32 Ford French Gray. While this roadster's high-mounted accessory headlamps (visible in other photos) are unfashionably (but then legally required) tall, the rest of its proportions are perfect.

As a quick aside, California had strict rules about headlamp height in the late 1940s and early 1950s. They had to be at least 28 inches above the pavement. This was later changed to 24 inches in the mid 1950s to accommodate low-lit cars like VW Beetles. Hot rodders of the period insist that cruel rule just gave the cops an excuse to stop them, as if loud mufflers weren't enough. Earlier photos of this car from the Nitti family show it with headlights mounted low on individual chromed stands, a polished stainless grille shell surround, and a neatly fitted white top. Joe drove his roadster to work, so there was no point in being stopped every day for an annoying but easily preventable light violation.

Other bodywork included filled door hinges, a rare modification in this era. Bob McGee pioneered them (see Chapter 3) back in 1948. The Nitti roadster had a liberally louvered four-piece hood, and a peaked and filled '32 grille shell. A chrome-plated front spreader bar – built by rodding great Hank Negley (his name is engraved on it) – tied together the boxed, filled, and rounded front frame horns. In the rear, the trunk handle was shaved, and there were widely spaced '39 Ford teardrop taillights, along with a custom license plate light made from a cut-down 1940s-era stock Ford unit. The rear spreader bar was plated, as well. Twin exhaust pipes ran neatly parallel to the rear frame rails, in proper roadster practice. The right side tailpipe is missing in some photographs (but it's clearly visible in an earlier shot taken at the lakes). We know now that prior to Medley's shoot, Joe backed into something and lost a foot or so of tailpipe. It was repaired after Tom's photos were taken.

Nitti's chroming bill must have been extensive. In addition to the headlamp bracketry, there are plated shocks – tubular, aircraft-style Gabriels in front and '41 Ford, lever-actuated 50/50 Houdailles in back – along with chromed radius rods, the aforementioned long lakes pipes made from '36 Ford driveshafts, the hood catches, and the front axle and spring. We'll learn very shortly why that didn't matter. The Ford

steel wheels mounted 6.00 x 16-inch front tires and what are probably 7.00 x 16-inch rears, with baby moon hubcaps. Interestingly, if you look closely, the whitewalls on the front tires are painted on – common in the 1950s.

Under the hood was a pretty hot '46 59A Mercury flathead with what's described in the old *HR* article as a "3/8" bore" (probably 3-3/8 inch), equipped with JE pistons and a stock stroke for 268 ci. Respected speed equipment manufacturer Earl "Pappy" Evans supplied the finned aluminum high-compression heads, a dual manifold, and a high-performance ignition system. The racing camshaft was a Weber, probably a 3/4-grind. Tubular headers from Sonny's Muffler Shop and the small air cleaners also received the chrome treatment, as did the generator and regulator covers, the upper radiator hoses, and a myriad of under hood nuts and bolts.

An Evans three-carb manifold was substituted when Nitti went lakes racing, which he did several times. By the standards of the day, this painted and plated roadster was a sanitary, relatively high-buck car. Fortunately for Nitti, he had two key sponsors – Earl Evans (for the speed equipment) and East LA's House of Chrome. Despite its fine finish, and all that chrome, this roadster was a runner. Early pictures taken at El Mirage show Joe's roadster (with solid hood top and sides, outside door hinges, and a trunk handle) with "Evans Special" painted on the cowl side, along with the

Here's Joe Nitti (standing) flexing his muscles, as his sister (behind wheel), and mother (holding door open) smile for the camera. Joe's ultra-sharp roadster won its share of awards, as can be seen from the trophy display. According to Pat Ganahl, who extensively researched the Nitti car, this picture was taken in 1950 in front of the Nitti home at 3036 Malabar, Los Angeles. The car appears hoodless here, with Joe's Evans triple manifold installed. He raced the car with the three-carb unit and used an Evans dual manifold on the street. (David Zivot Collection)

Joe Nitti fakes an adjustment on his roadster's Earl Evans-equipped flathead. I love this photograph. Nitti's slicked-back D.A. haircut and Vultures hot rod club jacket are classic. He was copping an attitude decades before the expression became popular. The Vultures of East Los Angeles were an active dry lakes racing hot rod club that was affiliated with the Russetta Timing Association. Joe drove his car on the street and occasionally took it up to the lakes. (Mark Mountanos Collection)

With his car stripped and the tonneau installed, a helmeted Joe Nitti is ready for a fast run at El Mirage in 1948. Note that the hood top and sides have not yet been louvered, the door hinges aren't hidden, and the lakes header pipes are not chromed. Those mods came later. The full hubcaps on the front were not used on the street and may have been an attempt at streamlining. David Zivot believes the roadster was black (possibly in primer?) when this shot was taken. (David Zivot Collection)

Lookin' cool, Joe Nitti poses with his '32 roadster in 1950, well on the way to completion. The door hinges are filled, and the hood sides are louvered, but the exhaust system and this early version of the headlight stands are not yet plated. We think the car is purple here, although the paint isn't completely rubbed out. Hubcaps are '46-'48 Ford – they were later replaced by "baby moons" in scriptless '40 Ford style. In the early days, guys worked on their cars at night and on the weekend, and drove them during the week, whether they were completed or not. (David Zivot Collection)

numbers 188-A on the doors. Running as the *Sunset Special*, number 394-A, in later pictures, the hood louvers are evident, as is a *Vultures Club* plaque on the rear spreader bar.

Inside, Nitti's car was a mix of both popular and unusual rodding styles. The steering wheel was the popular art-deco '40 Ford. Like so many of his fellow rodders in that era, Joe opted for "modern" column shift linkage for his '41 Lincoln-Zephyr transmission. The rear end came from a '41 Ford, and it carried a '32 Ford spring with reversed eyes and '40 Ford hydraulic brakes. The rolled and pleated seating was made of ivory leatherette (called "plastic" in the first *HR* feature).

Instrumentation was a high point of this roadster. Nitti installed twin functional accessory dash panels, one on each side of the modified '30 Ford dash, flanking a '48 Ford radio with a signal-seeking selector bar and a chromed cover plate. The effect was unusual, to say the least, and I can't recall anyone copying it. There's also a pressure pump on the driver's side. The radio antenna was located in front of the deck lid, just behind the seat. As noted, Nitti frequently drove his car to work at a parking lot he operated in downtown Los Angeles. *Hot Rod*'s feature writer wrote: (it) "…creates an impressive picture in city traffic and at the dry lake meets in which it is run."

For young guys reading *Hot Rod* magazine, the Nitti '32 was an object lesson in building a dual-purpose street and lakes roadster. It was beautifully finished and trimmed, its panels were stick-straight, and the proportions were true. Even in black and white photos, it made a lasting impression on all who saw it. The car's whereabouts in Los Angeles were well known from 1948 through 1951 or 1952, but then it disappeared.

Then it disappeared…but not for all time, as we'll see.

Pat Ganahl wrote a definitive story on the Nitti '32 for *The Rodder's Journal*, prior to its restoration. With all credit to Pat, who says he tracked this car for six years, I'll summarize its history as Pat described it, with annotations from David Zivot, the Las Vegas hot rodder (who tracked it even longer), and who subsequently found this lost relic.

It's believed that the Nitti car first took shape in East Los

Angeles some time around 1947, when Jack Mickelson, a '32 roadster owner and dry lakes racer, sold a '32 frame to his friend, Joe Nitti. Jack had apparently bought the NOS rails from a Ford dealer before the war. We're not sure where Nitti acquired his deuce roadster body, but they were certainly more plentiful in 1947 than they are today.

We think Nitti did much of the assembly work himself, although Nelson "Nellie" Taylor and John Ryan, two Evans shop stalwarts who built competition engines and also raced their own roadsters at the dry lakes, may have built the engine. Early speculation suggested that the Daleo brothers, Jim and Joe (they founded the *Vultures Club* and operated a garage located behind a Chevron station in LA's City Terrace neighborhood), may have helped with mechanical work, and might have even painted Nitti's car. But Ganahl found people who didn't think the Daleos were capable of that high a painting standard.

Pat further speculates that Gil and Al Ayala, whose shop in East Los Angeles turned out several great customs (the Wally Welch Mercury, for example), and who worked on the beautiful Eddie Dye roadster, probably painted Joe's car, at least one of the two times it was sprayed. Sadly, with the Ayalas gone, we have no way of proving that rather likely hypothesis. Joe's sister told David Zivot that she thought the Ayalas were responsible. But when you consider how well this car was done, it's plausible that Nitti would have taken it to the most talented refinishers/customizers in East LA. In that era, that meant the Ayala brothers.

Speaking of paint, several articles have speculated that Nitti was inspired by the purple and cream color scheme of Union 76 Royal Triton, a purple-dyed motor oil that enjoyed some notoriety in the 1950s. However, Zivot says he brought a clean sample of the color, taken from an extra wheel off the car, to ace refinisher, Stan Betz, whose keen eye noted that the deep purple paint more closely matched the oil itself, not the violet hue on the Royal Triton quart can. But we're getting ahead of our story.

Not surprisingly, Nitti won a number of awards with his car. The most important was probably a large trophy cup awarded for California's Most Beautiful Roadster, at the Los Angeles *Hot Rod* show in 1950. Although Ganahl's account in *The Rodder's Journal* discounts this trophy, and even hints that Nitti might have had it fabricated, David Zivot owns an actual photograph of Nitti's car at the show, pictured with the actual award. Other surviving photos of the roadster show a passel of trophies and attest to this car's winning ways.

As noted, Nitti drove, raced, and even commuted in his roadster. Zivot says that in 1951 or 1952, Joe had a tragic accident while driving his car. Sadly, a young boy on a bicycle was killed. Nitti reportedly served six months on an LA County work farm, and the presiding judge at his trial ordered him to get rid of the roadster. Instead of selling it outright, Nitti traded the car to Eddie Safire – a mechanic who worked at J.D. Coberly Lincoln-Mercury in downtown L.A – for a mildly customized 1950 Mercury Club Coupe. Surviving pictures from the Nitti family show Joe behind the Merc's wheel with the same "hood-y" expression that he sports in the earlier Medley roadster snaps.

Ganahl reports that Safire later sold the ex-Nitti roadster to Jack Sheldon, a salesman at J.D. Coberly. Leo Dempsey, one

of Safire's coworkers at Coberly's, didn't know why Jack Sheldon purchased the Nitti roadster because, in Dempsey's words to Pat, "he wasn't a roadster type." Sheldon let Dempsey drive the car at El Mirage, and a 1952 Russetta timing tag states that the Sheldon-Dempsey #348 B/Roadster turned 124.05 mph – a very creditable speed for a street car – on October 10, 1952. We're not certain when and to whom Jack Sheldon sold the Nitti roadster, but the next owner removed the flathead and sold the car to Eric Bodell, of the Sacramento area, who installed a Chevy V-8. Meanwhile, Joe Nitti moved to Las Vegas where he ran a Union 76 filling station and later drove a taxicab in that city's large fleet.

Sadly, Joe Nitti became a robbery victim while driving his taxi. Apparently, he died after being shot in the back of the head and robbed of a paltry $36. His son Roger, who also lives in Las Vegas, inherited a few photos of the roadster along with the *Vultures* felt patch from Joe's club jacket.

Joe ran a '46 59A Mercury flathead with a 3-3/8-inch bore, JE pistons, and a stock 3-3/4-inch stroke, for 268 ci. Earl "Pappy" Evans was his sponsor, supplying finned aluminum high-compression heads, an Evans dual manifold, and a high-performance ignition system. Evans also provided Joe with a triple manifold for racing. In return, Joe ran his car as the Evans Special, at the lakes. Weber supplied the racing cam, probably a 3/4 grind. The tubular headers (from Sonny's Muffler Shop), the small air cleaners, the generator and regulator covers, the oil breather cap, the upper radiator hose pipes, and most underhood nuts and bolts, were chromed. An enterprising Joe Nitti had convinced LA's House of Plating to swing for the chrome work. (David Zivot Collection)

Nitti's roadster epitomized the best street and lakes practice of its era. Although the original Hot Rod magazine "dry lakes" photo was faked in terms of its location, this car was the real deal. The quintessential '32 highboy, with a super straight roadster body, Nitti's purple chariot perched proudly atop a '32 Ford frame.

Roger wasn't born until after his dad sold the roadster, so he has no youthful memories of the car.

Now it's time we formally introduce David Zivot, a 30-something hot rod enthusiast who had been following the Nitti car's story since he was a kid. David's dad was a Las Vegas physician who bought gasoline at Joe Nitti's 76 station. David Zivot's daily driver is a chopped, full-fendered '32 Ford coupe, and he also owns a chopped '51 Merc, a '51 Ford Victoria, a '54 Olds, and a '41 Indian. Very interested in hot rod history, Zivot has a large collection of car club plaques, and he's been keen on hot rods since before he could legally drive. After his dad told David about Joe Nitti and his purple '32 Ford roadster, Zivot met and became friendly with Joe before his tragic death. At one point, Nitti even gave Zivot some old photos of his roadster along with a few trophies. And he said he had no idea what had become of his old car. Pat Ganahl notes that he looked for the Nitti '32 for some six years. As we'll see, David Zivot was even more persistent.

"I did some old-fashioned detective work," Zivot told me, "I even retained a private investigator. One call led to another. Finally, I found a truck driver who knew Nitti and Dempsey, and who had moved the car. After some more research and many more phone calls, I located Eric Bodell in Sacramento, and was able to get a photograph of an unrestored '32 Ford roadster that he owned."

One look and David Zivot knew he had found the Nitti car.

"It was definitely the worse for wear," Zivot told me. But he recognized the roadster's peaked spreader bar. "The dash was intact, but most of the gauges were missing," he says, "but the hidden hinges on the doors were evident. And the peaked grille was okay. But the headlight stand was gone. The hood top panels were in the trunk; the side panels were missing."

Zivot says Eric Bodell knew he had an old roadster, but he apparently did not know much about its history. And he didn't want to sell it. "One of these days," Bodell told David, "…he'd get around to restoring it."

Joe's roadster had filled door hinges, still rare for this time period, although the Bob McGee '32 (see Chapter 3) also had them. Louvered hood side panels were a big deal. No one repopped them 50 years ago – you had to make solid side panels, and then punch them.

Joe won a lot of show trophies with his roadster, which probably made his two sponsors, speed equipment manufacturer and tuner Earl Evans, and LA's House of Chrome, very happy.

"The car was stored indoors for many years," Zivot noted, "then it was moved outside, by the side of the garage and his wife's new Oldsmobile was moved inside." Sadly, the Nitti roadster languished under a tarpaulin alongside Bodell's garage for years.

Keeping the car's whereabouts to himself, and believing the owner would probably never restore it, David Zivot tried for seven years to get Bodell to sell him the car. "Finally," David said, "in 1999 he called me and said he wasn't going to get around to restoring the roadster. He wasn't a historian, so while he knew the car had value, he just didn't know what it was. Still, the price wasn't an extreme bargain. (Reportedly, Eric Bodell used the sale proceeds to buy a motor home.) But I knew I wanted it," Zivot says today. "For me, getting the Nitti roadster was the fulfillment of a dream."

As we've noted, the dream was in rough shape. Years of indifferent storage had taken their toll. The '32 frame had been altered to accept the small-block Chevy. Many parts were missing, although some important pieces had been removed and carefully stored in cardboard boxes. A profound restoration was in order. After some searching for the proper restorer, Zivot located Dave Crouse, of Custom Autos in Loveland, Colorado. "He told me he and his son Rob were starting a shop," says Zivot. "They'd restored classics and sports cars, but they wanted to get into restoring

original hot rods. They said if I let them do the car, they'd 'make it worthwhile' to me in terms of restoration costs."

That was an offer that Zivot couldn't refuse. While the restoration was underway, Zivot reports that the Crouses were very conscientious, carefully finding or making parts where they had to. David Zivot even measured the louvers from photographs in order to make the correct louver die so the Crouses could get the new hood exactly right. As mentioned, painting wizard Stan Betz mixed up a batch of perfectly matched Royal Triton-hued paint. When the body was sanded, it was evident that the '32 had earlier been painted black, then purple, and subsequently a final, deeper shade of purple. Mike and Jeff Johnson, owners of Past Times, Inc., in Estes Park, Colorado, did the finish paintwork.

David Zivot is a stickler for details. He discovered that the hidden hinges came from the rear doors of a 1940 Dodge four-door sedan. The compact Dodge hinge melded perfectly with the '32 Ford's doors, but the old, worn hinges needed replacing. The indefatigable Zivot scoured old wrecking yards and turned up the correct hinges.

Zivot found proper Stewart-Warner convex-lensed instruments (10 in all), and helped to carefully restore them. Dave and Rob Crouse gas-welded repairs to the body and frame, just the way it would have been done originally. Zivot

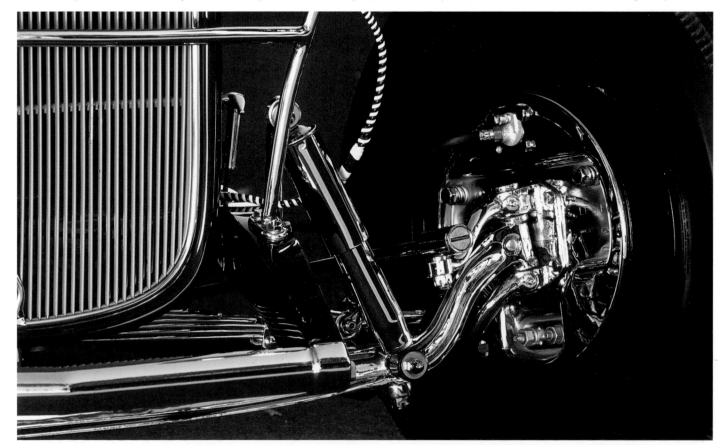

That dropped front axle may be a MorDrop, a popular period LA piece. Brakes are '40 Ford hydraulics. If it wasn't purple on this car, most likely it was plated, thanks to LA's House of Chrome. The rounded front frame horns and V'd spreader bar were subtle mods not done by everyone. In popular 1950s vernacular, Nitti's roadster was "sanitary."

restored the '40 Ford steering wheel and the Stromberg 97s, helped complete the generator, and polished the intake manifold, heads, fuel pump, and other parts.

Although the restored engine, by Red Hamilton of Red's Headers, looks very much like the original, it's a 286-ci flathead with an Isky 400 Jr. camshaft and a Kong distributor, which closely resembles the Evans unit. The headers were carefully matched, as were the myriad plated lines and accessories, right down to the plastic bicycle accessory wrapping over the wires and fuel lines. Credit Todd Herman and Rob Crouse for replicating the cream tuck-and-roll pleated interior. Many of David's friends worked on restoration details, helping to ensure the roadster made its successful comeback at the 2000 Grand National Roadster Show. Freshly restored, the ex-Nitti '32 won the coveted Bruce Meyer *Hot Rod* Preservation award, taking home the beautiful trophy – a Steve-Posson-designed, cast, and polished '32 roadster on a walnut plinth.

I saw the Nitti car for the first time at that show, and it was like being reunited with an old friend. Although I'd never seen the roadster in its heyday, like so many traditional hot rodders, after I'd looked at those pictures for decades, I felt I knew the car well. Although the car was close to perfect, the lakes headers had been completed hastily to make the show deadline, so Zivot subsequently had the Crouses redo them.

Overall, the completed Nitti '32 evidenced why this roadster had been such an icon. It had immense presence, and it

still does. Its deep purple paint and cream interior really pop. In a sea of primered, black, and occasionally red roadsters, it must have been a stunner in 1950.

Not long after the car was completed, David Zivot reluctantly sold it to Mark Mountanos, who also bought the Schaeneman '32 (see Chapter 15) from Kirk F. White. Zivot chose to give the car up as the result of several close calls in the heavy Las Vegas traffic.

Although he couldn't attend Deuce Day at the Petersen Museum in 2002, Mountanos sent both roadsters. "These guys were coachbuilders in their own right," he says. "The craftsmanship on many hot rods was excellent. With things like the hidden hinges and the antenna in the deck lid, Nitti was ahead of his time. And Joe, in those old pictures, could have been the inspiration for the Fonz, on *Happy Days*."

Mark Mountanos has no plans to sell the Nitti roadster. In fact, he'd like to take it to an AACA National Meet at Hershey Pennsylvania, for certification in Class 24-A as a racecar.

Today, the Joe Nitti roadster has joined the recognized ranks of significant restored historic hot rods. If you learn little else from this chapter, be aware that there are still a lot of great cars out there. They may have been altered, often extensively, from their original guise, but they're out there, just waiting to be discovered. If you have a favorite hot rod from the past, perhaps it's time you started looking for it – with or without a private eye.

This roadster had a feature no other car, before or since, seems to have duplicated. There were two Stewart-Warner panels, separated by a '46-48 Ford radio. The steering wheel was the popular art-deco '40 Ford unit, painted black.

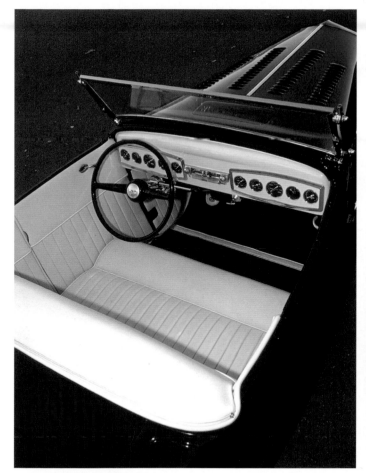

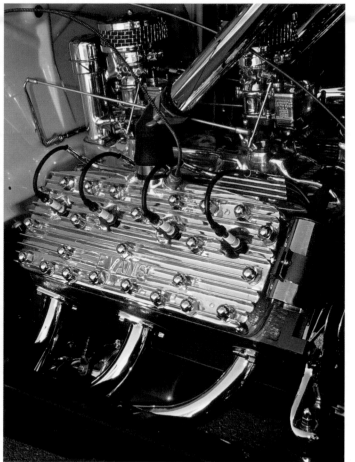

Ivory tuck-and-roll leatherette interior doesn't look too practical for a hot rod, especially a car that raced occasionally at the dirty, dusty dry lakes, but that was the style. And style was everything.

Under the hood was a pretty hot '46 59A Mercury flathead with what's described in the old Hot Rod magazine article as a "3/8 bore" (probably 3-3/8 inch), equipped with JE pistons and a stock stroke for 268 ci. Respected speed equipment manufacturer, Earl "Pappy" Evans, supplied finned aluminum high-compression heads, a dual manifold, and a high-performance ignition system. The racing camshaft was a Weber – probably a 3/4 grind. The tubular headers, from Sonny's Muffler Shop, and small air cleaners, received the chrome treatment, as did the generator and regulator covers, the upper radiator hoses, and myriad under-hood nuts and bolts.

Postwar Ford radio with signal-seeking feature bar looks great frenched into the customized dash. Joe probably never got bored reading all those gauges. When restorer Dave Crouse first saw this car, in its unrestored state, he took one look at those twin panels and realized – this was the long-lost Joe Nitti roadster.

Doane Spencer was the kind of hot rodder we all want to be. But very few guys possess all the skills. Doane could fabricate with the best of them, as you'd expect from any guy whom his friends called "Mr. Bracket." A self-taught mechanic, Doane could do it all – from welding and painting, to machine work and engine assembly. He also had a highly developed sense of styling and engineering. His legacy, this superb car, is arguably the consummate '32 Ford highboy roadster.

(5)

"**M**r. Bracket" built a hot rod. Doane Spencer's '32 Ford roadster is one of those very special cars where just the mention of it conjures up a distinct, timeless image in the minds of serious hot-rodders. For over half a century, this picture-perfect, jet-black '32 Ford highboy, with its laid-back DuVall split windshield, Schroeder racecar steering, hairpin wishbones, black steel wheels with skinny bias-plies, discrete plating, and integrated side pipes, has set a very high standard. It's been cloned and imitated, and its signature elements have been unashamedly copied by a legion of admirers.

Beautifully restored now, the roadster won the first Pebble Beach Concours d'Elegance Hot Rod Class, along with class wins at Amelia Island, Meadow Brook Hall, and Louis Vuitton in New York. Today, the ex-Spencer '32 is usually on display at the Petersen Automotive Museum in Los Angeles when its owner, Bruce Meyer, isn't out driving it. And drive it he does. In 2002, Bruce tooled the priceless Spencer deuce out to Pomona for the annual *LA Roadsters* Father's Day meet. A few

years ago, he drove it on Mark Morton's River City Rod Run, sliding around in the light snow we encountered in the San Gabriel Mountains. This roadster has even chingo-ed from Beverly Hills out to Bakersfield for the NHRA Reunion. Meyer, a man with a garage-full of Ferraris, 'Benzes, a 427SC Cobra, a Duesenberg, and a Bugatti, says "Driving it is wonderful."

There's a ton of history in this car. Old photographs show it at the Pasadena Roadster Club Reliability Run (where it won "Best Appearing Car" in 1947), and later that year it was shot at Pico Rivera, lined up alongside the best rods of its era, waiting to be chosen as one of the SCTA/Russetta entrants for the first big indoor hot rod show at the LA Armory. There are even shots of it running hard at El Mirage (where it turned 126.76 mph in 1950 with a relatively small displacement, 243-ci destroked flathead).

So it never won Oakland – big deal. This roadster epitomizes what hot rods were, and still are, all about. To learn its fascinating history, let's begin at the beginning.

Doane Spencer's '32 Roadster

As we've said, serious hot rods are always named after the guys who built them. Although Bruce Meyer owns it, this is still Doane Spencer's roadster. So who was he? Doane Spencer was the kind of hot rodder we all want to be, if only we had all the skills. Doane could fabricate with the best of them, as you'd expect from any guy whom his friends called "Mr. Bracket." A self-taught mechanic, Doane could do it all, from welding and painting, to machine work, engine assembly, etc. It's also evident from his surviving work and the fond remembrances of friends that he had a highly developed sense of styling and engineering.

Spencer believed you built a car using the best of what was available, and when upgraded parts came around, you fitted them. Like many great hot rodders, his goal was to make things better and faster. He never stopped improving this roadster, that is, until he switched to another project, his 1957 Thunderbird. And he never let that car alone either.

Interestingly, Doane's '32 roadster was already a hot rod when he got it. He and his friend, Jack Dorn, were students at Hollywood High School. Dorn first owned the roadster in 1941, when the then full-fendered '32 got a filled grille shell and shaved deck lid, along with a 21-stud, '37 Ford V-8. After Doane wrecked his Model A, he gave Dorn its genuine George DuVall split windshield. Jack then paid noted Hollywood bodyman, Jimmy Summers, $45 to modify the '32 cowl to accept it.

According to Pat Ganahl, whose story, "This Deuce is Wild" in Automobile Quarterly, Volume 37, #3, is arguably the best magazine article ever written about the Spencer '32, Doane paid Jack Dorn $500 for the roadster in 1944 when they were Navy shipmates. Spencer soon began modifying the car further.

We know from early photos of the car that the door handles were quickly deep-sixed. Initially, the hood and the solid

Here's Doane Spencer at the Pasadena Roadster Club Reliability Run in 1947, where his roadster won Best Appearing Car. Already a trend-setter, the car had a homemade headlamp bracket, filled grille shell, and solid hood sides, the DuVall split windscreen, and hand-fabricated hairpin wishbones. Note Glendale Stokers club plaque.
(Greg Sharp Collection)

Here's a famous trio. Left to right, Wally Parks presents the Best Appearing Car trophy to a flat-capped and smiling Doane Spencer. Ak Miller looks on. Wonder where that trophy is today? Note the split seat armrest, with the radio installed.
(Pebble Beach Concours d'Elegance)

hood side panels were smooth, but late 1940s pictures show two discrete rows of louvers on each side of the hood top. In front, a small nerf bar linked the easily removable (for racing) headlamps and provided a mounting point for the *Glendale Stokers* club plaque. Perhaps the most distinctive styling element of this roadster was its unique rolled pan with the inset license plate bracket, which covered the gas tank. Twin '37 Ford taillights were discretely mounted on either side of the tank, while '40 Ford hubcaps and beauty rims finished the 16-inch wheels. Doane Spencer would never use contrasting color wheels or whitewall tires. This car and everything that wasn't plated or polished, was black. All Doane's cars were black.

Doane's club, the *Glendale Stokers*, was a very active dry lakes racing group affiliated with the SCTA. Fellow *Stokers* member (and dry lakes legend) Barney Navarro recalled that Spencer's first modified flathead had Ord heads and a dual manifold, (Mal Ord was also a *Stokers* club member) and that the car was completed during the war. Pat Ganahl's search through dry lakes programs found Doane's car listed only with a postwar '46 Merc engine.

One surviving early photo shows what is probably the 258-ci engine with polished components. The flathead sports Ord finned 24-stud heads, a Navarro dual carburetor manifold, a converted Lincoln Zephyr V-12 distributor (though it occasionally ran a Kong distributor), a Winfield cam, and what look to be handmade but nicely shaped headers. There's a photo of the car on the cover of Don Montgomery's book, *Authentic Hot Rods*, and the racing numbers on the side are embellished with three letters that spell "SEX." Spencer apparently called one of his Navarro intakes a "Special EXperimental" unit, reflecting his wry sense of humor. This engine turned 112 to 114 mph on several occasions in 1947, but its displacement conceded too many cubes to others in Class C, where guys could run up to 350 ci under the prevailing rules.

Undaunted, Spencer decided to go the opposite way. He destroked his flathead by offset grinding a Ford crank and substituting shorter connecting rods. The result was 243 ci,

closer to the Class B ceiling of 250 ci, and the engine went 126.76 mph at an El Mirage run in July 1950. He was some 10 mph off the record, and it's fun to speculate whether he could have fiddled with cams, carbs, gears, and even alcohol fuel to go just that much quicker. But Doane already had other interests. In the spring of 1950, he was reportedly offered $100 in appearance money to drive his car to the first Indianapolis car show; so Spencer and his new wife Betty spent a month on the road in the '32, enjoying their honeymoon and hitting both the car show and the Indy 500. It took courage and mechanical skills to drive a hot rod cross-country in those days. Doane had plenty of both.

Steady improvements to the car included a 1940s-era Cadillac rear seat with a folding armrest to replace the Ford front seat. Cleverly, Doane incorporated the radio knobs on the armrest. Earlier, he had subtly reshaped the sides of the DuVall windshield to give it a sleeker shape. At one point, he took the roadster to Valley Custom, a noted Burbank restyling venue, where co-owners Neal Emory and Clay Jensen reworked the roadster's front cowl to form a continuous edge (like that of a '36 Ford roadster), which flared into the tops of the doors. It's another subtle trick, but when

its shape is still stunning. (It undoubtedly influenced the fiberglass example available today from Gibbon Fiberglass Reproductions, Inc.)

Doane Spencer was something of a rolling stone. He and his friend Jack Dorn often went on trips where they'd drive till they ran out of money, then work for a while in a Ford dealership, before moving on. Once when Doane was as far east as Latrobe, Pennsylvania, the local Ford dealer saw his roadster and offered Spencer a job on the spot. He took it, but only for a while.

The roadster remained Doane's road car and racer, and according to Ganahl, it was last listed in an SCTA program in September 1950. La Carrera Panamericana, the famed Mexican Road Race, began that year, and Doane Spencer was intrigued with the idea of entering his car. To do so, he'd have to modify it considerably, and he began in earnest on the task. Spencer Z-ed both ends of the '32's frame to help lower its center of gravity. He cut off the front and rear frame horns and relocated the gas tank inside the trunk. He bought a second K-member, cut it apart, reversed the pieces, and then welded them together to make an even stronger mount. Next he extensively boxed the frame and built a sturdy center X-member of heavy-gauge sheetmetal, which he also drilled liberally to save weight. Spencer was working at a Ford dealership at the time, so it was natural that he'd procure one of the big '52 Lincoln OHV V-8s.

The Lincoln was good for 205 hp @ 4,200 rpm and 305 ft-lbs of torque at 2,300 to 3,000 rpm. Clay Smith and Bill Stroppe adeptly tuned these engines to produce close to 300 hp, and Lincoln finished 1-2-3-4 in the 1952 La Carrera (using '53 engines). That was all Doane needed to upgrade his, but Lincoln engines were heavy, weighing over 700 pounds with accessories, so when Ford's Y-block replaced the flathead in 1954, Spencer elected to go with the lighter new Ford engine.

Meanwhile, Doane continued to modify his roadster for the Mexican race. He installed a Halibrand quick-change rear end and knock-off Halibrand magnesium wheels. At the same time, he built a sturdy brace under the cowl and fitted a Schroeder sprint car steering box and swung pedals for the clutch and brakes with twin firewall-mounted master cylinders. In a move that was never exactly imitated, though in my opinion, it should have been, he routed the exhaust pipes through the frame into handsome parallel

you see it, you can appreciate the eye for detail that Spencer possessed. In an era when most roadsters and coupes were usually more functional than stylish, Doane Spencer found ways to artfully customize and personalize his car.

Not long afterward, although the exact date is uncertain, Valley Custom also hand-formed a steel, coupe-like top for the roadster, using a portable air hammer, along with hammers and dollies. Later owner Neal East ran the car with a neat top occasionally, and Bruce Meyer still has it, completely restored. "I don't use it," he says, "because I like running the car open." While tops on chopped roadsters were somewhat rare in California, some folding and even a few padded examples were seen. This was the first example of a removable hardtop on a '32 that we can document, and

The Spencer roadster has one of the first split windshields George DuVall made for a '32 Ford. Later, Doane modified the flared sides and reshaped them for a cleaner appearance. He also had Valley Custom's Neal Emory and Clay Jensen rework the front cowl to form a continuous edge, like that of a '36 Ford roadster, which flares into the tops of the doors. When you see it, you can appreciate Spencer's eye for detail. In an era when most roadsters and coupes were usually more functional than stylish, Doane Spencer found ways to artfully customize and personalize his car.

An accessory license plate light from Cal Custom, '39 teardrops, and a plated and arched Model T rear spring to clear the Halibrand quick-change and '40 Ford axle bells. The rear brakes were adapted from a '41 Lincoln. It's all beautifully conceived, simple, and yes, we'll say it, elegant.

Anticipating hard stops on the grueling Mexican Road Race course, Doane liberally drilled his brake backing plates, fabricated a slick cooling scoop, added lever shocks from a '33 Ford, and plated the works.

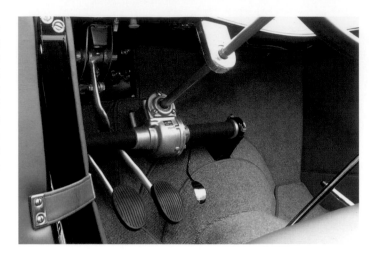

The location of the Schroeder steering box necessitates running the drag link through the cowl side. Doane fabricated an oval-shaped area behind the drag link mount. This shape is echoed in the plates below, which help anchor the hairpins.

lakes-pipe tubes, first with mufflers and later with spin-off end caps. This meant the car could ride low, but nothing would be lower than the frame rails.

The '37 tail lamps were replaced with '39 teardrops mounted in the lower trunk panel. Kirk White says the original, hand-formed rolled pan was deep-sixed after some lady ran into the rear of the roadster. "Doane told me he tossed it," Kirk says. "He was always moving on to what was next."

At the end of 1954, after a considerable number of accidents, the Mexican government permanently cancelled Pan American Road Races, so Doane never got to race his roadster in the event. Coincidentally, that's when Ford introduced the 1955 Thunderbird, and loyal Ford man Doane Spencer actually flew to Detroit with his young daughter, Doanna, and drove home a black one. The new 'Bird, extensively modified by Spencer, turned 149.53 mph at Bonneville in 1961. Spencer kept improving the car until he died, and it too spawned several clones. (Chuck DeHeras owns the original.)

At this point, the next two owners of the Doane Spencer roadster, Lynn Wineland and Neal East, entered the picture. Lynn Wineland built his first hot rod when he attended Coalinga (California) high school, before serving in the Army

Steady improvements in this car saw the adoption of a 1935 Cadillac rear seat, with its luxurious folding armrest, replacing the Ford front seat. Cleverly, Doane incorporated the radio's knobs on the armrest. Talented Tom Sewell, whose shop is in Cambria, California, was responsible for the artfully restored interior.

A vintage Harman & Collins distributor, with twin coils, handles the spark chores. Inside, the block is ported and relieved, with Lincoln-Zephyr valvesprings and Johnson adjustable tappets.

Air Corps and attending art school in Ohio. He first saw Doane Spencer's roadster at the LA Armory show in 1948, and later he and Doane connected at the 1950 Indianapolis car show, where Wineland's '32 was entered. Pick up an old copy of *Trend Book 102*, published in 1951 by Bob Petersen and Bob Lindsay, and you'll find photos of Wineland's sharp, channeled '32 roadster, with a split windshield. A member of the *Hoodlifters*, an Ohio hot rod club, Wineland ran a Navarro-equipped three-carb '42 Mercury engine with a Winfield SU-1R cam, rare Kinmont disc brakes, and a '42 Lincoln transmission with a column shift. (Doane Spencer's roadster, in lakes trim, is found on page 86 of the same book.)

When he returned to California, Wineland lived in a house on Spencer's street in Sun Valley. In January 1956, he signed on as graphics director for *Rod & Custom*, and three years later, he was the editor. In December 1959, Wineland put his friend Doane Spencer on the R&C masthead as technical editor, but Spencer seldom actually went to the R&C offices. Finally in October 1960, Neal East became an R&C associate editor. The stage was set for ownership changes.

Lynn Wineland purchased the roadster from Spencer sometime in 1958. Doane had bought a new house and needed the cash. Reportedly, the car was completely apart with no engine and running gear; Spencer had been selling the parts

The sanitary, full-race Mercury engine is devoid of plating. Note the fire-wall mounted brake and clutch master cylinders. Those lovely three-into-one, hand-built headers were done at PC³g.

Spencer also fabricated. Valley Custom apparently extended the hood top, fabricated the louvered hood sides, and did some repainting of the body and the hardtop.

Wineland's plans included a 348-ci T-Bird engine built by Les Richey. We couldn't find photos of the 3-71 GMC blower that was mentioned as part of the program, but the two-port FI shown could be the Scott unit. Although some parts were missing from the car, Wineland was able to get Doane's custom-built timing cover and lightweight housing that accommodated the water pump. Spencer had whittled and machined this handsome piece from aluminum alloy.

Sadly, Lynn Wineland never drove the Spencer car during his ownership. By 1968 or 1969, he was getting a divorce and was about to lose his house and his garage. He called Neal East, who'd sold his own roadster, but who did have a garage. Lynn offered East the Spencer '32, sans the Y-block that had been installed, but with a few important conditions: the car had to remain black, always be Ford-powered, and Lynn wanted the right of first refusal if it was going to be sold. Neal says he replied, "It's not getting sold, so don't worry about it."

Interestingly, in a letter to R&C in September 1995, Wineland wrote, "I never perceived nor claimed the car as being mine – I was just a custodian and I always consulted with Doane before proceeding with a change." Interestingly, Wineland closed his letter with this prophetic thought; "I'd prefer it to go to some place such as the Petersen Automotive Museum."

A talk with Neal East confirmed that the '32 never ran with the Lincoln or the Ford Y-block. "It's never had anything but a flathead in it," he says. "It was a smooth car, long before we knew what they were." After Neal got the roadster, he and his fellow R&C staffers were organizing a sort of nostalgia revival through the pages of the magazine. The cover of R&C's Street Rod Quarterly for Winter 1971 shows a quartet of historic flathead-powered roadsters. The cover features Jake with the Niekamp roadster, Bud Bryan and his '29 on '32 rails, the ex-Dick Kraft, Highland Plating Special, and the Spencer '32, now with a flathead installed. The other visible change is a set of orange Kelsey-Hayes

piecemeal to raise money. Wineland paid him just $300 (!) for what was left and moved it to his garage. But Spencer was still in the picture, still working on the car. Doane and Lynn are shown with the roadster on the cover of the December 1960 R&C, fabricating front nerf bars for a story. The Y-block engine is fitted, along with a beautiful set of four-into-one headers. In the eighth edition of Floyd Clymer's popular *Handbook of Engine Swapping*, there are two pages of photos showing how Spencer hand-formed and welded those headers, as well as how the exhaust pipe extensions were built to pass through the frame.

A close look at that R&C cover, and in the continued story in January 1961, reveals a beautifully finned valley cover that Doane built for the Y-block, along with what appears to be a two-port fuel-injection system. By this time, the front hair-pins have those distinctive teardrop-shaped mounts, and the front axle is a plated '37 Ford tubular item. The Lincoln brake backing plates are liberally drilled, and two beautiful-ly formed front air scoops are evident. The Halibrand quick-change was secured by a matching set of rear hairpins that

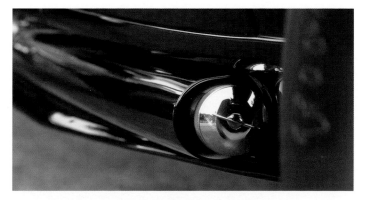

In a move that was never exactly imitated, though in my opinion, it should have been, Spencer routed his exhaust pipes through the frame into handsome par-allel lakes-pipe tubes, first with mufflers and later with spin-off end caps. He did this to ensure the car could ride low, but not have anything protruding below the frame rails. Reportedly, the wheelbase was extended from stock 106 inches to 108 inches. It was all done brilliantly.

wires with bias-plies. The hardtop is on, the hood sides are off, and the side pipes have the mufflers inside them, with the exhausts exiting in front of the rear wheels.

Neal hadn't disturbed much of Doane's work. The sturdy X-member was modified so the flathead could be hooked up to a longer '48 Lincoln overdrive transmission. "I actually found a side shifter for it in the J.C. Whitney catalog," East told me, "and it's spring-loaded from first to second. Because the shift mechanism is back and off to the left, the floor shift handle has a weird kink in it," he adds, "but at least it's close to the driver." East changed the driveline back to a torque tube, axed the outside rear hairpins, and installed traditional Ford 'bones. In front, he replaced the tube axle with an un-dropped '32 Ford truck axle. "Doane changed axles the way you'd change shirts," East recalls. "This axle fit perfectly with the hairpin wishbones, despite the frame kick-up, and there was no binding when you turned." The original paint needed touch-ups in a few places, but that was all.

"I put those Kelsey-Hayes wires on it to keep the nostalgia theme," he says, "but the pre-war Lincoln drums required special spacers (made by Eric Vaughn) before the wires would fit over them. That set up a violent oscillation, and I overcame it with a steering damper. I was proud of the way the car looked, so I took it up to Doane's shop in Eagle Rock to show him. He came out, kicked one of the rear 7.00 x 16s and said, 'Get those stupid wheels and tires off. It'll never handle with those on there.' I was crushed."

Later Neal installed "kidney bean" Halibrands and radials, as Spencer had intended, which changed the handling completely and for the better. "People have to understand," East says today, "Doane was always on the front edge. He had no interest in nostalgia. He was always thinking ahead. And he was right. The lightweight Halibrand wheels and radial tires made the car."

East drove the roadster a great deal in the early 1970s, making an 80-mile daily round trip from his home in Alhambra to work at Challenge Publications in Los Angeles. He did a long haul in 1976 to the Street Rod Nationals in Tulsa. On one occasion, the Vintage Auto Racing Association (VARA) invited him to run laps at Willow Springs in the car. "It was really fun," he recalls. "You could hang the tail out and just slide it like a racer. The reinforced frame meant there was almost no body roll, and the quick Schroeder steering worked perfectly. On the way home, I hammered it over Angeles Crest and hung the tail out whenever I pleased. One thing people should know about this car. It really handled well."

From 1985 to 1995, the Spencer '32 was relatively dormant. Neal East had Pete Eastwood and Bill "Birdman" Stewart freshen up the chassis and body, which included a hood repair that saw a full inch added to ensure the sides squared perfectly with the grille shell. The modesty panel inside the

shell was also reworked to hide the axle. They also remade the exhaust pipes out of stainless; Doane's steel side pipes had rusted. Then East moved to the Denver area, and work slowed to a crawl.

Spencer and Bruce Meyer spoke at the Hot Rod Reunion in 1995, and apparently Doane himself suggested to Bruce, who had earlier commissioned the restoration of the Pierson Brothers' coupe and the So-Cal belly tank, that he buy the car and complete it. Wendy Spencer, Doane's youngest daughter, who lives in Denver, asked Neal if she could see the roadster, and he brought it, unfinished, but assembled and in primer, to a local event so she could. Sadly, that was the same day her father died. Many hot rod enthusiasts, including Kirk White, Don Orosco, Gordon Apker, and Bruce Meyer, as well, had tried to purchase the car. East had refused every offer. But now he reconsidered.

"Tell me what you're going to do with this car," East asked Bruce. When Meyer told him that he'd make it available for everyone to see and admire, East agreed to sell. By now the time was right, even to the coincidence that "Birdman" and Pete Eastwood were working at Chapouris' shop, then called PC^{3}g, so they helped complete the roadster. The Doane Spencer roadster was delivered to the restorers in much the same form as it exists today. Pete Chapouris told me that they deliberated bringing it back to the way Doane had originally built it, but then decided that since he'd done most of the later modifications, even if he'd never driven it that way, that they'd restore it as it was. It was a logical decision.

The car had only ever run with a flathead, so that was the understandable engine choice. Rodding legend Tom Sparks built the strong flathead engine that powers the car today. It's a 59A Mercury block with a .030-over 3-5/16-inch bore, with a 4-1/8-inch Merc crank, for a total of 284 ci. The cam is a Winfield R1, and a pair of 2100 Holleys on an Offenhauser manifold handle the stroker's carburetion needs. The heads are also Offys. A vintage Harman & Collins distributor, with twin coils, handles the spark chores. Inside, the block is ported and relieved, with

Lincoln-Zephyr valvesprings and Johnson adjustable tappets. Those lovely three-into-one, hand-built headers were done at PC3g. There's not a lot of polish, but this motor is strong and reliable, and it sounds and runs the way Doane would have liked it.

Bruce Meyer knew Doane well; he understood the significance of this roadster, and knew what its disposition had to be. Meyer promised Neal East and Lynn Wineland, (who still had a sincere interest), that the completed roadster would be displayed at the Petersen Museum (where Meyer was Board Chairman) and that it would be shown at the 50th Anniversary Grand National Roadster Show.

He also exhibited it at the Oakland Museum, and as you've read, it won hot rod classes at Pebble Beach, Amelia Island, Louis Vuitton, and the Meadow Brook Concours d'Elegance – an unprecedented feat. It actually came within a whisker of winning "Best of Show" at the Louis Vuitton Concours d'Elegance at Rockefeller Center. Considering all the luxury and sports cars entered in that event, a hot rod win would have been really something!

Bruce Meyer sponsors an annual Preservation Award at the Grand National Roadster Show for the best restored hot rod. This trophy, a plated Steve Posson casting of the roadster on a wood plinth, is a lasting tribute to Doane Spencer, a remarkable, original, and talented hot rodder.

Says Meyer today, "this car has to be the holy grail of hot rodding. I never thought I'd own it. It was so complicated. I had to convince Neal I'd do the right thing with it, and we had to get Lynn's (Wineland) blessing, too. But I love having it, because I had a connection with Doane. He was an artist and a genius. That's why this roadster still inspires people."

One evening, Bruce Meyer kindly let me drive this car from his home in Beverly Hills, to the Petersen Automotive Museum on Fairfax Avenue. It fires with a loud bark, thanks to Tom Sparks' handiwork on the stroker flathead. It shifts crisply; once you get the hang of the offset floor shift and its spring-loaded second gear throw. The steering is heavy at low speeds, more precise, even sharp, as you increase speed. Thanks to the hefty frame reinforcements, this is the most rigid early deuce chassis you'll ever experience. The car tracks perfectly, despite its squirrelly bias-plies.

And it has soul. Peering through the DuVall windscreen, enjoying the flathead's deep rumble, seeing the dim glow of the instrument lights, and enjoying the whispering rush of the wind, you feel that Doane's spirit is riding with you…and he's insisting you go even faster.

The running gear on this car all flows rearward on the same plane – the drag link and hairpins are perfectly horizontal, the frame-extruded header picks up the line, and the rear is uncluttered by exhaust pipes or bumpers. That racy DuVall windscreen echoes the continuous speed theme.

6

Here's one of our favorite lost-and-found stories – a car that's been a classic since its creation. When you flip through the faded pages of early 1950s hot rod magazines, a few feature cars really jump out at you. For me, the Eddie Dye '29 Ford roadster is one. It's also a very complex story. Lost and found, then lost and found again, some of its construction and much of its life remains a mystery. To paraphrase Donald Rumsfeld, "here's what we think that we think we know…."

Low and sleek, the Eddie Dye '29 was easily one of the sharpest rides of its day. It features a hand-formed track nose and louvered hood, an extensively reworked cowl that erased the signature '29 "coach reveal," filled doors, a belly pan, a DuVall split windshield, a Stewart-Warner eight-gauge instrument panel, a Crestliner steering wheel, and a full-on, Earl Evans-built flathead engine. A distinctive, cleaver-shaped club plaque between the car's Pontiac taillights humorously reads, "Auto Butchers, ELA." (East Los Angeles.)

We don't have many period photographs of this car. It's shown in the January 1952 issue of *Hot Rod*, when it was on display at the Second Annual Los Angeles Motorama, held at the Pan Pacific Auditorium, in November 1951. (By the way, the pioneering show producers were *Hot Rod* founders, Robert E. Petersen and Robert R. Lindsay.) The *Hot Rod* magazine photo caption stated that the car was painted "Cherry Orchid," by Gil Ayala, the body was channeled seven inches, and the owner was Edison Dye. We know the frame was a much-modified '32 Ford unit that had been bobbed in front, fitted with a suicide front spring perch, and kicked up very high in the rear. With its dropped beam axle, the Dye roadster sat snake-belly low.

Not long afterward, in a March 1952 cover story, the original *Hop Up* magazine ran the first four-page magazine feature on the Dye roadster. That piece included a cutaway drawing by Jim Richards. Interestingly, the car's drag link, clearly visible in the January 1952, *Hot Rod* photograph, is missing. And there are no front brake hoses. A nicely

Eddie Dye's '29 Roadster

shaped nerf bar now connects the front headlamps and offers protection for the attractive track nose.

A year later, in Fawcett's *Best Hot Rods* #189, the roadster appeared again, and Fawcett's editors simply reused some of the same photographs. The *Best Hot Rods* story called the car "The Dye Hard," and included a photograph of its modified flathead. While the engine in the picture wasn't all spit and polished, the Edelbrock Super dual carb manifold, tubular headers, and finned Edelbrock high-compression heads are evident, as is the firewall-mounted sending unit for an electric tachometer. A caption notes that Earl Evans built the engine, but if that were true, the Edelbrock speed equipment would seem to be incongruous. Interestingly, the front wheels appear to be 16-inch, with '46 Ford caps; in back, there are 15-inch steel wheels with '50 Mercury flat caps. Tires are 3-inch whitewalls all around.

There was no mention of an earlier life or another constructor, either in *Hop Up* or the Fawcett book. According to *Hop Up*, Gil's Custom Shop in East Los Angeles built the roadster over a six-month period, for a then-high $3,400. Brothers Gil and Al Ayala were the East LA equivalent of the Barris brothers, primarily turning out cool customs, and in this case, a righteous roadster. The Barris duo issued "Kustoms" plaques with many of their cars; the Ayala brothers did the same thing with their "Auto Butchers" hatchets. Neither organization could be construed as a car club; it was just for publicity.

Car collector and hot rodder Duncan Emmons who worked for the Ayalas when he was 19 years old, told me, "Gil and Al are both deceased now. Gil was the paint expert; he had a great eye for color. Al was the metal man. They put those Auto Butchers plaques on all the cars they built. I still have an original one." Duncan Emmons told me he remembers the Eddie Dye car in the Ayala's shop. It was candy red," he said, "and they had it on its side, actually laying on its wheels, while they did some work on it."

Dye was listed in *HR* as the owner of the EDM Lumber Co. in Los Angeles, so we can assume he must have had the means to commission a high-buck custom roadster. For years, there was no reason to suspect the *Hop Up* article was anything but

correct in attributing the car to the Ayalas. I've always liked this roadster, and over time, I wondered where it had gone. It was too nice a car for someone to have trashed it. Until a few years ago, no one seemed to know who owned it.

But as we'll see, it was always around. I had begun to suspect something was amiss when I developed an article on metal wizard Whitey Clayton for the fourth volume of Hop Up, for Mark Morton. Whitey Clayton handcrafted the nose, grille, hood, and belly pan on the Niekamp roadster in his small shop in Whittier, California. He also fabricated parts for many other well known racecars and hot rods – noses, belly pans, dashes, and so forth.

Niekamp solid hood panels were one of Clayton's specialties, along with rounded blisters to cover a protruding head or generator. According to one eyewitness, "he could turn 'em out in no time." We're very sure he did the nose, the hood, and the belly pan on the Eddie Dye roadster. In magazine features, its construction was credited to Gil and Al Ayala. But our photographs clearly show the work-in-progress Dye roadster at Whitey's shop.

Now the plot thickens a bit. As Mark Morton wrote: "Here's the Eddie Dye '29, apparently under construction at Whitey Clayton's." The indentation behind the drag link

Here's the Eddie Dye '29, apparently under construction at Whitey Clayton's shop. The indentation behind the drag link (which is mounted upside down) is a clever touch, as is the way the lower hood panels flare out to meet the racecar nose. The louvers haven't been punched yet, but the headlight holes are already drilled. As well, the distinctive '29 Ford carriage reveals have yet to be removed. But it's clearly the Eddie Dye car. Based on these photos from Whitey's old scrapbook, we're pretty certain the aluminum panels are the work of the very talented Mr. Clayton. (Larry Clayton/Mark Morton, Hop Up)

Note the distinctively shaped hairpin radius rods on the Dye car. Whitey liked to take pictures of his work when it was done or close to completion. We know of only one case where he engraved his name on a metal panel (see chapter 11), but his extensive scrapbook, saved by his son Larry, was filled with pictures like this one, which while often unlabeled, were a remarkable tribute to his late father's skill. (Larry Clayton/Mark Morton, Hop Up)

(which is mounted upside down) is a clever touch, as is the way the lower hood panels flare out to meet the racecar nose. The louvers haven't been punched yet, but the headlight holes are already drilled. As well, the distinctive '29 Ford "carriage reveals" have yet to be removed. But it's clearly the Eddie Dye car. Based on the photos from Whitey's old scrapbook, we're pretty certain the aluminum panels are the work of the very talented Mr. Clayton."

The distinctively shaped hairpin radius rods on the Dye car were identical to those on the unfinished roadster you see in this chapter's photographs. Whitey liked to take pictures of his work when it was done or close to completion. We know of only one case where he engraved his name on a metal panel (see the chapter on Harold Osgood's T in this book), but his extensive scrapbook, saved by his son Larry, was filled with pictures that, while often unlabeled, were a remarkable tribute to his late father's skill.

The old photos of the Eddie Dye car under construction at Clayton's stirred up a bit of a fuss. The car's current restorers commented that they believed the handsome nose piece was fabricated by a different craftsman than whoever did the hood and side panels. They said they could tell this was true from style and quality of the metal work itself. Then, another person stepped forward to say that Reuben Miranda, who apparently owned a muffler shop in East Los Angeles near the Ayalas, did the nose on the car...but he offered no conclusive proof. It was also rumored that California Metal Shaping may have worked on the car. They apparently assisted the Ayalas with specialty pieces. We checked with a former CMS employee, Red Tweit, but he didn't remember the car.

Mark Morton decided to dig a little deeper and uncovered two remarkable photographs of the Eddie Dye car. They were taken at the lakes, it's believed, back in 1948 or 1949. The roadster wears the number 617, and at this time it's got the reshaped cowl profile, the sleek track nose, and the louvered hood top and sides – it's very close in appearance to the way it looks in the shots taken at Whitey Clayton's shop. Whitey closed up in 1950-51, so that's consistent.

It's important to note that the route to really fast roadster times at the lakes or Bonneville was a low, smooth silhouette. While not quite as slim in profile as a '27 or earlier T, '28/'29 Model A bodies could be made quite "slippery" when they were channeled and fitted with a track roadster nose and a full belly pan. Two of many such examples are the famous Bill Niekamp and Dick Flint '29 roadsters, both of which turned more than 140 mph at the lakes. That full frontal streamlining was worth an easy 10 to 15 mph versus a traditional '32 highboy's blocky silhouette. Whitey Clayton was the guy many people turned to for sleek track noses, and he received some acclaim for the Niekamp '29, so it's likely the Ayalas retained him to do the work on this '29 roadster, as well.

The Ayalas completed the Dye car in their shop, probably in late 1951 or early 1952. Gil and Al elected to finish the car with Orchid Cherry lacquer and white upholstery, and that's the way it appeared at the Pan-Pacific Auditorium Show in LA. The seats were constructed with a slight center peak in the seatback center, and two separate thin squabs were mounted to the floor. Channeled cars don't give you much legroom or vertical seat height. As it turns out, this lit-

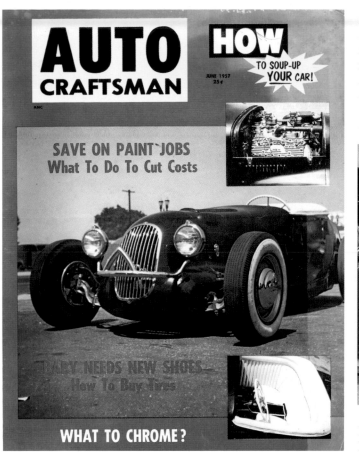

its distinguishing features were lost after Brousseau's extensive modifications. Before you shake your head and mutter, remember this. In the 1960s, hot rodding was on a very different path. People tried to achieve what they felt was a much more modern, contemporary look with older cars. As a consequence, overhead valve engines, tufted upholstery, external exhaust headers, alloy wheels, and metallic paint soon became prominent additions.

In keeping with the trends, Roger Brousseau deep-sixed the DuVall windshield and replaced it with '32 stanchions, along with a new windscreen that omitted the top portion of the windshield frame and was supported by a pair of chromed braces. He also removed Whitey Clayton's hand-hammered nose and hood side panels, thus exposing the unusual canted shocks, the 1937 Dodge shock mounts, the suicide spring perch, and the front axle. A '46 Ford steering box was installed, and a deep-dish Covico accessory wheel replaced the lovely Crestliner steering wheel. Thankfully, the Stewart-Warner 8-gauge panel remained.

The new upholstery by Kizer's was black, button-tufted Naugahyde, and there was a white top, as well. A chromed, three-point roll bar was mounted behind the driver's seat.

tle seat peak would be another identifier for the car in the future. It's also likely that the paint, upholstery, and plating were done on a contract basis for Eddie Dye. The Ayalas and Dye showed the nearly completed car at the Motorama, before the headlights and front nerf bar were done, then had it photographed for *Hop Up*, and the same shots found their way east to Fawcett Publications in Connecticut.

We also don't know how long Eddie Dye kept the roadster. It was shown on the cover of *Auto Craftsman* magazine in June 1957, but there was no article about it inside. It's believed the car changed hands at least once before it was discovered, languishing in a garage in Southern California in the early 1960s, by Roger Brousseau.

A transplanted Rhode Islander, Brousseau had moved to Santee, California, in the late 1950s. According to a cover story in the October 1964 issue of *Car Craft*, he had owned "a show-winning custom and three other rods." He told *Car Craft*'s reporter he wanted to build a "beautiful street roadster." He told me that when he first acquired this car, he had no clue to its previous history.

If you looked at the *Car Craft* article back in the day, you simply wouldn't recognize Brousseau's roadster as the Eddie Dye car. Its personality was completely changed, and

Auto Craftsman magazine featured the Dye car, sans DuVall windshield, on its June 1957 cover, but there was no feature, just a few lines attributing the car to the Ayala Brothers.

Roger Brousseau changed the Dye car substantially. He deep-sixed the DuVall windshield and replaced it with '32 stanchions and a new windscreen that omitted the top portion of the windshield frame and was supported by chromed braces. He removed Whitey Clayton's hand-hammered nose and hood side panels, exposing the unusual canted shocks, their 1937 Dodge shock mounts, the suicide spring perch, and the front axle. A '46 Ford steering box was installed, and a deep-dish Covico accessory wheel replaced the Crestliner wheel. The Stewart-Warner eight-panel remained. (Roger Brousseau)

New upholstery by Kizer's was black, button-tufted Naugahyde, and there was a white top, as well. A chromed, three-point roll bar was mounted behind the driver's seat. The belly pan was axed. Louvered side valences – all that was left of the original belly pan – covered the frame rails. A three-carb-equipped Chevy 348-ci V-8 was crammed in front of the now-modified firewall. The entire Ford driveline was trashed. The wheels are five-spoke Americans. This is substantially the way the car appeared in the movie, The Lively Set. (Roger Brousseau)

Tom Branch understood that as long as Jim Fuller had the original nose and hood, on his limited budget, he'd never be able to redo the Eddie Dye car as it had been in '52. Branch elected to make his own statement, rebuilding the roadster with elements of both the Dye and Brousseau versions. He fitted a chopped and filled '32 grille, leaving the unusual '37 Dodge shock mounts and canted shocks exposed. (Aaron Kahan)

The belly pan was axed. Louvered side valances (all that was left of the original belly pan) covered the frame rails. In the engine compartment, a three-carburetor-equipped Chevy 409 V-8 was crammed in front of the now-modified firewall. The entire Ford driveline had been trashed. The gearbox was a '62 Chevrolet 4-speed with overhead clutch and brake pedals, which in turn drove a contemporary Chevy rear end. Four-branch, parallel-chromed headers ran over the frame rails into large, capped collector pipes. From there, the exhausts ran under the car and emerged through a pair of tailpipes under the rear of the body. The brakes remained early Ford.

When Branch owned the roadster, he installed an Auto Butchers hatchet plaque. That's how I saw the car at Long Beach one Sunday, and subsequently at a number of West Coast events. Tom drove the wheels off it. (Aaron Kahan)

The car's lovely nose was now just a memory. A filled, chopped, and squared-off '32 truck grille shell with horizontal bars and accessory headlights on alloy brackets made up the new front end. The car had lost its low-slung appearance, thanks to the new front axle, the late-model rear end, and the replacement wheel and tire combination. Viewed today, with the clear hindsight of history, this car looks like a hodge-podge of parts compared to its original well-integrated appearance.

But in that era, nobody really cared. History wasn't a consideration. Nowhere, in any previous magazine, was there a mention of the car and its lakes and Bonneville history, and in this case, the Ayala history was omitted, as well. Brousseau had rebuilt the roadster, by himself, in his home garage. The *Car Craft* article said it was re-sprayed (in a deep shade of red) with a homemade air compressor. Hey – that was the 1960s!

Tom Branch and Jim Fuller lined their cars up for an historic one-time shot at Pomona in 1999. Remember, the Eddie Dye body and chassis are Branch's car; Fuller's "clone" has the nose and hood of the original Dye roadster. Soon after this photo was taken, Branch sold his car to Don Orosco, and Orosco copied the Fuller-owned Whitey Clayton-built nose and hood, so he could correctly restore the roadster. (Diana Branch)

We tracked down Roger Brousseau in Dudley, Massachusetts. "I bought the car in San Diego," he remembered, "from a guy who was a painter. It had the track nose, the hood, and the DuVall windshield, as well as the body and the bobbed '32 frame, but there was no firewall, engine, or transmission. It was mostly all apart. I think I paid $650 for it."

"I did everything myself," Brousseau continued. "I found a '32 truck grille shell and made the horizontal grille bars out of brass tubing. I made the headers too. And I got a '36 Ford tubular axle ([*sic*]…it's from a '37 Ford V-8/60, the only year Ford offered that axle) and installed it. That car handled great," he remembers. First he put a three-carb 348-ci Chevy in it, a new 335-bhp engine from an Impala. Later he installed the 409.

Brousseau was a member of the *San Diego Prowlers*. "I was young, and I didn't know the car's history," he said. "I eventually found some old pictures of it, the way it first was, but that wasn't until a year after I got it." Roger Brousseau had all the original body pieces. He could have restored the roadster back to its Eddie Dye configuration, but that's not what people did with old hot rods in that era. They built cars with then-contemporary features, and with Roger's redo, the roadster was considered cool enough for a *Car Craft* cover feature. "I could kick myself now," he commented. "I'd love to have it today."

Shortly before its *Car Craft* appearance, the roadster had a starring role in a now long-forgotten B movie, *The Lively Set*, with James Darren and Doug McClure. It was depicted on many of the movie posters, without the top, and with its chrome roll bar. "Romance and racing are in their blood," the film's promotion read, "and the faster the action, the more the fun."

"I took the roadster to a car show in Los Angeles, and it won first place in the Street Roadster class," Brousseau says. "Universal had someone there. They were looking for cars for an upcoming movie. They'd talked to some of the *LA Roadsters*, but those guys wanted too much money. A friend of mine, Joe Perinella, had an early Dodge roadster with a Chevy engine, and they used his car too. We spent a month at the Studios while they did the film."

After the movie was over, the old beam axle was replaced with that 1937 Ford V-8/60 lightweight tube axle. Thankfully, as they were key to this car's lasting identity, the unusual hairpin radius rods stayed as they were. About that

time, D-spoke American mags were installed with fat Firestone Darlington rears and smaller Pirelli fronts. It's likely Roger earned a few bucks for the car's movie appearance, so he may have used that income for the later additions.

In 1969-70, Roger Brousseau moved back east. He told me that, contrary to earlier stories, he actually gave away the roadster's old DuVall windshield, plus the original aluminum nose and hood, to a good friend who was building a car. "I know it would be worth a lot of money today," he told me, "but back then, I just wanted him to have it." Roger then sold the roadster to his dentist, a man named Colladinado, whose offices were in Temecula.

Next, Curt Holmquist acquired the roadster. He was also a member of the *San Diego Prowlers*, and he knew Roger Brousseau. Curt had actually ridden in the roadster when Roger owned it. "That car was really fast," he remembered, "with that 409. It could really scare you. I think Roger bought that engine complete, as a kind of early crate motor. With the top up, and the doors welded shut, it was very hard to get in and out, and you had to be kind of short to drive it. We called it the doorless wonder."

In an odd quirk of fate, Curt Holmquist actually bought the car's Clayton-built track nose, the louvered hood, and the DuVall windshield, *before* he was able to get the roadster itself. The pieces were offered some time earlier. "I'd had a friend," Holmquist says, "who did body work and also worked on street rods. He had injured his hand, so I helped him paint a '50 Ford coupe. He had gotten the pieces from Roger – we didn't know where the rest of the car had gone – and in exchange, he traded them to me. I got everything from the cowl forward."

Curt Holmquist tried unsuccessfully to fit the old Eddie Dye roadster nose and the hood panels onto another '29 roadster he owned. That attempt failed because the original car's cowl shape had been changed, and the original Dye roadster body had been widened a bit when it was channeled. So he took the pieces to the old Long Beach Swap Meet, where he sold the panels and the windshield to Jim Fuller, of Santa Barbara. Jim believes he paid $350 or $400 for the pieces. (Hold that thought, for a moment, while we continue with the saga of this roadster.) "Then six months later," Holmquist told me, chuckling, "I ended up with the whole car."

The way he found it is the sort of thing enthusiasts dream about. "It was 1973 or 1974," Curt recalled. "I think Roger had given the roadster away to his dentist, or maybe sold it to him, then that guy got divorced, and somehow it ended up with the dentist's ex-wife. I was driving through this San Diego neighborhood to call on a customer of mine," he recalled, "when I saw this garage door was open. Like any car enthusiast, I slowed down to look. What I saw was Roger's old roadster."

Don Orosco's shop in Pebble Beach is the current home of the Eddie Dye roadster. Craftsmen Brad Hand and Ole Erickson have begun the painstaking task of bringing this one back. Virtually every piece will need massaging, but the end result will be a truly unique historic roadster, well worthy of a 4,000+-hour restoration.

Don Orosco and Jim Fuller devised an odd but workable deal for the Eddie Dye '29s track nose. Fuller owned the original, and wanted a quality repaint for his own '29. So, Orosco's shop repainted Fuller's car (in black, since you asked). In exchange, Fuller let Don and his team borrow the original Whitey Clayton-built track nose and hood so they could make an exact copy. Here's the result.

Look closely; the nose and side pieces form a perfect circle. The grille is standard sprint car practice, hand-made of brass, with each bar carefully fitted, and the louvered hood has a bubble to clear the flathead's offset generator. It doesn't get any better than this. Whitey Clayton was truly a magician with metal.

"Of course," he recalls now, "stuff was stacked up all over it. But I recognized the color and could see a little of the chrome roll bar and one rear taillight. It was just dumb luck. I parked in the street, looked over, and there it was. A woman was standing there, arguing with her son. I asked her if I could just look at the car. The woman said yes, but she was really looking for someone to take it away. I gave her a deposit on the spot. I think I paid $1,000 for it. Someone had tried to push start it, and they'd run into the back and damaged the right rear. It still had the 409 in it, and now it had dual quads. But the motor wasn't any good any more."

Along with a friend, Curt tore the roadster apart. They installed a 283-ci Chevy (a low-mileage engine from an El Camino) and a Powerglide, because it was smaller than a 350 Turbo-Hydromatic and it fit nicely. Holmquist knew about the car's previous Ayala/Dye history, and even better, he knew where the parts were to bring the car back, at least in appearance, to the way it had looked in 1952-53. So he called Jim Fuller and asked if he could buy back the nose, hood, and windshield, and Jim Fuller said yes.

"So I drove all the way up from San Diego to Santa Barbara," Holmquist recalled, "and then Fuller said, 'I've changed my mind.' I can't tell you how angry I was. It was a 500-mile round trip for nothing. Why he changed his mind I'll never know."

Curt Holmquist installed a chopped Model A grille shell, completed the car in just two weeks, and drove it for several years. He didn't have the top, but admits he was too tall to get in the car with it on. "It was a sonofabitch to get in and out of, anyway. If you spent much time in it," he remembered, "you weren't walkin' too good. Only Roger could drive it."

Curt sold the roadster in the mid 1970s. "But afterwards, I tried hard to get it back. I lost track of it, then I saw it for sale at the *LA Roadsters* swap meet one year." He hung around looking for the owner, "...and when I went away for a few minutes, the last thing I saw was the car going out the gate."

Obviously, this car had a hold on people. Roger Brousseau told me "every time I went back to California, I tried to find

it, but I never did." The car's history for the next two decades is unknown, but perhaps someone reading this will be able to fill us in.

Fast forward to 1997. Tom Branch, of San Gabriel, California (coincidentally a member of the born-again *Auto Butchers* car club), was looking for a hot rod. By chance, he spotted what looked to be an interesting candidate at a cruise night at Frisco's Burgers in Downey. It was a channeled '29 Ford, by now painted yellow, with a Model A grille shell, a tube front axle, a straight windshield, a corduroy interior, a wood-grained dash insert, and American mags.

Tom thought it was a 1960s-era car that had been updated in the 1970s; until the owner told him it had once been in a movie. The car's curious front suspension intrigued him, as did many other details. He immediately decided to sell his roadster pickup and buy the yellow roadster. He called his friend, Kevin Preciado, who manufactures Cyclone speed equipment, to tell him he'd bought an old hot rod, and that it was formerly a film star.

"I had just come from Jim Jacobs' where he was restoring the Niekamp '29," Kevin told me. "And I was thinking about old hot rods. When I saw the hairpins on Tom's 'new' car, they looked oddly familiar. I mentally photographed it and went home to look. About the same time, Eric Madrid, a mutual friend of Tom's and Kevin's, pointed out the Eddie

Dye car in *Best Hot Rods*. A check in the old Fawcett #189 confirmed Kevin's suspicions. The unique hairpins and the closely mounted front shocks were the giveaways. "The windshield was gone," Kevin said, "and there was no nose to go off, but when we looked under the cowl, you could see where the bolt holes were for the DuVall."

The Eddie Dye roadster had surfaced again, but it no longer looked much like a Motorama star attraction. Branch learned what he could about the car. As he told *Hop Up*, for an article in the 2000 issue, "the Eddie Dye period is kind of a mystery; in the early 1960s, a man named Roger (Brousseau) owned it, put in a 409, a four-speed, changed the front end, interior, and wheels and tires. That's the way it appeared in the film *The Lively Set*."

Tom Branch did a lot of research on his car. He located Roger Brousseau, Curt Holmquist, and Jim Fuller. Fuller decided to do his own version of the Dye roadster with a '29 body, doors that opened, the DuVall, and a number of other changes. Branch understood that as long as Jim Fuller had the original nose and hood, he'd never be able to redo the car as it had been in 1952, on his limited budget. So Branch elected to make his own statement, rebuilding the roadster with elements of both the Dye and Brousseau versions. He fitted a chopped and filled '32 grille. Then he trashed the old corduroy upholstery and had Tito's of San Gabriel, California, reupholster the roadster with a pearl white tuck-and-roll, marine vinyl interior.

For running gear, Tom installed chromed reversed Mercury steel wheels front and rear, with Firestone bias-ply 5.60 x 15s in front and 8.20 x 15-inch slicks in the rear. He dressed up a 1968 Chevy 327 with triple carbs on an Edelbrock manifold, finned valve covers, and external headers by Lobo. He also redid the rest of the mechanicals as needed. Rick Grindle of Reseda, California, tastefully pinstriped the body and grille shell, and as a crowning touch, once again the car wore an *Auto Butchers* hatchet plaque. That's how I saw the car at Long Beach one Sunday, and subsequently at a number of events – Tom drove the wheels off it.

Tom Branch met Jim Fuller at the LA Roadster Show in 1999. That's when Branch decided he wouldn't be able to complete his car as the Dye roadster. Jim Fuller, who'd built a car around the pieces he'd bought, was unwilling to sell the nose and hood from the original car. They did park their two roadsters side by side for a historic photograph.

Just over a year later, in August 2000, Don Orosco, owner of the Pebble Beach hot rod class-winning Dick Flint roadster and the So-Cal '34 Ford coupe, made Branch an offer he couldn't refuse. Orosco then made a crafty deal with Jim Fuller. In exchange for copying the Dye car's real nose, Don's master craftsmen, Ole Ericson and Brad Hand, would paint Fuller's car. Jim decided he wanted it black, and

The Dye roadster's '32 frame was kicked up considerably in the rear, and then channel iron was used to form new crossmembers and body supports. This late-model rear end, installed by Roger Brousseau when the car received a Chevrolet V-8 engine transplant in the 1960s, will be replaced by a correct early Ford rear. Lacking construction photos, Orosco's team has to be archaeologists of sorts, deciding what is in fact original, and how the car's builders first created it.

as he said to me, "it's the equivalent of a $10,000 paint job." Jim's track-nosed '29 now runs a bored and stroked flathead, and it has doors that open. It's not quite a Dye clone, but it's a car many people would love to own.

Don Orosco plans to completely restore the former Eddie Dye roadster to look as it did in 1952. Robert Genat photographed the restoration for this story. Even in its unfinished state – but with a stunning new nose, louvered and blistered hood, and front nerf bar, precisely copied from the original pieces – you can easily see it will be dynamite when it's done. As this is written, Don is waiting to learn when there will be another roadster class at Pebble Beach, (perhaps in 2007) and then he plans to do a ground-up restoration. Knowing the quality of Don's previous cars, when the born-again Eddie Dye roadster is rolled out in Cherry Orchid lacquer at last, there will be a lot of people smiling.

Sometimes the fun of these historic hot rods is all the interesting detective work that's needed to trace a trail. The "Eddie Dye" roadster was unquestionably one of the neatest-looking early hot rods, and knowing that it had lakes racing history makes it more interesting and significant. And it's wonderful that it has surfaced and survived. Perhaps the publication of this book will encourage anyone who knows more of its early life to come forward, so the complete story can finally be told.

Looking down into the cockpit, the scope of work needed is enormous. Some re-creating will be necessary, as the car was changed substantially in the 1960s. That was a period when many early cars were "updated" and "improved." Precedent insists this car be restored to the way it was when it was first built.

7

Bob Petersen purchased the Ray Brown roadster for his collection, and it's usually on display in the Bruce Meyer Gallery. This great roadster's career has spanned half a century. It will be remembered for its fine racing record under Ray Brown's auspices, and for its pioneering efforts at Hershey with Kirk White.

This roadster defines "Historic Hot Rod." At the huge Antique Automobile Club of America Annual Fall Meet in Hershey, Pennsylvania, in October 1992, a curious crowd was packed four deep around a bright green '32 Ford highboy. When I edged closer for a look, I saw an old friend, Kirk F. White, holding court. Along with the car's restorers Jim Lowrey and his son Jim, Jr., Kirk enthusiastically talked about the restoration of this neatly proportioned, authentic dry-lakes racer.

A coveted SCTA plaque on the dash informed us that on September 21, 1947, with Ray Brown at the wheel, this same car had turned an impressive 123.62 mph at El Mirage. It doesn't get more authentic than that. The judges agreed, confirming the roadster as a bona fide racecar, eligible for AACA Class 24-A, and they awarded it a First Junior badge. The following year, White returned to Hershey to snag the roadster's AACA Senior award.

I didn't know it at the time, but this roadster would have a

big effect on my hot rodding life – it was a key inspiration for my own '32 Ford highboy. Seven years later, along with then-museum board chairman Bruce Meyer, I was able to help arrange its purchase, by Robert E. Petersen, so it could become an important artifact in the Petersen Automotive Museum's ongoing tribute to hot rod pioneers like Ray Brown. These men who raced at the lakes as youngsters, and then went on to hold important positions in the aftermarket performance industry, were the backbone of hot rodding, as we know it today, and roadsters like this one played a big part. But we're getting ahead of our story again.

Ray Brown was born in Sioux Falls, South Dakota, in 1928, but he began his '32 roadster at age 16, when he attended Loyola and then Hollywood High Schools in Los Angeles. The car first took shape in Ray's backyard, just after Word War II ended. Early pictures show a rough roadster body in various stages of completion. For three years, as a high school student, Ray had what many budding rodders would have considered a dream job. He worked for notoriously

Ray Brown's '32 Roadster

strict but talented Eddie Meyer in West Hollywood. Young Ray toiled at a variety of tasks: porting, machining, relieving blocks, and helping to build engines at the small, highly respected Eddie Meyer Engineering shop. In those days, Ray worked closely with Eddie's son Bud, and with hot rodding great Tom Sparks. In order to save the money he needed to build his roadster, Ray also worked evenings, parking cars at the Florentine Gardens in Hollywood.

Brown acquired his earliest racing knowledge from two of the best guys in the business. Working from their small shop at 645 North Robertson Blvd., in West Hollywood, Eddie and Bud were pioneers in the large-scale manufacture of flathead speed equipment. The Meyers, father and son, fielded a fast team of Midget racers and went on to dominate their classes in powerboat racing, with both Eddie and Bud driving. Distinctive, well made, and topped with that memorable racecar/powerboat logo, the Eddie Meyer dual intake manifolds, finned high-compression heads, and dual-coil/dual-point distributors were considered top-of-the-line. They were used on V-8/85s and V-8/60s by successful racers like Ray Brown, Jack McGrath, Jack Calori, Doug Hartelt, and Manuel Ayulo, to name a few.

The '32 roadster was Ray's everyday transportation, and it would become his first racecar. He drove it to work almost daily, even while it was under construction. Vintage photographs show a very young Ray in the '32 pulling into the Meyer shop driveway, with the car in various stages of completion. Even before it was painted, Ray raced the roadster successfully, and he continued competing in it in 1946 and 1947. Ray earned 11 timing tags with the car, helping to amass points for the competitive *Road Runners* hot rod club.

The roadster was typical in appearance for cars of that era, but its construction and finish were tops. The '32 shell was neatly filled. A three-piece hood with a very distinctive louver pattern, "lunch box" latches, and Dzus fasteners wore twin teardrop-shaped aluminum Eddie Meyer badges. The windshield was chopped 2-1/2 inches, the cowl was filled, and the door handles were shaved (but the trunk lid handle was retained).

In the rear, twin horizontally-mounted '40 Chevrolet taillights lent a different touch. Inside, there was a '40 Ford wheel, a column shifter, and an emergency brake, also from the '40 Ford. Under the steering column, a discrete pull cable allowed the driver to change the advance of the Eddie Meyer distributor. There was a Bell pressure pump to the left of the wheel.

The car's frame was neither boxed nor modified. In front, an Ed Stewart "Dago" dropped axle, stock (but plated) split wishbones, and tube shocks anchored the front suspension. In the rear, a Model A spring was used to clear the Halibrand quick-change. Lever shocks, twin tailpipes running parallel to the frame rails, and a chromed spreader bar completed the rear.

A two-gallon tank in the trunk and a parallel fuel system allowed Brown to convert his roadster to alcohol fuel at the lakes, where he'd switch fuel systems and install reworked and re-jetted twin 97s. After removing the windshield and headlights and fitting a snug tonneau cover, he was ready to roll. Consistent speeds in the mid 120s were a creditable achievement for a flathead-powered, distinctly non-aerodynamic highboy in that era. His fastest time in that car was 125.70

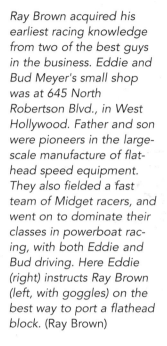

Ray Brown acquired his earliest racing knowledge from two of the best guys in the business. Eddie and Bud Meyer's small shop was at 645 North Robertson Blvd., in West Hollywood. Father and son were pioneers in the large-scale manufacture of flathead speed equipment. They also fielded a fast team of Midget racers, and went on to dominate their classes in powerboat racing, with both Eddie and Bud driving. Here Eddie (right) instructs Ray Brown (left, with goggles) on the best way to port a flathead block. (Ray Brown)

It's 1946. These guys are back from overseas and they're building roadsters in Ray's mom's backyard. Ray's '32 is on the right. The frame on the left has been Z'd, and check out that low front crossmember. Both engines are Eddie Meyer equipped; the car on the left has Eddie's famous exhaust-heated hi-rise intake. (Ray Brown)

mph, a competitive result for a very streetable, largely home-built roadster on a buggy-sprung chassis that was 15 years old. Perhaps even more remarkably, in late 1947 Ray took the '32 to Lake Arrowhead near Crestline, California, where it was photographed shortly before he sold it. While there, the car was caught in a snowstorm. Ray's plucky open-wheeled highboy sported tire chains on the rear wheels, along with a snug top and side curtains. In the early days, guys used their hot rods for everything, and that wonderful photograph is proof positive.

Ray painted his car in a fashionable 1946 Buick color called Sherwood Green. It was an unusual and distinctive hue for a hot rod in that era, and the shade subtly changed depending upon the lighting. Most rods of that era were unfinished in gray primer or left in original Ford black. Popular rodding repaints were Vermillion Red, Bright Green, or Washington Blue. Ray recalls that he saw a then-new Buick convertible in that color and immediately decided that was the shade he wanted for his roadster.

With its well-tuned, bored and stroked 284-ci flathead, running a snappy Winfield SU-1A cam, Ray's roadster wore the

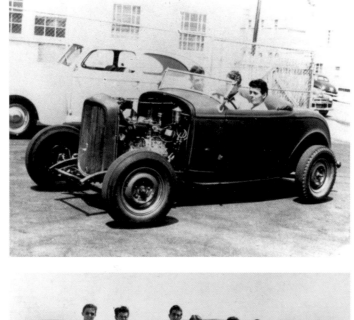

numbers "99C" and was a contender in Class C whenever it ran. But like every serious racer, after earning some 11 timing tags at SCTA and Russetta meets, Ray felt he'd reached the car's potential, and he wanted to go faster. He sold the roadster in 1948 for $850 to Bob Hutchinson of Pennsylvania. Hutchinson picked up the car on a rainy evening, and Ray says he never expected to see it again. Besides, he was ready for a new challenge.

Flush with cash, working in his mother's garage again, Ray had already begun on a more aerodynamic, potentially faster '27 T lakester. The resulting snake-belly low, mid-engined T ran a 156 ci, highly modified V-8/60 using all the tricks Ray had learned in the Meyer shop. Ray raced it in Class A, where it turned 134.73 mph in June 1949, at an SCTA event at El Mirage dry lake. The well-engineered little car was featured on the cover of Hot Rod magazine in May 1950. Inside, a Rex Burnett cutaway drawing emphasized its clever construction. The "new" car's highest speed at El Mirage was just over 137 mph.

Ray and his new racing partner, Alex Xydias, of So-Cal Speed Shop fame, were now competing for SCTA points for the Glendale Sidewinders, and the successful T was featured in

So-Cal Speed Shop ads. With his Meyer days behind him, Ray's swift 60 ran Evans heads and dual manifolds, Kong ignition, and a Harman & Collins cam. The V-8/60 engine was capable of an astonishing 6,800 rpm. About this time, Ray started his own company, Ray Brown Automotive, on Western and Lemon Grove in Hollywood; Alex's shop was in Burbank, and these two pioneering hot rodders are still friends to this day.

In 1950, Ray began competing in the "T" at Bonneville, and set a record with a two-way average speed of 133.33 mph. He later built a de-stroked and sleeved, 302-ci, Chrysler Hemi-powered belly tank lakester that dueled with Alex Xydias' 296-ci, Edelbrock-equipped, flathead-powered So-Cal tank. Ray hit a two-way record-setting average of 197.88 mph. To this day, Ray and Alex still argue in a friendly way over who went fastest in an aircraft belly tank. Alex's Bobby-Meeks prepared, nitro-burning flathead, incorporating every trick the talented Meeks could muster, managed a one-way run of 198.340 mph. Ray's Hemi-powered tank, running on alcohol, with a Chet Herbert roller tappet cam, edged out the earlier Meeks/Xydias two-way record of 197.17 by 0.71 mph, and eventually turned over 200 mph. Perhaps more importantly, Ray's results, with a Hemi that was not yet tuned to its full potential, showed racers that Chrysler's new engine had the ability to permanently retire their beloved flatheads.

As we noted, Ray sold his roadster in 1948 to Bob Hutchinson, who drove it back east to Mount Lebanon, Pennsylvania. Interestingly, in his research on the Brown '32, Kirk White found that Bob Hutchinson had been working at a local Ford agency there in early 1949. About that time, Hutchison purchased a used set of 1932 Ford fenders there, which he installed on the Ray Brown car. Incredibly, those fenders came from the Doane Spencer roadster. On

one of his cross-country trips, Spencer allegedly had sold the fenders off his car, reportedly for $18 (!), to Ed Lowther. Bob Hutchinson held onto the Ray Brown roadster for years. In 1973, he moved to Las Vegas, and, of course, the '32 was taken along. Kirk White reports that Ray's old roadster, now full-fendered and repainted black, "was in good dry storage from 1948 to 1991, and had very little use."

Ray himself gave little thought to the fate of the roadster. He occasionally found himself wondering what had happened to it, but he was very busy. Hot rodding was Ray's springboard for a remarkable career as one of hot rodding's living legends. Brown's speed shop soon evolved into his own company, Ray Brown Automotive, and began making seat belts back in 1951 under the Impact Auto Saf-Tee Belt brand. Eleven years later, he became the country's major supplier of belts to the U.S. government. Ray helped coin the slogan, "The life you save may be your own."

Along the way Ray was one of the first to realize the potential of Chrysler's Hemi OHV V-8s. After showing the way with his own belly tank, Ray and his company built Chrysler racing engines for the 236-mph multiple record-setting Shadoff Special Streamliner, (designed by Dean Batchelor, built by Carl Fleischmann, and driven by Mal Hooper), the 203-mph Bonneville record-holding Guy and Joe Mabee Oil Drilling Co. Special, Mickey Thompson, and many others. Ray was elected SCTA president in 1953.

Ray's engine wasn't pretty, but it ran like a scalded cat. Dual fuel taps on the firewall alternatively access the two-gallon alcohol tank in the trunk or the regular fuel tank. Ray would switch fuel systems right at the lakes. He'd install reworked and re-jetted twin 97s and after removing the windshield and headlights, and fitting a snug tonneau cover, he was ready to roll. Consistent speeds in the mid 120s were a creditable achievement for a flathead-powered, distinctly non-aerodynamic highboy in that era. His fastest time in that car was 125.70 mph, a competitive result for a very streetable, largely home-built roadster on a buggy-sprung chassis that was 15 years old. (Ray Brown)

Ray Brown's '32 roadster (right) and an unidentified '29 on '32 rails wait their turn at El Mirage. Ray raced for the SCTA Road Runners club. Note the lady in rolled-up jeans chatting up the guy in the '29. (Dean Batchelor)

It was hot, dirty, dusty, and dangerous, and you sometimes waited in line for hours. But when the big moment came, and you nailed the gas, and streaked across the hard-packed alkali surface at 120+, it was all worth it. Ray Brown gives 'er the gun at El Mirage in 1947. (Ray Brown)

He initially retired at age 39, but couldn't stay away from the speed equipment game for long. Returning to the business world, he became senior vice president of Superior Industries, helping that firm to become a major aftermarket and OEM supplier of safety equipment and alloy wheels. Ray was elected a member of the SEMA Hall of Fame in 1991. With his busy life unfolding, Ray Brown had no idea his old roadster was languishing in a lock-up garage in Las Vegas.

Kirk White takes up the story here. "For most of 1991," Kirk says, "I had been advertising in *Hemmings Motor News* for genuine early racing hot rods from the 1940s and 1950s. Most of my responses missed the mark widely. Then in early September, a gentleman named Robert Stamper called on a Sunday evening and said that he had a car that…was what I was looking for…but he didn't know

much of the car's history. We talked for quite a while, and finished with him promising photographs…. Finally, near the end of October, the pictures arrived, and I looked carefully at the three-piece hood."

Kirk White was pretty sure he'd "…seen that distinctive louver pattern somewhere…I checked one of Don Montgomery's books," he said, "and there it was. In fact it was in all three of his (early) books, and Tom Medley's *Hot Rod History* had a chapter on Ray Brown." Kirk says today that when he learned the car's dry lakes history, he realized "this was the opportunity I'd been looking for." Luckily, White was coming to Las Vegas for an auto auction. Bob Stamper picked him up at the airport and they drove to the storage garage that held the roadster.

"There it was," Kirk White says, "looking pretty good for essentially being in storage since 1949 [*sic*], albeit now in black, full-fendered, and a bit down at the heels. I was really getting nervous. There was a major auction in Las Vegas that weekend, and the town was filled with dealers and collectors, so we put the car back in the garage, went through our purchase arrangements, and I flew home to Philadelphia."

Kirk had the '32 shipped to Jim Lowrey Sr. and Jim Jr.'s shop, which was then in Chelmsford, Massachusetts. The three men talked about the roadster and decided "since it was virtually intact, that it should return to its 1947 racing configuration."

"To really cement the car's history," White continued, "we elected to certify the car with the AACA as a Class 24-A racing car. The AACA is extremely careful about certifying a car, and your vehicle has to have a bulletproof provenance. Gaining certification is a lot like getting a master's degree…it's a painstaking effort."

Fortunately, with the '32 so complete and well preserved, the restoration was in White's words, "pretty straightforward." The roadster still had the engine that Ray had used when it raced in 1947, with all the original Meyer equipment on it, and Ray's name was stamped on the front of the Meyer twin-carb intake manifold. "I called (the late) Dean Batchelor," Kirk said, "and asked him what he could tell me about Ray Brown. 'Here's his phone number,' Batchelor replied."

"And I had the pleasure," Kirk recalls, "of telling Ray that we had unearthed his great '32 dry lakes car."

Ray Brown takes up the story here. I asked him how he felt when he got the call from Kirk. "Naturally, I was thrilled," he said. "Kirk and I got to know each other, and we began to talk on the phone and correspond about the details he needed to restore the car."

By the spring of 1992, the roadster's restoration was well underway. Kirk learned that during its Las Vegas sojourn,

Meyer speed equipment.) But after considerable effort, all the missing pieces were located.

Ray Brown helped via telephone and letters. His amazing memory for details and his extensive personal files ensured the '32's restoration was correct and accurate. Kirk explains, "When I asked Ray about the tonneau cover snaps, he told me exactly where each one was located. The caramel brown leather upholstery and a new black tonneau cover were done by Dave Emory at LeBaron Bonney."

Ray also described the squared-off porting technique that Manny Ayulo used. "When we took off the heads and intake manifold, it was obviously Ayulo's handiwork." Incredibly, after all those years, Ray's car still had its "original" 1946 Mercury engine.

The car debuted at the Ty-Rods Old Timer's Reunion in Hudson, Massachusetts, in September 1992. "We were thrilled," White remembers, "and so were the rodders who got to see it and spend some time with the album filled with early racing photos, restoration progression, etc."

The following month, Kirk and the Lowreys brought the

the '32 had actually been stolen for a brief period of time. When it was returned, a few instruments and some other parts were missing. In the "as found" photos, the headlights are not mounted. He had to find replacements for some of the rare curved-glass Stewart-Warner gauges, and he needed a set of "fresh" Eddie Meyer heads, as the old ones were unusable. (This was before Don Orosco began reproducing

Ray painted his car in a fashionable 1946 Buick color called Sherwood Green. It was an unusual and distinctive hue for a hot rod in that era, and it changes shade slightly depending upon the lighting. Most rods of that era were unfinished in gray primer or left in original Ford black. Popular rodding repaints were Vermillion Red or Washington Blue. Ray recalls that he saw a new Buick convertible in that color, and immediately decided that was the shade he wanted for his roadster.

Ray Brown helped the restorers via telephone and letters. His amazing memory for details and his extensive personal files ensured the '32's restoration was correct and accurate. According to Kirk White, "When I asked Ray about the tonneau cover snaps, he told me exactly where each one was located." Dave Emory at LeBaron Bonney did the caramel brown leather upholstery and a new black tonneau cover.

car to Hershey. Although it was not the first time a hot rod had appeared at the fall AACA Meet (Ron San Giovanni had shown his ex-*Cam Carriers'* altered T drag roadster earlier), it was the first time a dry lakes racing roadster was shown in Class 24-A. "At 6:00 A.M., we rolled the car out of the trailer, fired it up through the open lakes plugs, and rolled it onto the show grounds. The crowd loved the car, and along with the other roadster we had there (the Bob Schaeneman '32; see Chapter 15), you couldn't get near the cars for the throng. It was a major step for hot rodding in the world of the AACA. Someone commented that it looked as though we were handing out $100 bills all day, the crowds were that thick around the cars!"

After Hershey, White was able to drive the car for the first time. "What's it like? It couldn't be any better," he told *Hop Up* magazine's Tim Gavern in an interim issue of that magazine, published in 1994, "with an incredibly smooth and strong push of power from the flathead, and the whine of the Halibrand. It's an amazingly good ride in the '90s," Kirk reported, "it must have been out of this world in 1946." (If you have a copy of that magazine, there's a "letter to the editor" from me, and a picture of my "just-started" '32 roadster. Seeing Ray's old car was the prime impetus for my six-year project.)

A few weeks later, in November, Kirk brought the '32 to the NHRA's inaugural meet in Bakersfield, California, and reunited Ray Brown with his car. "It was a pretty special moment," Kirk recalls. Ray told me that seeing his old car there, after 44 years, was quite an emotional experience. He said, "I thought, oh God, there it is. And I spent a wonderful day visiting with Kirk and Dean and all the other people who had come to see it. It was great." In 1994, the ex-Ray Brown roadster received the AACA Past President's Award, the highest honor an AACA-certified competition car can earn.

Kirk White continued looking for other historic hot rods, and he turned up a few of them. His long, well-written descriptive advertisements were a highlight in *Hemmings*.

Some of the cars he found are in this book. They include the '32 roadsters of Tommy Foster and Bob Schaeneman.

White's pioneering efforts at Hershey paved the way for the "Pebble Beach invasion." By painstakingly restoring a historic vintage street and dry lakes-driven hot rod roadster, and presenting it as an authentic American racing car in AACA Class 24-A, White had neatly circumvented traditional rules and attitudes. Remember, the first time this deuce was shown to a possibly hostile AACA audience, those potentially adverse attitudes turned on a dime. When we all saw that people were packed around the little green roadster, BS-ing and bench racing, it seemed natural to present the idea of historic hot rods to Pebble Beach Concours d'Elegance co-chairmen, Lorin Tryon and J. Heumann.

Bruce Meyer, John Mozart, Glenn Mounger, Gordon Apker, Dennis Varney, and I all talked about an historic hot rod class at Pebble. After patiently listening to our case, one night during dinner at the Hershey Hotel, Lorin seemed ready to make the decision. Hot rod historian Dean Batchelor had just passed away, and it was the right time to create a Concours award in Dean's name. I spoke with Ford West Coast PR boss, John Clinard. Thanks to his initiative, Ford Motor Company offered to underwrite the Dean Batchelor Award, and a permanent Stanley Wanlass bronze trophy was created in Dean's name.

For the inaugural hot rod class at Pebble Beach, nine great historic cars were assembled. Bruce Meyer's ex-Doane Spencer '32 took top honors, the Ray Brown '32 was second, and the ex-Tony La Masa, "Ricky Nelson," channeled '32 was third. They were all winners that day, as far as I was concerned, and the sight of old 99C, with Kirk White at the wheel and Ray Brown riding shotgun, was one for the history books.

Late that year, I became the Director of the Petersen Automotive Museum in Los Angeles. Dave Simard continued to work on my '32 roadster back in Leominster, Massachusetts. It was completed just in time for the 50th

clutch at 3,000 rpm resulted in a long screech from the 7.00 x 16s, and a snap-shift to second gear caused a loud chirp of rubber. The Ray Brown roadster let British show goers see what a true American hot rod was all about.

Back in California, I was privileged to have the opportunity to take the roadster to a number of hot rod events, including one where Ray rode alongside me in his old car. On the way home one afternoon, we ran out of gas. With the modifications for the quick-change, the altered tank only holds about 10 gallons. Ray said, "This used to happen to me all the time."

When the Petersen Museum presented, "Speed: The World's Fastest Cars," Ray Brown's old roadster was on display representing the dry lakes and early Bonneville era. This '32's active career has spanned over half a century. It will be remembered for its fine racing record, under Ray's auspices, and for Kirk White's pioneering AACA efforts that helped to underscore the significance of historic hot rods. It's a great survivor, and an authentic glimpse into the past – just like its first owner.

Anniversary of the Grand National Roadster Show. Petersen sponsored a special four-roadster display at the show, which was held that year at the Cow Palace in South San Francisco. Our stand included my freshly done '32 highboy, Mike Russell's ex-Moomjean '32 roadster, the Miller Automotive Special, another historic '32 roadster from the Petersen Museum and, thanks to Kirk F. White, we also had the ex-Ray Brown car. Although we were located in the rear of an auxiliary building, the roadster display attracted a lot of attention. Shortly after the show concluded, Kirk told me that Ray's old car was for sale.

Bruce Meyer and I called Bob Petersen right away to suggest he purchase Ray's '32. "Pete" made the decision over the phone, and to my great delight, the Ray Brown roadster became part of the Petersen's permanent collection. I was able to drive the car on occasion, helping to publicize the museum, and I can confirm Kirk's impressions. It's very responsive, surprisingly quick, and the pipes have a delightful rap. In June 2000, I brought the '32 to the Goodwood Festival of Speed in England and hammered it up the long test hill in exhibition runs, sharing the driving "chores" with UK writer Andrew English. What a thrill! Popping the

The AACA badge signifies this roadster's provenance in Class 24-A for authentic racecars. The Antique Automobile Club of America doesn't encourage hot rods, but they will acknowledge a car with genuine racing history. The Ray Brown roadster holds both AACA Junior and Senior awards, and its success has helped encourage other hot-rodders to enter authentic cars in AACA competition.

The '40 Chevrolet taillights were unusual on roadsters. While driving this car one day, I managed to break one, and when I went to replace it, I learned there was a right side and a left side. Everything about this car is classic: the frame rail-hugging tailpipe, Halibrand quick-change, notched gas tank – and I can attest that it drives as good as it looks.

Compare Dick Flint's channeled, belly-panned '29 Model A roadster to its early upright 1950s contemporaries, and you'll realize the effect this extraordinary lowboy had. Its proportions are perfect; the racecar nose that some have compared to that of a Ferrari or Maserati Grand Prix car was very contemporary. The '39 teardrop taillights, plated Auburn dash panel, big-and-little ribbed/grooved rubber combo, and fashionably protective nerf bars are hot rod iconic.

This all-star car was built by an all-star cast. When you compare Dick Flint's channeled, belly-panned '29 Model A roadster to its early 1950s contemporaries, you begin to realize the effect this snake-belly low-boy had over half a century ago on enthusiasts and civilians alike. Its proportions are well nigh perfect. The racecar nose, which some have compared to that of a Ferrari or Maserati Grand Prix car, is still contemporary. That notable nose wasn't just a pretty face – Dick turned 143.54 mph in this car at El Mirage in 1950. The '39 teardrop taillights, plated Auburn dash panel, big-and-little, ribbed and grooved rubber combo, and neat nerf bars are hot rod iconic. Though it idled for a time, the Dick Flint roadster is now beautifully restored. It has been copied and cloned – it was and is, a hot rod classic.

Ask Bob Petersen about this car, and the famous May 1952 *Hot Rod* magazine cover that showed Flint and an actor companion, stopped at a crosswalk, ogling a chesty coed, and "Pete" replies without hesitation, "that was the first issue where we sold over half a million copies."

The red rod on the cover must have helped. Dick Flint's A-V8 was the Hot Rod of the Month in that notable issue, capped with a full photo shoot by Felix Zelenka and a Rex Burnett cutaway drawing. The car's contours were perfect, and its full belly pan, which we learned was functional (hence the car's high trap speed), was beyond the capability of the average mid-century rodder. It turns out the hand-formed aluminum pan was done by none other than Dean Batchelor, working with Valley Custom's Neil Emory and Clay Jensen. The Valley boys also fabricated the car's sleek nose and hood, complete with inverse louvers and smooth, generator-clearing side blister.

Flint, like so many 1940s-era rodders, was overseas during World War II. Stationed in the Philippines, between Navy duties he fantasized about building a Model A to replace a car he'd left behind. Soon after the war ended, he left harm's way for a spot in a hotbed of hot rods. Flint worked for Alex Xydias at the original So-Cal Speed Shop in Burbank. A member of the *Glendale Sidewinders*, then a very active SCTA racing club, Flint went to the very first Bonneville meet in 1949

Dick Flint's '29 Roadster

with the So-Cal Speed Shop team. Working for So-Cal, Dick Flint could cherry pick their extensive catalog for the best in components. He was a frequent attendee at lakes meets, and he had a vision for a winning show-and-go car.

Dick started with three Model A roadster bodies, taking the best of each to assemble a sound example, then channeled the body over a Model A frame. He'd commissioned a local welder to do the frame welding, but the work wasn't up to Dick's standards. The Z-framing, done to further lower the

car, was crudely finished, but working on a limited budget, Flint elected to go with what he had. In those days, as Flint confirms today, "We didn't worry too much over what you couldn't see." By the time this car was completed, with its full belly pan covering everything underneath, the botched and crudely finished frame would be well out of sight.

Flint built the brackets that held the body to the chassis; he also made the engine mounts, shock brackets, those cool nerf bars, and every fixture needed to mount the battery, exhaust system, and the fuel tank. He then adapted hydraulic brakes from a '46 Ford and fitted a So-Cal dropped and filled front axle. Next, Flint brought the "roller" to Valley Custom for extensive bodywork while he began building the engine.

Working with Neil Emory, and with advice from Dean Batchelor, Flint envisioned a wind-cheating track nose reminiscent of those on prewar Indy racecars. As was so often done, Dick and Neil chalked out the shape of the nose on the shop floor. Using 18 pieces of welding rod, partners Emory and Jensen developed a supporting framework and then they hand-formed the lovely nose section out of aluminum. Emory made the grille out of round aluminum rod, as well. Flint filed it to perfection before it was buffed and, according to Batchelor's article in *Hop Up*, clear lacquered to protect the finish. They also fabricated the shapely three-piece hood and took it to Art Engles, who punched the louvers from the outside in.

Valley Custom did a great deal of custom bodywork on this car. The seams under the deck lid were filled, the side panels were flared inward, and the rear deck corner reveals were finished to look like those of a '32 Ford. The panels in the wheel wells had rusted out, so Valley Custom replaced them with new removable panels. The full belly pan was made in five pieces. One panel under each side ran the full length of the car. There was a center section held on with aircraft-style Dzus fasteners, a rear panel under the body, and a small panel under the rear axle, which could be removed easily.

As Dean Batchelor noted in an extensive article that was a cover story in *Hop Up*, June 1953, "By having the underpan made in sections like this, the driveshaft and rear-end assem-

Not sure where this was taken, but it's typical of the way shots were done before it was common to use a studio. The shooters picked an open area, with a neutral surface, and tried to photograph from a low position, or from a ladder or elevated position. The result was a clean photograph, devoid of clutter, and a chance to appreciate the clean lines and clever features of this remarkable roadster.

Dick Flint's channeled, belly-panned '29 Ford roadster was a Hop Up cover car in November 1951. Just completed, four years under construction, this low-slung beauty had topped 143 mph at the lakes. Features then were sparse in the "little books." One paragraph, a few photos, all black and white, and that was it. But this car would go on to more covers, and more color. (Ken Gross Archives)

• DETAILS OF ONE OF AMERICA'S MOST BEAUTIFUL ROADSTERS

Now it can be told. Look closely at those whitewalls, and then check out the left side front tire. Dean Batchelor told me that the whitewalls were added to "brighten up the picture." There's a jack under the axle on the left side of the car because the whitewall was a taller tire and the car needed to be level for the photograph. That said, the Flint car was always a star whenever it appeared.

bly can be removed from the car by removing two panels instead of the whole belly pan." Dean modestly omitted mentioning that he worked part time at Valley Custom, and he did a great deal of the belly-pan work. He did write, "the rear, or easy part, now completed, they started on the front. The word 'easy' here, means only in comparison with the rest of the work. No custom work is easy."

To complete the car's smooth appearance, Valley Custom welded and filled the joint where the Model A cowl met the body. The hole in the cowl for the original Model A fuel tank was filled, and a new tank was relocated under the deck lid. Inside, a '32 Ford dash panel was extended downward and gently, and peaked to accommodate an inset Auburn panel. Convex lensed Stewart-Warner instruments replaced the original Auburn units (originally made by S-W), while two additional gauges, a fuel pressure gauge and an ammeter, flank the Auburn panel. Flint retained the Auburn's original 100-mph speedometer. He trimmed the fluting off an art-deco '40 Ford wheel, cut down a '39 floor shift handle for the transmission, which was fitted with a 26-tooth close-ratio Zephyr cluster, and soon afterward, retained Floyd Tipton, in Burbank, to upholster the car in medium brown co-hide, a synthetic but natural-appearing leather.

While Valley Custom's crew completed the bodywork, Flint began on the '40 Merc flathead. The engine was bored 1/8 inch,

and a 4-1/8-inch stroked crank was fitted (although one early source says this is a 4-1/2-inch stroker, we're certain that's not correct), bringing displacement to 286 ci. Flint installed one of the hot sticks of the 1940s, a Winfield Super 1A camshaft. The usual internal mods were performed, including Johnson adjustable tappets, three-ring racing pistons, full balancing of the internal moving parts, plus a port, polish, and relief job. Dick's friend, Karl Fleischmann, created the ignition. Three 97s on an Edelbrock manifold matched block-letter Edelbrock 9:1 high-compression heads. Tubular headers, with discretely hidden lakes plugs, rounded out the externals. In stark contrast to the car, the original engine finish wasn't particularly pretty. Both top radiator hoses had to be routed sideways to clear the generator and belt pulleys. But in this case, looks didn't matter. In the lower corner of the dash is an SCTA timing tag attesting to an El Mirage run of 143.54 mph. *That* mattered.

Interestingly, dry lakes enthusiast Dick Saillant photographed this car at a Russetta Timing Association meet in 1951. Following a practice done by top shops today, Flint assembled the entire car, and then ran it at the lakes in both RTA and SCTA meets, before disassembling it for plating and paint. The fully completed '29 was featured in Hop Up in the November 1951 issue, and again as a cover car for a larger article in Hop Up (which had transitioned from a pocket mag to a full-sized one) in May 1953. In the meantime, it represented the fledgling NHRA at several shows, and won awards at the Oakland Roadster Show and the third Los Angeles Motorama. Although some people believe the roadster depicted on the initial NHRA badge was the Bill Niekamp '29, I think you can make a good case that it was Dick Flint's roadster.

The final finish was Federal truck red. The car was featured with garish whitewalls and fake wire wheel caps on the '53 *Hop Up* cover, but if you look closely, you'll see the left side

Proof positive this car was definitely a goer – the Flint roadster at the lakes in 1950. Note that the roadster's cowl is even with the top of the Merc's fender. The small roll bar may not have helped much, but it probably satisfied requirements. The roadster's best time, in June 1950, was in excess of 143 mph. Reportedly, Flint ran it at the lakes in unfinished form, set his best time, then came home, disassembled the car, painted it, and finished it off.
(Don Cox)

front tire is a ribbed Firestone. Dean Batchelor told me many years ago that they temporarily installed those two whitewalls on the right side of the car to brighten up the cover shot. The roadster never ran with them. For the record, the front tires were ribbed 5.00 x 16s, while the block-tread rears were 7.00 x 16-inch Firestones. The Halibrand quick-change rear, with a 3.27:1 ratio, and relocated Ross steering, with that distinctive high-mounted drag link, came later. Curiously, a likeness of this car, painted blue, appears on the cover of the *Popular Mechanics Hot Rod Handbook* for 1954. I have a copy, and when you look closely at the illustration, it appears the three lads in the picture are removing a twin-carb intake for a Chevy six.

Dick Flint owned the roadster until 1961. In those days, *Hot Rod* magazine had a classified section, and the car was actually offered for sale. Don't you wish you'd made that call?

Duane Kofoed, a member of the *LA Roadsters*, acquired the Dick Flint roadster in the early 1960s. He drove the wheels off it, and it was photographed and filmed at many shows and rod runs. But the weak frame became weaker; Duane says that the doors would spring open if the car traversed a steep driveway. When Kofoed disassembled the '29 to rebuild it, he was horrified at the condition of the frame and he was stymied by the extensive work required to make the roadster right.

Fast-forward some thirty years. Don Orosco, a shopping center and hotel developer from Pebble Beach, and an enthusiastic vintage racer and hot-rodder, had been trying to purchase an historic '32 Ford roadster. Like many people, Orosco was unsuccessful in buying the Doane Spencer deuce from Neal East, but East graciously tipped Don off that there might be a significant '29 roadster available for restoration. Orosco contacted Kofoed, who was at first reluctant to sell. In fact, it took Duane two years before he even consented to send Don photos of the car. Orosco knew exactly what it was, of course, and after an inspection meeting at a garage in Burbank, Don wrote the check.

Orosco's company, DBO Development, is located a stone's throw from the Laguna Seca racetrack outside Carmel, California. He and his talented crew, which includes fabricator (and steam car enthusiast) Brad Hand, metal wizard Jim Allan, and body miracle man Ole Erickson, carefully studied the old car to see what had been done to it over the years.

Initially, they too, were dismayed. The original flathead and the Ford driveline had been replaced by a small-block Chevrolet and an Olds rear. The rear end assembly was connected with a set of hairpin wishbones and an added tubular crossmember. In order to make more space inside the car, the inner frame rails had been trimmed, weakening the frame still more, to the point where it bowed outward and sagged. It was unusable, and really not even salvageable.

Valley Custom filled the seams under the deck lid; the side panels were flared inward and the rear deck corner reveals were finished to look like those of a '32 Ford. The wheel well panels had rusted out so they were replaced with removable panels. The full belly pan was made in five pieces. One panel under each side ran the full length of the car. There was a center section, held on with aircraft style Dzus fasteners, a rear panel under the body, and a small panel under the rear axle, which could be removed easily. Dean Batchelor worked part-time at Valley Custom, and did much of the belly pan.

Working with Neil Emory at Valley Custom, and with advice from Dean Batchelor, Flint envisioned a wind-cheating track nose reminiscent of those on prewar Indy cars. Dick and Neil chalked out the shape of the nose on the shop floor. Using 18 pieces of welding rod, partners Emory and Jensen developed a supporting framework, and then hand-formed the nose section out of aluminum. That notable nose wasn't just a pretty face – Dick turned 143.54 mph in this car at El Mirage on June 11, 1950.

The track-influenced Ross steering setup was relocated to exit on the cowl side. The suspended drag link gives the roadster unmistakable racecar flair. The '40 Ford steering wheel was retained, and the ribbed front tires were a popular lakes choice.

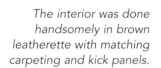

The interior was done handsomely in brown leatherette with matching carpeting and kick panels.

The track-roadster influence is very evident here. Cars like this one, with streamlined roadster noses, channeled bodies, etc., were in a transition in the early 1950s. They still could be competitive at the lakes, but they were evolving toward less competition and more of a great street-rod look. The track-nosed Bill Niekamp roadster is another example; it too turned over 140 mph, largely because of its slippery shape.

been done when the car was built. Don Orosco likes to joke that it would have been cheaper to build the car from scratch than it was to sensitively restore it. Dick Flint says that the final result was absolutely necessary, adding, "...it was the way I would have done it, if I could have done it over."

Credit Tom Sewell, from Cambria, California, with the upholstery; John Wolfe and Company from Willoughby, Ohio, with the extensive instrument restoration; and another John Wolfe with the engine machining and assembly work. This time, the flathead was a trusty 59AB block, bored and stroked to 3-5/16 and 4 inches, respectively, for 276 ci. The cam remains a Super 1A Winfield. The distributor is a restored Eddie Meyer unit, which resembles a twin-coil Kong, with a Pierce-Arrow distributor cap. For a time, Orosco ran a set of his reproduction Eddie Meyer finned heads, but presently a correct set of block-letter Edelbrock heads is fitted.

Everything about this engine is neater than the original, but Orosco & Co. resisted the temptation to over plate and polish. The radiator, an improvement over the original, is a custom Brassworks unit which, along with some belly pan

Orosco and his team thought about what to do for several years. They finally decided to re-engineer the frame and build an entirely new platform for the car, using construction techniques and materials that could have been available in 1950 and 1951. As Don says today, "We looked at the work of a number of period guys, including people like Frank Kurtis. We wanted to encapsulate the construction methods of that era into something that could have been done back then, if the builder had the requisite skills."

The resulting chassis was fabricated, beginning with an extensively cut down '32 Ford K-member (actually disassembled at first into 25 pieces) that was mated to Model A-type rails. The new frame was Z-ed at either end, and extensively boxed, with the lightening holes cut and flared over as though the Ford factory had originally done them. A Model A firewall was trimmed down to fit. Chrome-moly tubing was used to form a strong framework to support the cowl and the Willys-Knight steering box, as was 1950s-era racecar practice.

The team closely copied Ford factory welding style, frame rail forming, and riveting practice. The resulting new frame was strong, beautiful, functional – and "legal," according to Pebble Beach Concours d'Elegance restoration rules which permit, at the judges' discretion, judicious re-engineering and restoring, just so long as the work is such that it could have

mods, seems to have cured any tendency for the fully enclosed car to overheat. Mike Sanchez applied the Sikkens Honda Milano Red paint, which Flint says is very close to the original hue.

The roadster made its debut at the 50th Anniversary Oakland Roadster Show in 1999. Orosco had commissioned an award-winning display that featured a huge color blow-up of the famous *Hot Rod* cover. Dick Flint himself and some of the original *Sidewinders* were there to see it. Fittingly, the '29 received a great deal of critical acclaim. Still, a few details needed correction. Don and his team had fabricated the hood and incorporated a top bubble to clear the carburetors with air cleaners they had installed. That wasn't the way Flint built the car, so they redid the hood accordingly. The upholstery was redone again, this time with leatherette that more closely resembled the grained original material. Orosco had managed to locate an NOS set of Firestone block tread Ascot tires, at a "huge" expense, from a man in Southern California who'd been hoarding them for years. "At the end," he reflects, "the cost of this restoration didn't matter. We were striving for perfection."

The Dick Flint '29 was one of nine roadsters present for the second hot rod class at the Pebble Beach Concours d'Elegance in 2001. Bruce Meyer brought the freshly restored Bob McGee roadster, Blackie Gejeian was there with his "Shish Kebab Special," and other entries included the ex-Dick Williams T, the Highland Plating Special, and the ex-Rico Squaglia T roadster (the 1951 Oakland AMBR winner).

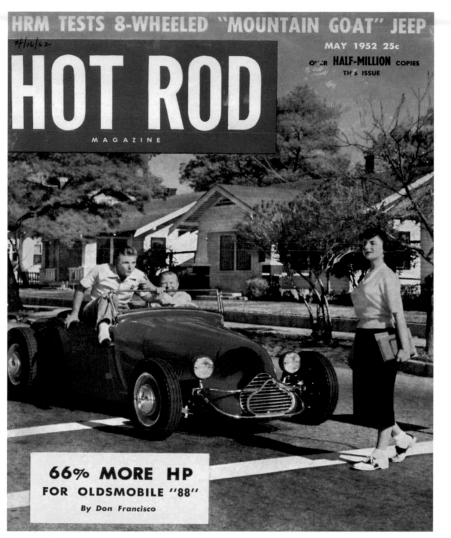

Ask Bob Petersen about this car and the famous May 1952 Hot Rod magazine cover that showed Flint and an actor companion, stopped at a cross walk, ogling a chesty coed, and "Pete" replies without hesitation, "that was the first issue where we ever sold over half a million copies." The red rod on the cover must have helped. Dick Flint's A-V/8 was the "Hot Rod of the Month" in that notable issue, capped with a full photo shoot by Felix Zelenka and a Rex Burnett cutaway drawing. The car's contours were perfect and its full bellypan, that we learned was functional (hence the car's high trap speed), was beyond the capability of the average mid-century rodder.

That Pebble Beach Sunday in 1999 dawned with an unusually overcast leaden sky that persisted for most of the day. Contestants wiped condensation off their cars continuously at first, bright finishes were dulled by the persistent early morning haze, and the initial crowd was a bit sparser than usual. But those people who did brave the cool weather were rewarded with another great Pebble Beach show. The hot rod display was simply terrific. Parked in a long parallel row, the lineup of nine multihued, impudent T's, A's, and deuces was a wonderful contrast to the more formal classics and swoopy sports cars. The class judges this year were Ray Brock and Don Montgomery once again. Tom Sparks replaced Alex Xydias who had been a judge two years earlier. We felt because of Alex and Pete Chapouris' connection with the So-Cal Speed Shop, we'd avoid any semblance of a conflict of interest if Alex skipped judging this year. We had about three hours to scrutinize all nine entries and we needed every minute.

Earlier, Jay Mays, vice president of design for Ford Motor Company, presented each entrant with a Steve Posson sculpture of the Doane Spencer roadster on a marble base. A Ford

Auburn panel was plated, with inserts removed. Dick retained the Auburn Eight 0-140-mph speedo, and substituted 2-5/8-inch convex Stewart-Warners for the original Auburn gauges. The Model A inner panel was extended downward to encompass the full width of the Auburn dash insert.

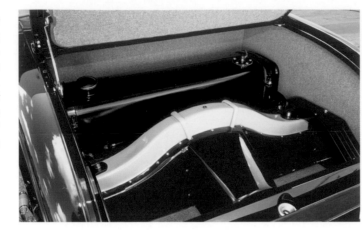

blue plate thanked everyone for participating. Mays summed it up pretty well: "the hot rod is a uniquely American form of automotive expression that, over time, has come to be appreciated as symbolic of high-speed, purpose-built vehicles. Like Italy's Ferraris and Germany's Porsches, American hot rods have become icons of a nation's inventiveness and culture. Today, around the world, the American hot rod represents originality, youth, and fun."

Jay told me that Ford Motor Company was proud to sponsor the hot rod class and the Dean Batchelor Memorial Trophy. "Dean understood the importance that the early hot rods and those who built them had on both the automotive industry and our culture." Mays couldn't help note that " ... virtually all historically significant hot rods are Ford-based, and most are Ford-powered, as are all the entrants in the hot rod class at this year's Concours." Then-Ford Motor Company Chairman and CEO Jac Nasser was one very interested spectator, too. He spent a few minutes inspecting the class and talking with me about his company's support.

Although each car in the class was deserving of an award, three roadsters emerged above the others, with very close tallies. At Pebble Beach, in order to receive a judged award, the car must be started and driven over the ramp in front of the Lodge under its own power. As they're staged to drive

over the ramp, one by one, winning contestants know they've won a first-, second-, or third-place award, but they don't know which one.

The chosen roadsters of Bruce Meyer, Don Orosco, and Blackie Gejeian remained static for a few moments, sitting side by side. The staging marshal tantalized everyone by making them wait. Then he beckoned to the Gejeian T, driven by one of Blackie's nephews, and it rumbled up for its trophy, accompanied by a burst of sincere applause. Both occupants looked a little disappointed. Blackie likes to win, and he had worked very hard on his car. I'm sure as a fierce competitor he was feeling let down with third place.

Then the real contest ensued. Bruce Meyer and Don Orosco are friends and rivals. Each wanted very much to win in 1999, and both had spent a great deal of time and money on their cars to reach this moment. Meyer sat still with Pete Chapouris in his car; Orosco had Dick Flint by his side. The marshal looked at one car, then he looked at the other, and then he looked away for what seemed like an interminable moment. The crowd collectively held its breath. Then the marshal pointed at Bruce Meyer, who with a classy, sportsmanlike gesture, waved to Orosco and accelerated up the ramp to receive his second-place trophy to a hearty round of smiles and applause. If Bruce was disappointed, you'd never have known it. He smiled and waved to the crowd, his hand above the neat tan top all the way back to his place on the lawn.

Don Orosco and Dick Flint resembled a pair of Halloween pumpkins; they were smiling so broadly. Don laid on the gas, the pipes snarled, and the knobby rear tires spun for split seconds in the soft wet grass. Then the Flint roadster and its two happy occupants blasted up the ramp to receive first place, along with the Ford Motor Company-sponsored Dean Batchelor Memorial Trophy.

Commented Orosco afterwards, "I liked winning. It was a hectic day because we were running two racecars at the Monterey Historics, and I had to race back to Pebble Beach for the award ceremony. It's the ultimate Concours and it was very meaningful for me to win the Dean Batchelor award, because Dean and I were friends, and he knew Dick (Flint) and had actually done some work on this car."

"To tell you the truth," Don continued, "I had steeled myself and I was comfortable with whatever would happen. There was nothing more that Brad Hand, my crew, and I could have done on that car. I mean all you can do, is all you can do. We made a few changes to stiffen the chassis, and when Dick saw them, he said, 'you know I paid a guy to do what you did, and he screwed it all up. I didn't have the money back then to change it. Now the frame is the way I wanted it originally.' "

"And I knew it was going to be a battle among Blackie, Bruce, and me. Of course, I'm flattered that we won. It was a great end to several years of turmoil to restore that car the right way. For me," Orosco continued, "one of the best things was getting to know Dick Flint. He was blown away by the crowd and the media response to an effort he'd made when he was back in his late teens. It was great to be able to share the weekend with him and his friend Roberta. Dick deserved to participate. We're just the caretakers of these old cars, and we should honor the guys who actually did the work."

A few days later, Bruce Meyer sent a characteristically gracious note: "Dear Ken, Am I glad I didn't have to choose between the nine historic hot rods last Sunday…an almost impossible task, but you made a good decision! It was a great day, and again, the response to hot rodding was overwhelming – definitely a growing trend."

The Flint roadster remains the pride of Don Orosco's multi-car collection. He took it to the Goodwood Festival of Speed in England in 2000, and blasted it enthusiastically up the tricky hill climb course that's euphemistically known as "Lord March's driveway." Earlier, Indiana's Joe Sievers cloned the car expertly and very closely, a process that took some 16 years. Today, that example resides in the John Koehnke collection. It closely resembles the original car, except for its 283-ci Chevy V-8, (as the original had been upgraded in 1957) dual quads, and a liberally louvered deck lid. It would be a kick to see the two cars together one day.

The Dick Flint roadster was also the inspiration for a more modern track-nosed T built in 2001 by the very talented Steve Moal of Oakland, California, for Gary "Goodguy" Meadors. It certainly goes without saying that the Flint car remains one of the most influential hot rods ever built. It's a lasting tribute to the persistence and talent of Don Orosco and his crew.

The Flint car was expertly cloned by Indiana's Joe Sievers, a process that took some 16 years. Today, that example, which closely resembles the original car, is equipped with a 283-cid Chevy V-8 (as the original had in 1957), dual quads, and a liberally louvered deck lid. It fools nearly everyone who sees it. (Paul Gommi)

A boxed and strengthened Model A frame, tubular crossmembers, a '37 Ford tubular axle, tube shocks, and a mixture of Ford and Lincoln brakes rounded out the running gear. Tiny headlamps were all that was needed, but all most people saw of this car were its taillights.

9

"TV Tommy's" blazing Buick-powered T was a street star and a drag strip demon. The story of Tommy Ivo's memorable T-bucket roadster really has to start with Norm Grabowski and his arguably even more famous "Kookie T."

Fifty-to-sixty somethings will remember a popular mid 1950s-era TV show called *77 Sunset Strip*. On the show, Ed "Kookie" Byrnes, while not the primary star, played a good-looking parking attendant who worked at *77 Sunset Strip*, a fictional Hollywood watering hole. Kookie, whose main affectation was whipping out a comb at every opportunity to arrange his "duck-tailed" hair, was involved in every episode in quick-to-solve, hardly serious, but amusing detective adventures.

Byrnes' own ride was far cooler than any of the cars he valet parked. For the show, he drove a radical T roadster that had been built and owned by Grabowski, then from Sunland, California, who at that time was an aspiring actor himself. Norm received several bit parts, thanks to his then-unusual car.

Although hot-rodded Model T's weren't unusual at the time, Norm Grabowski did his up with a twist, and in the process, he created a new genre of rods overnight. His bright blue bucket incorporated a number of signature items that soon became (you should excuse the expression) the norm where T's were concerned. They included a plated '37 Ford tubular front axle, with a transverse leaf spring mounted "suicide" style behind it. A Model A rear spring arched over the '40 Ford rear end, and tall slicks ensured the scratch-built car had a serious tilt. The result incorporated design cues from lakes modifieds in a cute, cartoon-like manner.

When Grabowski's T was first featured in *Hot Rod* magazine in April 1955, according to the article, a '52 Cad mill was present, and the intake was topped with a borrowed 3-71 GMC blower running a four-throat Rochester carb. There were no flames (yet) or rear exhaust stacks – but the basic shape was defined.

The car was a hit right out of the box, and if you'd missed it

HOT ROD MILESTONES

Tommy Ivo's '25 T Roadster

on TV, you probably saw it in a famous full-page shot in *Life* magazine's now highly collectible hot rod issue, dated April 29, 1957.

Sadly, according to rodding writer/photographer, Bo Bertilsson, Norm's old T is reportedly in a garage in Dayton, Ohio. The car was altered substantially in the 1960s, with twin superchargers and many other modifications. At this point, it seems unlikely that it will ever be restored to its original configuration.

Reportedly, a few pieces from Norm's car found their way onto a superb reproduction built by pinstriper Franco Costanza. There's also another well-built repop of the car that debuted at the 50th Anniversary Grand National Roadster Show in 1999. This one was built by Donn Lowe, and owned by Grand Pendergraft, of Portland, Oregon. But as the purpose of this book is to show significant cars, then and here, without any reproductions allowed, we've had to leave out the seminal Grabowski effort.

Tommy Ivo's T, while strongly influenced by Grabowski's, is pretty famous in its own right, with a number of interest-

ing parallels, including the owner's even more frequent TV and movie appearances. Here's the full story…

Ivo himself was a talented young actor who starred repeatedly in "B" movies. He may have appeared in as many as one hundred of these cheap-to-produce, quick-to-film, somewhat banal-plotted features.

By the time he was 16 years old, Tommy Ivo was able to realize every kid's fantasy. He went to his local Buick dealer, along with a friend, and began asking questions about the new 1952 models. Apparently, the salesman (who Ivo recalls was a Mr. Pansy), virtually ignored the two youths until Ivo produced a fat roll of one hundred dollar bills, and asked "How much for that red Super over there?"

The wad of hundreds apparently got Mr. Pansy's attention, and Ivo and his pal took the new hardtop home. Three years later, "TV Tommy" bought a new '55 Century hardtop, powered by Buick's still relatively new and powerful 322-ci V-8, took it to Pomona, and set a class record with it.

Tom told Prieto "he cruised and hung out at a well-known drive-in restaurant known as Bob's Big Boy in Toluca Lake, California. He received his share of attention from the local girls with his new Buick," wrote Prieto, "that is until Norm Grabowski came upon the scene with his freshly built T roadster with its gleaming chrome and polished aluminum, multi-carbed Cadillac engine sticking out in the breeze."

The local guys and gals dropped everything, gathered, and oohed and ahhed over the sharp little hot rod, with its bug-eyed driver who made his trademark funny faces. It wasn't long before Tommy Ivo engaged Norm in conversation about building a similar machine.

"Sure, kid," was Norm's curt reply while turning his attention back to the young, surrounding chicks.

Accepting what he saw as a challenge, Ivo set out to build a T-bucket of his own. He started by precisely measuring (with Norm's permission) everything about the Grabowski car. Ivo carefully checked the wheelbase, engine setback,

Tommy Ivo found his truck in five pieces out in the desert. Trial assembly looked like this, but the finished product was infinitely sharper. (Tommy Ivo Collection)

Popular teen movie themes included sex, hot rods, high school happenings, rebels, and monsters. Tommy Ivo cut it both ways. He had a successful TV and movie career, and, for a brief time, his car was virtually unbeatable. (Tommy Ivo Collection)

"I removed the front end, the rear end, springs, etc., really everything I thought I could use. I started with that Model A frame and Randy and I modified it extensively – he did all the welding. I never trusted my own welding," Ivo admits today.

He arrived at the overall ride height he wanted by kicking up the frame in the rear to lower the car. The resulting frame step made his T sit more level than Grabowski's car. Ivo undoubtedly knew he'd be drag racing, and if his chassis had an extreme rake, it might look cool, but it wouldn't hook up as well. The engine was originally installed with two four-barrel carburetors, just to get it running. Once it was clear that the little hot rod would run and drive to his satisfaction, it was disassembled for plating and painting.

Like most hot rods, as soon as it was finished enough to be driven, it was off to the drive-in. Sure enough, Norm Grabowski soon made his appearance and spotted the Ivo car. He looked it over rather carefully and then inquired as to what was next in the way of modifications.

Ivo replied that he planned to add a top and then do some trick paint. "Wouldn't you know it," Ivo says today with disdain, "before I could get the top made, Norm had installed one on his car, and he also added flames. I was

ground clearance, etc., and he says he didn't miss a thing.

Because of the success of his '55 Buick at the local drags, and its smooth delivery of power, Ivo elected to use a Buick V-8 engine in his new hot rod, and he promptly found one offered for sale.

"It was a metal-sprayed stroker," Ivo told Prieto, "and while it was a fairly strong motor, I didn't expect it to last very long."

With the help of friend Randy Chadock, and members of his club, the *Road Kings* of Burbank, California, Ivo soon assembled all of the parts he knew he'd need. He gathered up a rusty hulk that was the front half of a '25 Ford Model T phaeton body. That came from a desert area wrecking yard. He located an abbreviated Model A pickup bed, and then picked up a Model A Ford frame of unknown vintage from a local scrap yard.

To shortcut the running gear process, Ivo bought a complete '40 Ford. He dragged it into the driveway of his mother's house, turned it up on its side, and stripped the usable running gear from the overturned hulk.

but they were renting the car, and I knew better than to interfere. They just about wore it out between running the snot out of it and letting it idle; it was fit for a rebuild when they were through. By the way, they were more than willing to pay for that rebuild."

"Knowing that they would pay," Ivo continues, "I stopped by Max Balchowsky's shop (called Hollywood Motors) in Burbank and inquired about getting him to give me a hand building a first-class engine. He agreed and proceeded to give me the advice I needed. That's how I got to know Max, and it was the beginning of our relationship."

Tommy's T wasn't just a movie star; when he showed up, the competition generally faded. In this photo, it appears Tommy was running his Weiand Drag Star six-carb manifold. Looks like it was a winner that day. (Tommy Ivo Collection)

"To the victor go the spoils." Ivo takes a victory lap with the trophy girl. Note the fenders; this car was a killer in street-legal trim. Those slicks took a bite and it was "Adios Tommy." (Tommy Ivo Collection)

gonna put flames on mine, but now that he had already done his that way, I had to find another route."

Like most works in progress, Ivo changed his T often, improving both the appearance and the performance. He added a chromed '37 Ford tube axle – replacing the I-beam '40 Ford unit. Cleverly, Ivo and his friend fabricated a four-bar front suspension setup using four Ford tie rods. He then convinced speed merchant Phil Weiand to cast a special six-carb manifold for a Buick. Phil agreed, and Ivo got the first one. It became known as a Weiand "Drag Star" manifold – quite prophetic, considering what the T would soon do in a quarter-mile contest. Other touches included windshield posts that were chopped three inches, then finished with a distinctive, tall folding white canvas top with a crescent moon-shaped rear window.

About this time, Ivo landed a part for himself and his car in the movie *Drag Strip Girl*. Between *77 Sunset Strip*, appearances in *The Choppers* and other films, and, of course, *Hot Rod* magazine, rod-minded guys all over the country saw these two impressive "Fad-Ts" as they soon became known, and more than a few imitators were launched. It's safe to say that both cars were the forerunners of a long line of shortened, smart-looking, powerful Ts. They still wield considerable influence, wherever Ts are discussed.

"During the filming, like between takes," relates Ivo, "they would leave the car idling for hours. They didn't want to shut it off for fear it wouldn't start again. I knew it would,

Tube axle, Lincoln Bendix brakes, hairpins...your basic mid 1950s hot rod setup. Just add Buick power.

As most people know, Max Balchowsky would become famous in his own right building and racing the series of *Old Yeller* sports-racing cars, all using "nail-head" Buick engines to great effect. Max's reputation was one of meticulous preparation and uncommon use of parts that his competitors viewed with disdain. If you wanted a hot Buick motor, Max was the man. Pretending to use recycled oil and used spark plugs, Balchowsky had a way of disarming his fellow racers.

"Much the same can be said of Tommy Ivo," says Prieto, him-

The "outhouse" half moon rear window came about when Ivo realized his tall T looked a lot like a privy on wheels. The name didn't stick, but the signature half moon window did.

The "IVO T" vanity plate isn't needed – you'd have to be brain dead not to know this ride. Tommy was a member of the still-active Road Kings of Burbank. The club's annual picnic is a not-to-be-missed affair.

self a Lions 200-Mile-Per-Hour Club member, "and both men were fiercely competitive."

After a lengthy discussion about what was needed, Max suggested Tommy run a welded stroker crank to raise the 322-ci engine's displacement. When completed, the finished product measured 402 ci, with 10:1 compression, Jahns high-dome pistons, Grant rings, a Scintilla Vertex magneto, a Winfield cam (Balchowsky only used Ed Winfield's camshafts) and –- alternating with the Weiand six-jug manifold – a Hilborn fuel-injection system with eight polished stacks.

"Max showed me how to port the cylinder heads," says Ivo, "and after I'd finished, he said, 'Oh, by the way, there are two more sets that you can do while you are at it.' What could I say? No? This, of course, was just after he had just showed me what to do."

Ivo then upgraded his roadster with a sturdy '37 La Salle gearbox, mounted behind the big Buick with an "Honest Charley"

adaptor. He welded up and locked the rear end's 4.11:1 gears and painted the whole package in then-popular Titian Red. He used reversed and widened 15-inch Mercury rims in the rear, as Norm had, with flat '50 Merc caps. Whitewalled slicks and small front tires on reversed rims preserved the rake. Brakes were Lincoln Bendix units in front and '40 Ford drums in the rear. The abbreviated bed accommodated the gas tank. The taillights were integrated into the car's rear nerf bars. Inside, a panel full of Stewart-Warner gauges was mounted in a slightly indented dash. White tuck-and-roll Naugahyde upholstery and black carpeting finished the car off nicely.

The T was blazingly quick. With Ivo behind the nearly vertical steering wheel (another smart copycat cue from Grabowski's car) the hot red T proved to be a draggin' demon. Using racing recapped slicks and a locked 4.11:1 rear end gear, Tom stormed the local drag strips, turning elapsed times in the 12-second range, achieving speeds in excess of 117 mph. His best was 125 mph in the quarter, and his e.t.'s were very competitive.

In 1957, this was exceptionally fast, and he not only won trophies in his class, but he often took home the overall Top Eliminator trophy. With his quick reflexes, Ivo won 21 trophies in as many weeks at several different drag strips, and soon caught the eye of the editors of *Hot Rod* magazine. They ran the T on the cover of their August 1957 issue. In a two-page photo feature entitled, "For Kicks and Cups," *Hot Rod* magazine's editors called Ivo's T a "...fascinating combination of ancient Ford and late overhead V-8."

While his accomplishments at the race tracks were considerable, Ivo likes to point out that he did meet Norm Grabowski on the starting line only once, "...and I won!" he quickly adds. "I turned 104 mph that day at Saugus Drag Strip," he recalls. Enjoying his "revenge," he says, "I had a grin from ear to ear."

The T ran in the Street Roadster Class, and Ivo had little trouble beating everything and everybody around the Southern California area. It was only the all-out racecars and some hot motorcycles that could take him, and then

only if they made a very good run. For a short time, he was a threat to win the whole meet everywhere he went. Ever in search of hot competition, Ivo ventured out from the San Fernando and San Gabriel Valley drag strips of Saugus, San Fernando, and Colton, to the hotbed of dragdom known as Lions Drag Strip, then run by Mickey Thompson.

Don Prieto says, "It was here that he encountered 'the rules Nazis.'"

Said Ivo: "Some guy named Cassidy was running a street roadster down there and I was wiping the floor with him and he protested me – first because I had no windshield wiper. Well, I ran the car without the windshield, why should I have to have a wiper? 'Well the rule says....'"

"So I added a wiper. Next it was fenders; they said I needed fenders, so I added fenders. I still wiped 'em out. Then it was the pickup bed was too short. It needed to be three feet in length. So I made a bracket that bolted to the back that made the bed the legal length. Then it was a roll bar. This stuff went on for weeks. Then one day someone got hold of Mickey, and told him the engine was set back too far for the class (it was more than the allowable 25 percent). Well that's why it got such a good bite," Ivo explains, "but then they were on to me and they drove me out of the class."

"It didn't end there," Ivo recalls. "I went home and built the absolute rattiest rig I could build with a dented-up rusty body, and I even welded a hatchet stuck in the trunk. I put on a Squirrel tail on an antenna – all the clichés of hot rod squirrel-bad taste – but I put my strong engine in it and I reduced the weight by about 150 pounds and went back at 'em just to prove a point." Pictures exist of this ratty T. Ivo actually stuck a meat cleaver into the deck lid, painted on crude numbers, passed inspection and, you guessed it: "I won again. It made them craaazzy!"

"That didn't last too long, though," Ivo laments, "as I had decided to build my first dragster. It too had a Buick engine,

The white Naugahyde, black rugs, Titian red body, and black wheels work well together. The instruments are Stewart-Warner; the dash slightly indented. That Bell three-spoke steering wheel is nearly horizontal. The too-tall windshield was removed for drag racing.

Von Dutch's infamous over-and-under "barefoot" logo... nuff said!

The handsome Buick V-8 was a torque powerhouse. High compression, Hilborn injection, a hot Winfield cam, careful porting, and assembly thanks to Buick boss Max Balchowsky, meant that competition never had a chance. The only way to beat Ivo was to change the rules. And even when that happened he managed to win.

and (he says modestly) it was quite successful, winning its fair share and setting many records in the process."

"I sold the T to Bill Rolland," Ivo remembers. "He hacked it up and changed it all around. I was upset, but I had had my fun with the car. It then sat around for years after that and was finally sold. Jack Rosen, the new owner, decided to restore it. I was pleased that it was returned to its original state."

"When it was finished in 1988, Rosen invited me to an *Early Times* Rod Run where the car was to make its debut, and a film crew was to make a documentary of the whole event. I agreed, and wouldn't you know, the day before I was to go, he sent me a 14-page script to memorize. Needless to say, I winged it – I'm too old to remember lines like I did when I was a kid. But all in all," Ivo says, "things went well and I have a copy of the film that they made. It was a nice tribute to the car."

To be fair to Bill Rolland, who earlier owned a famous '29 A on '32 rails built by Don Ferrara, his "changes" earned the ex-Ivo T another *Hot Rod* magazine feature (and cover spot) in the January 1960 issue. Rolland apparently strengthened the car's frame, redid the exhaust system, took the crescent rear window out of the top (and replaced it with a circular opening), removed the Merc caps, and painted the car (himself) metallic Cobalt Blue. In keeping with the "retro-rod" fashions of that early 1960s era, the car was extensively pinstriped, and Rolland added vintage cowl lamps along with a Boyce Motometer radiator ornament with flared wings.

Jack Rosen apparently got the Ivo T from his father, who'd previously had it rebuilt by George Barris into a show car that appeared from the 1960s through the 1970s. In the late 1980s, Jack Rosen had Ron Jones build a new frame for the roadster and restored it to look the way it did when Tommy was showing it and winning drag races, week after week. Fortunately, most of the original pieces were intact, facilitating the restoration.

Tommy Ivo was enshrined in the National Hot Rod Association Museum of Drag Racing in Pomona, California, in 2002. At that time, all four of his most famous racecars were displayed, including his double- and quad-engined dragsters. In pride of place was the Titian Red roadster that he so meticulously built over four decades earlier.

Ivo's and Grabowski's Ts have remained two of the most famous hot rod icons of all time. Their influence on the "Fad-T" element is unquestionable. To my mind, both were great looking, eminently drivable cars. Many later "T-based" imitators used spindly wire wheels, dangerously trick and fragile suicide front ends, and even omitted front brakes. The Ivo car was always a top performer on the drag strip; Norm's "Kookie T" was a road-going car as well – Norm claimed to have driven it from LA to Las Vegas on one occasion. They captured the look before anyone else, and they became the standard. Perhaps one day, both of these great cars, in their original guise, will be reunited. Until then, we have photos, films, and old TV shows of Grabowski's car, and you can see the Tommy Ivo T on permanent display at the NHRA Museum in Pomona.

Buick nailhead (some said nailvalve) engines had small vertical valves, were noted for stump-pulling torque, and were perfect for drag racing. The Hilborn injection system was problematical for the street, but worked great at the drags. The handsome headers were easily uncorked.

Still ready to rock and roll, Dave Simard's (East Coast Custom, Leominster, Massachusetts) picture-perfect restoration of the Jim Khougaz roadster is owned by Dr. Mark Van Buskirk of Crown Point, Indiana. It's arguably the best-looking, channeled, period racing '32 roadster, ever.

Bringing back the "Blue Bullet" – here's living proof that channeled cars are cool. In hot rod speak; channeling is the term for dropping a body the full width of a car's frame rails, then remounting it. This major surgical procedure effectively creates a low silhouette. Of course, floor space and seat height are lost, but you look cool. Very cool.

If you're an East Coast hot rodder from the 1950s, chances are you saw a lot of channeled cars, and you probably didn't like many of them. There were a few standouts, like Bill Neumann's '31 Model A roadster, Norm Wallace's '32, Jack Lentz' New Jersey deuce (better known as the *Golden Rod*), and Fred Steele's slinky purple roadster. All four of those cars appeared in magazines on both coasts. And you better add Andy Kassa's '32 coupe and Tommy Foster's '32 roadster to that short list, too.

Still, most attempts to channel cars on the right coast produced butt-ugly results. Channeling affects every aspect of construction. If you simply removed the floor, spread and

10

remounted the body (probably with a lot of quickie welding and homemade angle-iron brackets), the result was a crude-looking car. The rest of the job was often cobbled together quickly, so typically a channeled car's grille and radiator were mounted too high, the engine was often insanely tilted, the seats were reduced to thin cushions, and the altered floors became too flat for comfort or practicality.

On the West Coast, where highboy roadsters ruled, channeling produced a clean silhouette. But in dry lakes racing, channeling kicked your car up into the highly competitive Modified Roadster class; so channeled '32 roadsters weren't very common at the lakes. To minimize wind resistance, most modifieds, or lakesters as they were renamed when they had streamlined grilles, used '29 Model A bodies, or even better, '27 or earlier Model T roadster bodies, which were narrower and lighter.

Here's a story about a seriously channeled, beautifully proportioned '32 roadster that was campaigned successfully at

Jim Khougaz's '32 Roadster

El Mirage from 1946 to 1950. At first, it was a dual-purpose street and lakes car, serving its owner/builder, Jim Khougaz, as a wicked street ride and a weekend racer. Running on methanol in July 1949, Khougaz achieved a best-ever speed of 141.95 mph in SCTA's C Lakester Class at El Mirage. That engine was a 286-ci flathead with a Winfield SU-1A cam, Edelbrock heads, and a four-carb manifold, backed by a three-speed, column-shifted '40 Ford box with Zephyr gears. An early *Outriders Club* member, Khougaz helped start the Van Nuys *Roadmasters* in the San Fernando Valley.

Back in the day, Khougaz's radically chopped and dropped '32 looked much the way you see it on these pages. How this original roadster came to be restored is quite a tale.

Jim Khougaz is your prototypical hot rod founding father. He was tooling around Hollywood in a '32 roadster in the late '30s; before he served with distinction in World War II as an Army Air Corps tail gunner, top turret gunner, and flight engineer in a B-17 bomber. After hostilities ended, he was up at the dry lakes most weekends, setting fast times in his channeled, belly panned, and remarkably aerodynamic modified deuce roadster. Later, he raced a Chrysler-powered '27 T at Bonneville. He went on to a successful career in the speed equipment industry with his own Van Nuys, California-based company, Khougaz Balancing, until he retired. Bright, alert, and blessed with a remarkable memory, he likes to recall his hot rod days.

Khougaz told me that he was barely 14 years old in 1938 when the exhaust rumble of roadsters heading out Sepulveda Boulevard to the Cajon Pass en route to the dry lakes hypnotized him. "I'd sit out as a kid on Friday and Saturday nights," he remembers, "and all the cars would be heading for the lakes. I said I wanted to go out and see what was goin' on out there. When I finally got to go, I was tickled pink."

As soon as he could legally drive, Jim Khougaz was right in the game. "I've been interested in hot rods all my life," he admits. "Before the war, I had a couple of '32s and a '34, and they were all roadsters. This particular car was my third. I bought it in really bad shape. You see, I'd had another '32 Ford at the same time. But my sister and brother took it to

the movies one night. It had mechanical brakes, so when somebody stopped short in front of them, they couldn't stop, they turned sideways, hit a pole, wiped out the axle, and put a great big dent in the cowl. But I had enough parts laying around to build another car."

Modestly, Khougaz recalls the interruption that took him and thousands of young men away from their lives to fight in Europe. As an air crewman, he flew 34 combat missions out of Italy. "We trained in Sioux City, Iowa, in late '43," he says. "I wanted to be a pilot, but we were told there were too many pilots. I could have gone to Officer Candidate School for something else," he continues, "but I wasn't interested in being a Lieutenant. I wanted to fly."

Jim soon got his wish. He went to crew training center, and then attended gunnery school in Las Vegas. "We flew our brand new B-17G overseas. I thought we'd join the Eighth Air Force in England, but we went down to Italy to the Fifteenth Air Force. I flew in every position. Later on I was the top turret gunner/engineer."

Like many lucky veterans, Khougaz couldn't wait to resume hot rodding. "In 1946, after I was discharged, I took the roadster all apart, cleaned it up, and I was back in business. First I ran it as a highboy at the lakes against the '27 T mod-

Khougaz readies his lakester for speed runs. Note the belly pan has a bulge to clear the '32 radiator, and that flat wheel discs replace front brake drums for better aerodynamics. It should be noted that Jim's channeled '32 is lower than the door handles on the adjacent Mercury coupe. (Jim Khougaz/Mark Van Buskirk)

Jim Khougaz campaigned his '32 roadster successfully at El Mirage from 1946 to 1950. At first, it was a dual-purpose street and lakes car, but by 1947, with a tank full of methanol and a full belly pan, it could top 140 mph. Here Khougaz streaks across the lake bed at El Mirage in a period photo that captures the excitement of lakes racing and preserves it for all time. (Jim Khougaz/Mark Van Buskirk)

ifieds. There was no way in the world I could compete with them because of their (small) frontal area. But that's the way classes were set up by the SCTA."

"So in '47 I decided I'd better channel the car. It really didn't take that long, less than a month of part-time work. I cut the floor out and picked up the same mounting holes, except for the bottom ones, drilled the frame, Z-ed it in the rear to clear the '46 Ford rear axle, and put the body back on it. But," he admits now, "it looked like shit."

"In hindsight," Khougaz feels, "it was poorly built (at first). I had limited facilities. When I look back on it, it was a helluva poor job, but it was all I could do at the time. I didn't have a machine shop (then) or the know-how. So it was cut, weld, and learn, cut, weld, and learn." Later, he redid a number of things to get the body as low and sleek as possible.

Fortunately, several photos survive of the Khougaz roadster in its heyday. We looked at one where Jim's '32 is waiting in line to race. "That photo, with the big wire wheels on the back," he recalls, "is probably the first time I ran it as a channeled car. SCTA's Roadster classes were either for highboys or modifieds. After I channeled it, it became a Modified Roadster. That 'C' with the number referred to the engine size. The first few runs were on gas, but by the time I got it channeled, I had converted one manifold setup to methanol. We would switch carburetors when we got up to the lakes. We'd go up on gas, then change manifolds. I had two tanks, both mounted in the car, so you could switch. And I used a pump to pressurize the tank. We had to bring methanol with us in 55-gallon drums from the warehouse. You couldn't buy it up there."

Jim Khougaz understood that horsepower, or its equivalent, could be obtained in several ways. For the most part, he used a series of ever-increasing, big displacement flatheads with hot cams and multi-carb manifolds, culminating in the 286 cubic incher you see in this book. But some of Jim's contemporaries, lakes racers like Don Waite, Paul Schiefer, Randy Shinn, and Jack Avakian, to name a few, realized early on, that a sleek silhouette, as found in a modified '27 T body, often with the engine mounted amidships, cut through the air more cleanly and ran considerably faster with the same sized engine. These low-slung roadsters were classified as modifieds. Strictly race-cars, they were unsuitable (and unintended) for street driving.

Khougaz stuck with his '32 roadster body, but he maximized its airworthiness perhaps better than any of his deuce driving rivals. The body, of course, was channeled over seven inches,

even more than the depth of the shortened frame. A '32 grille shell was smoothed, peaked, and sectioned several inches. The custom three-piece hood and louvered side panels were about two inches longer than stock to clear the twin Wico magnetos. The hood sides were shortened (versus a stock hood) to accommodate the deep channel.

If you're wondering about the missing louver on the left side hood panel, of course, there's a story behind it.

"When he (one of Jim's friends) was punching the louvers, something came up, and he was interrupted. He went ahead and started punching them again, and all of a sudden, we looked down and he had missed one. You should have heard me scream. I said, 'I'll be damned. I don't know if I want to go through all that bullshit again, because those were special panels. I had to have them specially made, and you couldn't buy them off the shelf.' But we all make mistakes and you cannot go back. There's no way in the world you can go back."

The good part here is that, although the Khougaz '32 raced many times, often with different numbers, it's easily recognizable in old photos when you spot that errant left hood side. To complete the streamlining, Jim neatly faired the lower edge of the body right into the frame rails on each side of the lower cowl. Khougaz ran the channeled car for

two years. "Then, about 1949," he recalls, "I made the complete belly pan out of sheet aluminum, and by 1950, we didn't drive it on the street anymore. Now it was strictly for the lakes. I was running 130+mph; the '27 T's were going up to the 150s, and most of 'em were still flatheads. The belly pan worked," he still notes with pride. "I picked up six to seven mph."

That belly pan is an extraordinary piece of work. It runs from the front frame horns, under the engine, all the way to the rear, ending in a rolled pan with the twin exhausts protruding through it. There's a small opening for the lower portion of the crankcase and a cutout to clear the rear-end pumpkin. When Khougaz originally made it, he formed "some bumps for the differential and the pan." In the rear,

the corners were covered with a contoured piece on each side. When you look under the rear of the roadster, there's a virtually unbroken flat surface from front to back, like an aircraft wing. In front of the grille, there's an aerodynamic filler panel to prevent the front end from lifting.

Remarkably, Jim Khougaz did this work without the benefit of a wind tunnel. A proponent of the "if it looks right, it is right" school of engineering, he took what he understood of aircraft principles and, acting within the SCTA's rules, applied them to his car. Khougaz later sealed the cockpit with a tonneau cover, leaving a small opening for his head. The result was an increasing series of lakes times culminating in a 141+ mph dash in 1949.

The channeled body was actually welded to the frame in front. For further stiffness, Khougaz says, "I used a big heavy piece of quarter-inch-by-quarter-inch strap steel to give it some strength and welded it to the body, following the door contour. That gave the doorjambs some rigidity. Before that," he says, "it was pretty flimsy. You could feel that when you slammed it (the door) shut." The frame is boxed between the K-member and the rear crossmember. And there are custom brackets to accommodate a roll bar.

The proportions Khougaz achieved are quite beautiful. The completed car sits better than any channeled historic roadster I could think of, including the Tony La Masa '32 that took a third place at Pebble Beach in 1999. I complimented Jim Khougaz on his work, so long ago. "I tried to keep the lines of the hood as original as possible," he said. Although he extended the hood nearly two inches, the revised proportions work very well. What was his influence for the belly pan? "I wanted to pick up every bit of speed I could," he says. "I even made new motor mounts for the front, so I could get the car down as low as I could. I wanted to cut through the air as easy as possible."

Once he had dialed in the car's shape, Khougaz finished the bodywork and plating to a high standard. He painted the car a distinctive shade of metallic blue. "The paint was a special color," Jim remembered. "H. F. Parker had the DuPont line of paints, and the man who mixed the paints was a friend of mine. He went out of his way to create the dark blue color I wanted using DuPont lacquer. We must have taken two weeks of trying before we came up with that shade. At first it didn't have enough metal flake in it. We kept matching paint back and forth until we got it."

With the car's low height, the King Bee headlights were mounted high alongside the grille on specially made flat brackets. There was a headlamp height rule in those early days – just another way the LAPD had found to harass hot rodders. "The cops were out there with tape measures," Khougaz recollects, but it didn't stop him, as vintage pictures show, from using his car on the street.

To improve high-speed aerodynamics, Khougaz fabricated an aluminum belly pan for his sleek roadster. It ran from the front frame horns, continued under the full length of the car, and ended in a smooth tail panel.

Handsome dark brown pleated interior contrasts neatly with this car's metallic blue exterior and cordovan wheels. Comfy bench seat permits three cozy passengers thanks to the '40 Ford column shift.

The ex-Jim Khougaz roadster was a star at El Mirage dry lake. Running on methanol, against much-modified T-roadsters with cleaner, smaller, even lower silhouettes, Jim hit a high of 141.95 mph at an SCTA meet back in July 1949. "I wanted to see how fast I could make a '32 roadster go," he said, and proceeded to prove it.

The 286-ci flathead in the Khougaz roadster runs a Lincoln-Zephyr distributor conversion, Edelbrock heads and 4-carb manifold (with four Stromberg 81s), and homemade headers. Inside, pop-up pistons, big valves, Johnson adjustable tappets, Lincoln valvesprings, and a Winfield cam do the serious work. Mark Kirby and his talented crew at Motor City Flathead, Dundee, Michigan, built the engine.

The channel job was just part of the lowering process. In front, a three-inch dropped and filled axle did the deed, along with a "de-arched" '35 Ford spring mounted in front of the axle. In the rear, the frame was Z-ed. Finally, the windshield was chopped 3-1/4 inches. This car sits very, very low.

The completed interior has a '47 Mercury steering wheel on a '32 Ford column with a '32 Ford steering box. There's a Stewart-Warner mechanical tach on the left side of the wheel, and the dash is a complete unit, panel and all, from a 1932 Auburn. Those gauges are all early S-W curved glass units. "I was very, very lucky in getting that Auburn dash," Jim recalls. "A friend of my dad's named Perkel owned a junkyard in Van Nuys. Ours was a small community, and the junkyard was right down the street from the auto parts houses. I was working there before the war, off and on. We'd always go down to the junkyard and scrounge around for parts, and that's where I saw this old Auburn. It was in pretty good shape and it had that dash."

"So, in those days," he continued, "everyone went after the centerpiece with the instruments. I said, 'bullshit, I want it all.' I didn't have much money then, but I said 'Perk, can I have the whole thing?'"
"He replied, 'if you want to take it out yourself, you can have it for two dollars.' We worked on that car, on our lunch hour, for three days, and finally got the whole dash out of this junk car. Then we cut it very carefully, we just cut a little amount, to fit in the same contour, but we reversed it; we made it concave on the front. Everything fit. We spent a helluva lot of time welding it in. I never mounted SCTA timing plates, because I didn't want to drill any holes in the dash. I have 40 something tags…all those memories, in my toolbox." Why didn't he mount a tag? "Every time you run, you get a better time," said Jim. "I thought, well, 'I'll put one in later,' but I never put one in."

The wheels were 16-inchers, painted a dark cordovan shade of red. "They were brand new Ford wheels on the front and wide-based Lincolns on the rear." I asked about the tall wire wheels shown in one of the lakes photos. "Those were not my wheels," said Jim. "I didn't have a quick-change. I had a 3.54:1 rear end. And I needed more gear, so the only way I could get it was to put bigger tires on. I never could afford a quick-change in those days. They were $180; it was a lot of money," he laughs. "You could build two engines at that time for that price."

Like a surprising number of racing old timers, this spry 80-year-old has a great memory for details. "My second engine, bored to 3-3/8, also used a 3-7/8 stroke," he noted. "Later on, we got a 4-inch Merc crank and stroked it to 4-1/8 for 296 ci. When we ran at Bonneville, I wanted to stay back a class, so I de-stroked an engine, to 3-5/8-inch stroke, and that one had a 3-5/16 bore. With it, we could easily turn 5,600 to 5,700 rpm. My engines were always carefully balanced, with a chopped flywheel and just enough weight to just dump the clutch. There was no ring gear; we just pushed it to start."

"I used Winfield camshafts," Khougaz continued. "I met Ed right after the war. He did my first cam and even showed me a little (about it). We became good friends.

"Where ignition was concerned, I never used a Vertex," Jim recalled. "Instead I used twin Wico industrial magnetos, using a split casting mount specially made for a V-8. There was no advance; you preset the timing using a lead plate with markings. I ran 27, 28, or 29 degrees of advance. I also used a converted Lincoln-Zephyr V-12 distributor (as the car is now equipped). Manuel Ayulo, who went on to be a famous CRA (California Roadster Association) and Indy driver, did my block relieving. I saw how he did it, tried it myself, broke through the casting, and had to weld the block up again. It was a lot of work."

Constant experimentation was the norm in those days, as Khougaz and his friends tried to run faster and faster. Everyone was seeking an edge, no matter how small. "I started with a two-carb manifold. First I used (an Eddie) Meyer, then had an Edmunds, but I never used it. Later I tried an L&S manifold and heads; their fin work looked good but we had to re-contour the chambers; really we re-domed 'em. We almost always used domed pistons, not flatheads. Every time you'd mill the head to raise the compression ratio, you had to re-cut the domes. L&S heads were around for a very short period of time. Every time any manufacturer came out with a new item, all us young kids that didn't know any better would jump on it, thinking it was better than what was available."

"At first we simply used stock valves, but when we increased the size of the intakes, more (fly-cutting) work was needed. We always used Lincoln-Zephyr valvesprings, and then we increased the size of the intakes. In those days, you'd build an engine, and two or three runs later, you'd change cams, change compression, and change carbs. You might start out

The Ford drag link and parallel split wishbone are artfully plated. The front spring is a late Ford setup located in front of the dropped beam axle; with reversed spring eyes, the Khougaz car sits belly low.

the course of a day, with adjustments, four to five runs were pretty adequate. The wind would come up, and by 1:00 to 2:00 P.M., it could be blowin' hard. It was hot when the sun came out. And there was always a tailwind. We'd run west to east, you'd get two to three extra miles per hour with the wind. When it was too strong, they'd just stop running. If there were 10- to 15-mph tailwinds, there'd be too much dust. Before the war, they ran several cars at once, and it would get very dusty. But there was always a slight crosswind," he remembered, "so in 30 seconds, the dust would clear, and you could run the next car."

Once the car was painted, plated, and very smart looking, Jim Khougaz took it to driving events and car shows. He entered one of the early Pasadena Roadster Club Reliability Runs. The car is pictured in a photograph in Don Montgomery's *Hot Rods as They Were*, where he finished fifth overall. In the February 1949 issue of *Hot Rod* magazine, Jim Khougaz, in his channeled '32, and Ted Miller, in a '29 highboy, took on seven sports cars in a "challenge sprint race" held on an impromptu course at the Davis Motorcar factory in Van Nuys. The event was called "Sports Car vs. Hot Rod." Phillip Payne, in a Mercury-powered Special designed by Willis Baldwin, had the fastest time of 1 minute, 11 seconds.

Interestingly, Payne had timed his car at a Russetta Timing Association meet at the lakes, so its appearance begged the question: was this a hot rod with sports car attributes or a hot rodded sports car? Second place of 1 minute, 13 seconds, was taken by a young Phil Hill in a supercharged MG. Khougaz's '32 had the third fastest time of 1 minute, 16 seconds. In August 2003, at the Pebble Beach Concours d'Elegance, hot rods returned for the fourth time in a class called "Road Racing Rods." Both the Khougaz '32 and the Phillip Payne Special were reunited when Stephen Payne brought his late father's Special over from the UK.

with two carbs, then build up to three or four. As flathead engine technology progressed, you'd try to keep up with it. Nothing was ever the same twice running."

Why the column shift in a racecar? "That column shift worked good," he said; "remember, we weren't drag racing, so you didn't have to speed shift."

What was it like to run at the lakes? "They'd pick a new course every month," said Jim. "By the end of the day, the course would be torn up. Sometimes we'd have to change the course in mid-day, and run adjacent to it, because the surface would only last for 200 to 300 cars running, then you'd have to change positions. We had a lot of roadsters, but we ran 'em pretty quick, about 30 seconds apart. Over

Although the Khougaz roadster was never a feature car in *Hot Rod* magazine, it was pictured in a July 1949 article by Walt Woron, as a fine example of channeling in his "How to Build a Hot Rod" series.

Jim Khougaz ran his '32 roadster from 1946 off and on until 1950, when the Korean conflict broke out. He was called back in the service during the Korean War, and that stopped his racing career for several years. On active duty once again, Khougaz flew in a converted air/sea rescue B-17 with lifeboats lashed underneath its wings. "I had Herbie

Papazian, my friend and next-door neighbor, drive the car when I went away to Korea," says Jim. "I came back in '53 and ran it half a dozen times after the Korean War, between 1953 and 1957. By then, I was starting to build a modified T roadster. The T was mine, but Herbie and I were together on it. I had bought it before the Korean War, and it sat in my dad's backyard until after I came home. I took the body off – that was all I wanted – and I started working on it; it was finished in '57."

Khougaz was involved with SCTA for years. "I was elected president in '54-'55, shortly after I came home from the Korean War. I also became secretary-treasurer of the Bonneville Racing Association." He'd moved up from running at the lakes to the salt flats of Utah, and the new car was ready to double the speeds of his old '32. Pick up an old January 1959 copy of *Hot Rod* magazine and the Khougaz D modified roadster commands a four-page spread with a cutaway drawing under the heading, "T Masterpiece."

So what became of the channeled '32? "Herbie ran the car till about '56-'57, then I parked it," said Jim. "I was busy working on the T. I had a family, but I didn't want to sell it. Later, my kids were too busy. They didn't have the same interest. But they took the car apart, and were going to make it into a street machine. For one reason or another, that project was sidelined. The '32 never ran on the street or lakes again. It sat in Jim's shop for nearly 40 years.

In April 1995, Jim Khougaz ran an advertisement in *Hemmings Motor News* offering both of his roadsters for sale. Dr. Mark Van Buskirk, a Dentist (and hot rod enthusiast) from Crown Point, Indiana, happened to be in Las Vegas, when he read Khougaz's ad. "I jumped on a plane to Los Angeles with a $49 round trip ticket," Van Buskirk recalls. "I was the first guy who got there. The ad mentioned this was a hot rod with real provenance, and I liked that. Earlier I had planned to build a '32 Ford roadster, and here was a real one for sale."

Was it sad to sell your car? I asked Jim Khougaz. "It broke my heart," he replied. "Even my son asked, 'are you sure?' But I said if he offers me $25,000 I'll sell it." Mark paid the price and soon the Khougaz roadster was on its way to Indiana. Van Buskirk talked to several people about restoring his car. In 1997, he and I met at Mark Kirby's Motor City Flathead shop in Dundee, Michigan. At that time, Kirby was building a flathead race motor for Van Buskirk. And later, in a 1940 Ford pickup, with Van Buskirk driving,

that same engine set the course record for the Newport, Indiana, Antique Auto Hill Climb. After we met and talked, I suggested to Van Buskirk that Dave Simard would be the best person to restore his roadster.

Mark and his late father brought the Khougaz roadster, then really just a pile of pieces, to Dave's Leominster, Massachusetts, shop, East Coast Custom, in May of 1997. After a five-year, comprehensive, ground-up restoration, the completed Khougaz/Van Buskirk '32 made its debut at the Grand National Roadster Show in San Mateo in January 2003. There it won the Bruce Meyer Preservation Award and competed for the title of America's Most Beautiful Roadster. A few weeks later at the Oakland Rod and Custom Show, the '32 won several more trophies, including

Best Engine, Best Rod, The Nostalgia Award, and second place in the Altered Street Roadster Class – a class comprised totally of modern street rods. And at the Amelia Island Concours d'Elegance in March, the born-again ex-Khougaz roadster won the *Street Rod Builder* Most Significant Hot Rod trophy.

"It's taken five years," Van Buskirk reflects, "but I've enjoyed seeing the progress on visits to Dave's shop. My dad was a patternmaker, and when we visited Dave's clean but-hardly-sterile garage, he looked around and said, 'this is a craftsman; he's a good guy.' That made *me* feel good."

"I had a picture in my mind's eye," Van Buskirk adds, "and the finished roadster came out exactly the way I'd pictured it. I'm thrilled and totally satisfied."

Simard's shop has turned out some remarkable vintage-style rods. He's built and restored a lot of cars. Was this one a challenge, we asked? "Not really," he replied, "but we did do a few things differently. First of all, when the pile of parts arrived, I thought to myself, 'I should really put this car together, with all the original pieces, to best evaluate what we'd have to do.' So we did, and we took plenty of pictures."

"For a channeled car, " says Simard, "it's good looking and well proportioned. Typically, I don't like channeled cars. But after we put it together and installed the belly pan parts, I thought it looked like a little Rodzy racecar – you remember those motorized model hot rods manufactured in the 1940s by Cameron Precision Engineering Co., in Sonora, California?"

"Our biggest challenge in restoring this car," Simard reflected, "was assembling the body and chassis. The body is actually welded to the chassis in front, so we had to paint it, and then weld it back together perfectly – there could be no adjustments – and then we repainted the areas that were blistered by the welding. We painted the complete interior and carefully welded it together with the chassis. Everything had

to be perfect so the doors, hood, radiator, and grille would fit just right. There was no second chance to adjust anything."

If you look closely, you'll see they succeeded. The fit is razor sharp and probably much better than when the car was built. Is it over-restored? Not really. Racecars of that period were very well built. Out of respect for Jim Khougaz's vision, this roadster is as good as they get today, and it's a great example of bringing back an historic hot rod with fine credentials.

"The hood is a good example of Khougaz's work," says Dave. "In an era where most guys used simple lunch box latches, he developed a unique three-piece hood system using a support rod on each side to secure the panels. The support rod fits neatly into a small hole in the frame. It's secured by a knurled nut, and it's very nicely done."

"And that belly pan," he chuckles. "We must have 400 to 500 hours in fabricating it. Mark Szmyt in my shop probably did half of that. It was a lot of work. Stan DeCoste, another one of my guys, did great detail work on the car. Kevin Olson and Phil Austin, from Viking Auto in Vernon, Vermont carefully matched the blue paint from samples we took off the original panels where it hadn't faded. Steve Pierce from OneOff Technologies in Gilford, New Hampshire, did a superb job on the brown leather upholstery and the tonneau cover. I want to credit Joe MacNeil and Bob Hilton of J&B Metal Finishing for their perfect plating. And thanks to Skip Readio, of course, for the wiring."

Simard punched a few louvers in the belly pan so the car could "breathe" on the street, and he wrapped the exhaust pipes underneath it so it wouldn't slow cook one very happy Indiana dentist on the many rod runs he hopes to complete in the future.

Jim Khougaz was reunited with his old roadster at the Concours on Rodeo in June 2003. He was very impressed, as was his family. The crusty old ex-AAF machine gunner was moved to reminisce a little. "I'm delighted to see that Mark's got that much interest," said Khougaz. "A lot of people will buy something and not do (anything with) it. But he did everything he said he'd do. Of course, I wanted to see it, and I took my son and his family along and showed it to them." His friend Herbie Papazian came to see the car once again, as well.

"You'd be surprised," Khougaz reflected wistfully, "how attached you get to something like this. This car was just a thought when I was a kid. I'd always wanted a '32 roadster. I didn't like '29s. I wanted a '32. It's just something you grow up with."

Then he paused, and shook his head, saying, "I get shivers thinking about all the good times we had in that car."

Classic roadster cues: '39 teardrops, twin pipes through the deck panel, and tall 7.00 x 16-inch rear tires. Missing is the Roadmasters, Van Nuys, car club plaque that Khougaz occasionally mounted above the license plate.

11

Chester Osgood began building this '26 T in the late 1940s, raced it until 1958, and kept it for over 40 years. The legendary Whitey Clayton did much of the metal work. It's had only two other owners. Frozen in time somewhere back in the late 1950s, never changed, updated, or even painted, it's a survivor. John Koehnke, who bought it in 2004 from Jim Busby, will keep it unfinished.

Chet Osgood never finished this remarkable roadster, and John Koehnke plans to leave it just the way it is. Historic hot rods with a pedigree are rare and valuable. Here's one that qualifies in spades. Chester Osgood began building his '26 T in the late 1940s, raced it until 1958, and kept it for over 40 years. It's had only two other owners. The legendary Whitey Clayton did much of the metalwork. The T was frozen in time somewhere back in the late 1950s, and has never been changed, updated, or painted. It's a great survivor – and if its present owner, John Koehnke, has his way, it will stay unfinished.

But before we tell you about the Osgood roadster, you should know about the man who crafted its most memorable features. He was a talented metalsmith who practiced his art in Los Angeles in the late 1940s and early 1950s. His name was Dwight Clayton, but everyone called him Whitey.

Clayton crafted significant parts of several of the historic hot rods in this book...like the low-slung, track-nosed, Bill

Niekamp '29 roadster that won the first Oakland AMBR trophy in 1950; the Bob McGee/Dick Scritchfield '32 roadster; and the channeled and belly-panned Eddie Dye '29 with its racecar-inspired nose and split DuVall windshield.

Whitey also made the track nose on the sleek, record-setting '27 T lakes roadster of Don Waite; and built the three-piece hood and side panels on Lynn Yakel's devilishly chopped and channeled '32 five-window coupe. Along with countless roundy-round racecar bodies, Whitey Clayton built the body for the famed Marvin Lee, *City of Pasadena* streamliner.

Although he barely got a line of credit in *Hot Rod*, Clayton handcrafted the nose, grille, hood, and belly pan on the Niekamp roadster. It's unclear as to whether he also did the vertical section that shortened the body. We know Clayton reworked a track-nosed grille from one of Joe Gemsa's sprint cars for Don Waite, widening and flaring it to fit the T's wider dimensions. He also fabricated the engine cover

Chester Osgood's '26 T Roadster

and belly pan for Waite's mid-engined T, considered the best-proportioned lakes car of its day.

For Bob McGee's *Hot Rod*-cover '32 roadster, Whitey Clayton fashioned a unique extended dash, highlighted with an oversized tachometer that was intentionally reminiscent of the panels in the ill-fated 1935 Miller-Ford Indy cars. He also made the McGee car's innovative three-piece hood, with its unique latching mechanism, along with the car's unique sweeping deck lid that runs down to the bottom of the tail.

Around the same time, Clayton hammered out a sexy three-piece louvered hood for Lynn Yakel's ultra-low '32 channel job, and fabricated a few side pieces in aluminum for that car, as well. "He reworked the side moldings on my car so they stopped just short of the hood side panel separation," Yakel recalled, saying, "Whitey was a quiet, understated guy who worked by himself." Yakel's coupe was done about the same time as the Niekamp car, and Lynn remembers seeing Bill's roadster under construction. His coupe ran Russetta meets in 1950, turning over 122 mph. Later that year, he clocked 128.02 mph at Bonneville, helped no doubt by Clayton's sleek bodywork.

Solid hood panels were one of Clayton's specialties, along with rounded blisters to cover a protruding head or generator. According to one eyewitness, "he could turn 'em out in no time." We're very sure he did the nose, the hood, and the belly pan on a famous *Hop Up* cover car, the Eddie Dye roadster (see Chapter 6). Its overall construction is credited to Gil and Al Ayala.

For a time, ex-racer and keen hot rodder, Jim Busby, owned our chapter feature – a largely unrestored, track-nosed, center-steered '26 T with a four-carb Ardun-Ford engine. Chester Osgood built this low-slung, competition-oriented roadster in LA in the late 1940s. Whitey Clayton fabricated the Osgood car's sleek nose, hood, and belly pan.

When I first looked closely at it in Busby's shop I saw that the name "Chester Osgood" is etched on the radiator tank, and under it, are the words, "Clayton Metal Shop." I had missed that inscription at first. When I spotted Chester

Osgood's name engraved on the radiator header tank, I stepped back and admired the flow of the aluminum body panels. Standing alongside, a colleague of mine, Lou Ann Hammond, pointed out Whitey's name, etched in smaller type, just below the owner's.

"Look right there," she said. "Aren't you hunting for someone named Clayton?"

"How did you find that?" I asked.

"I was looking for it," she said. "An artist always signs his work."

Sadly, that wasn't always true. Osgood told me he asked Clayton to engrave both their names on the header tank. Whitey never signed anything, so far as we know. His work itself was his signature. Luckily, the aluminum on Osgood's car was never painted, so you can still see every hammer mark Whitey made. The hand-fashioned aluminum panels are eggshell thin. They're perfectly curved and matched side to side; it's sheer artistry in metal.

Whitey Clayton's little shop was located at the corner of Lakewood and Artesia Boulevards in Bellflower, California, from 1949 to perhaps early 1951. He rented the space, about the size of a three-car garage – from a talented German machinist named Lou Madis. Exact details are sketchy, because

Lou Madis, a machinist whose shop was next to Whitey's, helped Chet convert a junkyard steering box find into a center steering setup. The steering wheel is a four-spoke Bell racer that Chet purchased from Roy Richter at Bell Auto Parts. This car oozes history.

Chet's lakester had a distinctive shape, center steering, and a low silhouette that, along with a full belly pan and tonneau cover, guaranteed minimal wind resistance. The cowl was artfully cut back for a more streamlined shape, and the body was securely attached to a rigid framework of chrome-moly steel tubing.

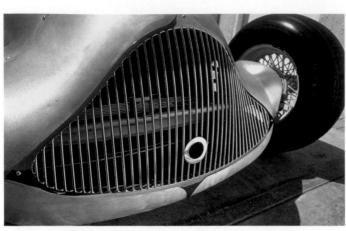

He did all his work painstakingly with hammers and dollies."

"Whitey was one of the first guys to develop what we thought of as an 'Indy car nose' for hot rods," Lean continued. "He also built racecar noses, hoods, and belly pans. He could fabricate nearly anything. He was one of the most sought-after craftsmen, and he was as nice as he could be. Mostly he worked on show cars and cars that competed at the lakes."

The Don Waite roadster was an exception for Whitey. In its case, he rebuilt and widened a nose he'd previously built for a racecar owned by Lou Gemsa. "He made a pie cut or two, spread it open, and made it wider," said Don. "Whitey gas welded everything and finished it with files and hammers."

Whitey passed away some 20 years ago. Apparently, he liked to take pictures of his work once it was completed. A few grainy, black and white photos, taken in front of his small shop, constitute a remarkable record of one man's patience and skill.

Whitey Clayton's father was a fine finish carpenter and furniture maker, but he chose to work in metal. Larry Clayton, who was "six or seven years old" when his dad was shaping tin, believes his father started as a "body and fender man. In those days," Larry says, "people didn't replace fenders after an accident. Someone pounded them out. After my dad died, we had a stack of hammers and dollies that he'd used. Many of them he made himself."

"My uncle worked with aircraft," Clayton continues. "And dad worked with him in the early '40s in Wisconsin. Whitey may have picked up his aluminum experience at that time. He had no formal training, but he had tremendous natural ability. Larry Clayton never became a body craftsman. He said his father told him, "I don't want you to have to work the way I did.""

Norm Lean, a well-known lakes racer for the *Dolphins* car club, who went on to become the American CEO of Toyota Motor Company, told me: "Whitey was a master at creating panels out of aluminum. The sheet aluminum he used was rolled flat in several harnesses," Lean continued. "Whitey used SO gauge. It's very malleable, so you can bend it easily.

Waite told me he was proudly bringing the nose home from Whitey's shop, in the seat alongside him, in his '32 roadster, when he was T-boned by a cement truck. The passenger side of his roadster, and the racecar nose – which was perched on the seat – were badly damaged, and the nose absorbed part of the impact.

"When I got out of the hospital," Waite said, "I brought the damaged grille back to Whitey's. 'What did you do to it?' Clayton asked. After I told him, he wasn't at all perturbed; he just got to work and straightened it all over again. And he only charged me 10 bucks."

Norm Lean remembers a '27 T roadster with an Indy nose and a full belly pan that was built for Dan Busby (no relation to Jim) of Long Beach. "It was really a work of art," Lean remembers. "I must have been in Whitey's shop 20 or 30 times," says Lean. "I couldn't afford his work, but I loved to watch him. He (probably) wasn't expensive by today's standards, but there was no money in those days for this sort of thing. Most people built their cars without spending much on appearance. The Pierson brothers were an exception because they had Edelbrock as a sponsor."

Jack Calori, whose distinctive '32 roadster, with twin pipes running up each side and chopped '36 Ford three-window, were models for many rods and customs in the late 1940s, told me, "Whitey was a fantastic bodyman. But he was expensive. I couldn't afford his work."

"Whitey's shop was probably about 30 feet wide," Norm Lean recalled, "and about 60 feet deep. There was a grinder in front. Lou Madis, (from whom Whitey rented his shop) was a great machinist, and he reground crankshafts. I don't think he metal-sprayed the cranks there," said Lean, "but he offset ground them to build stroker cranks. Lou also align bored the main bearings too, matching the surfaces perfectly so you could turn a crank with your finger. Guys'd do anything to reduce friction. Whitey stood around a lot," said Lean. "And he'd spend a lot of time talking. I think there were times when he didn't have much business. He was a heavy smoker, but then, in those days, many people were."

Chet Osgood described Whitey's small shop in similar terms. "The Niekamp car was first," he confirmed. "When my car was there, Whitey was working on Marvin Lee's (*City of Pasadena*) streamliner that flipped on its last run. He'd worked at Bert Letner's T, too." It's likely Whitey fabricated the side panels and belly pan on Letner's Elco twin plug roadster with its unusual eight-spark-plug cylinder heads. There's a racing picture of it in the Clayton photo collection. He also did Mel Leighton's sprint car. "It had a Riley motor and it needed bubbles on the side. Whitey did them all by hand," said Osgood, "as neat as you please." Osgood confirmed that working with Whitey was "…a pleasure. He had real vision. I just told him what I wanted.

Sometimes he'd sketch it out first. He really knew how to pound metal. He'd start with flat sheet stock, without using any jigs or bucks. He was a real artist, really easygoing. The grille in my car is formed by hand and it fits neatly in the shell with a little groove all around. They go together perfectly. It was incredible to watch him do that work. I just wish I'd gotten a photo of him (doing it)."

"Whitey made all his own tools," Osgood continued. "After he closed his shop, he worked as a body and fender man at R. L. Gould Chrysler in Long Beach. You had to be a certain kind of person to make this (fabrication) business work. Whitey worked on a lot of nice cars, but it wasn't enough. He had a large family; he needed a steady income." He later went on to work with Clay Smith and Bill Stroppe. Whitey helped on the Lincoln La Carrera Panamericana team, and he's visible in many of the team photos. Later, he built the bodywork and finned headrests for Pete De Paolo's famous '57 Ford *Battle Birds* that ran at Daytona Beach.

Chet Osgood credits Whitey Clayton with a lot of work on his unique roadster. "You'd tell him what you wanted him to do and he'd take it from there. My car had a modified '28 Chevy frame. Under the cowl and the body, Whitey fabricated chrome-moly steel tubing to strengthen it. He hand formed the hood sides. He used a brake to get a little offset when he made those hood panels, so everything fit together beautifully. Whitey made a lot of hoods and grille shells. He really had it down."

"We were always friends," Osgood says wistfully. "Whitey was the sort of person you never forget. He smoked way too much. But you'd never forget watching him do his work."

"Dad struggled to make the shop pay," Larry recalls. "He never had business cards. But there's a photo of Tommy Smith's roadster at the Pan-Pacific Auditorium (where they held the first two SCTA/Russetta hot rod shows and *Hot Rod* magazine debuted) and next to the car, there's a sign that reads, Clayton Metal Shop." Larry remembers having appendicitis as a child. "Dad built the front and tail for a Midget racer to pay for my surgery," he says.

Word quickly got around in the hot rod community that a quiet, unassuming man in Bellflower could build anything you wanted out of aluminum. Hot rod enthusiast and historian John Brown unearthed a reader letter in "Walt's Shop Talk" in the October 1949 issue of *Hot Rod* magazine. One Eugene M. Anthony of Madison, Wisconsin, noted that some cars depicted in coverage of a major show, "seem to have a grille and shell of commercial make [*sic*]." Anthony wrote to ask where he could purchase one. Walt Woron's answer was: "…most grilles of this type are manufactured by Kurtis-Kraft. The shells are usually handmade; those in the Los Angeles area are generally made by (Emil) Diedt and (Lujie) Lesovsky or Whitey Clayton."

The serious cockpit has an aluminum pan for a single seat. The car's aluminum lower hood sides fair rearward and perfectly complement the belly pan sides, which neatly cover the frame rails. Chet Osgood purchased his Ardun heads from Fell Auto Parts. "It was the test set that they had in their shop truck." this 296-ci engine has Chet Herbert's first roller tappet cam.

Despite his reputation, without steady business, amidst the tough economic years of the Korean War era, Whitey's shop didn't last long. After a few short-term positions, he went on to a great career at Bill Stroppe's. But like a fine sculptor, whose statues are admired long after his passing, much of Clayton's beautifully fashioned metalwork endures.

"He was the best metal man I ever knew," normally taciturn Bill Stroppe told the Clayton family at Whitey's funeral.

"He could leave the Italians (metal crafters) for dead," adds Chet Osgood.

"He was a marvelous individual," says Lynn Yakel. "He never felt pressure. When I walked into his shop and looked at the parts for the Niekamp roadster, I was awed. I'd never seen anything like that."

"You wouldn't believe what this man could do with a simple sheet of aluminum," Norm Lean added, "He was a great craftsman and a fine person."

Bodywork by Whitey Clayton gives an historic hot rod a special cachet. The Niekamp and McGee roadsters were finished, raced, altered over time, owned by other people, and then artfully restored. That's not exactly the case with Chester Osgood's lakester.

Chet's car was first pictured in *Hot Rod* magazine in March 1949 in an article that showed racers preparing for the 1949 dry lakes season. The barely finished racecar nose is clearly shown, although the vertical grille is not yet installed. The car's '29 Chevy rails are not visible. Prophetically, the caption reads, "The familiar '32 grille and shell is fast becoming obsolete with builders going all-out for streamliner fronts."

The cars shown in the *Hot Rod* article include the combination street and track roadster of Harold Miller, Don Waite's T, Eddie Miller Jr.'s streamlined, Pontiac-powered lakes coupe, and a '34 Ford competition coupe being built by Bill Phy. The cover car for that issue was the 1948 SCTA top point-getter – the Spurgin-Giovanine Chevy 4-powered lakester, also a track-nosed job.

Osgood was in fine company. Serious lakes racers may not have understood every aerodynamic principle, but they knew that a racecar nose cut through the air better than a vertical T or deuce grille. That's why cars like the Flint and Niekamp roadsters had them, and everybody wanted one.

"I'd bought the car, a '26 T, a few years earlier in Lomita, California," Osgood told me. "And I actually drove it as a T for a while before I started building the frame by hand. We used to drive it to the races at Huntington Beach Speedway. Then I took it all apart and started building it. It sat for two years during the Korean War while I was in the service."

Chet's lakester had a distinctive shape, center steering, and a low silhouette that, along with a full belly pan and tonneau cover, guaranteed minimal wind resistance. The cowl was artfully cut back for a more streamlined shape, and the body was attached to a framework of chrome-moly steel tubing. Even the hood has a tube framework underneath it. The car's aluminum lower hood sides fair rearward and perfectly complement the belly pan sides, which neatly cover the frame rails. In front, a thick stock '32 axle, with a suicide transverse spring arrangement, keeps the racecar nose low to the ground.

The quick-change rear center section was purchased new from Pat Warren. The rear end is locked, in lieu of a limited-slip differential. Lou Madis machined a set of chrome-moly steel bars to a Hudson axle pattern for the rear axles, which are housed in '34 Ford bells. (Osgood told me those early Hudsons were "known for their strong axles, so everybody copied them.") The hand-formed aluminum interior would do credit to a period racecar, but that was Clayton's specialty, of course. Inside, there's a selection of Stewart-Warner and war surplus instruments on a hand-made panel.

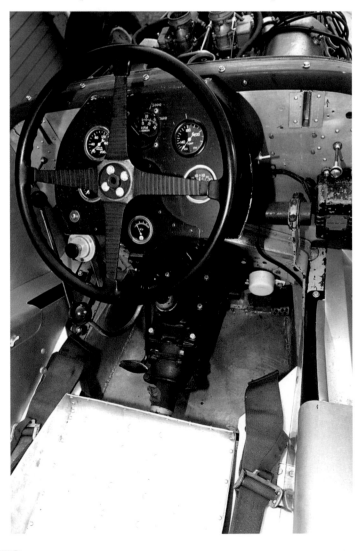

This cockpit means business; big Stewart-Warner dials are easy to read. Center steering location means the Bell steering wheel is right above the transmission lever.

The roadster's full-length belly pan flows rearward and finishes in a rolled, rounded section below the tail. The exhaust pipes are enclosed under the pan and they exit under the turtle deck. A racecar-inspired flip-up gas filler tops the deck just behind the passenger compartment. Knock-off wire wheels by Dayton round out the four corners. "I purchased four 18-inch wheels brand new from Dayton," Chet recalls. Then Pico Rim Co. cut down a pair to 15 inches, slightly reversing them for the proper offset. Lou Madis helped Chet convert a junkyard steering box find into a center steering setup. The wheel is a four-spoke Bell racer that Chet purchased from Roy Richter at Bell Auto Parts.

There's no headlights, no top, no windshield, or curtains – this car is a racer, pure and simple.

Under the hood was one of the first Ardun overhead valve conversions for the Ford flathead. The engine displaces 296 ci, with a 3-3/8-inch bore and 4-1/8-inch stroke. "Originally I ran it as 268 ci, with a 3/8-inch bore and a standard 3-3/4-inch stroke, " Chet recalls, "but when we started drag racing, I went for the big stroker."

Chet purchased the heads from Bell Auto Parts. "It was the test set that they ran in their pickup," Chet recalls. "But it never ran very well. They were getting out of that business (selling Ardun conversions), so I bought their shop truck heads." (The shop truck also ran a set of Kinmont disc brakes – Bell Auto Parts was a distributor for those, as well.) The Ardun valve covers have lifting handles at each end. "They had a brand new set of small Ardun heads for a V-8/60 for sale," he says. "I sure wish I'd bought those, too."

Osgood told me, "Chet Herbert made several different camshafts for it. It was the first time he ever ground a roller tappet cam for a flathead V-8. We couldn't make it run at first, but we figured it out. He gave us these GMC lifters and they were smaller than Fords, so we had to metal spray them for increased clearance. You did everything yourself in those days," Osgood recalls, "or your friends helped."

A Kong distributor handles the ignition. The handsome, side-by-side four-carb log manifold was handmade from the original Ardun setup by milling off the original carb risers and making new ones; the quartet of Stromberg 97s faces outwards. Years ago, the engine had an Addis oil pump and a dry sump oiling system, (but Osgood kept that setup for an engine he's currently building). Initially, the '39 Ford box had first and reverse removed to save weight, and Chet just ran second and third. Jim Busby replaced the missing gears, so the transmission is intact today. Cook Machine (the makers of Cyclone rear ends) did the roadster's modified driveshaft.

Dry lakes racing was starting to wane when Chet was ready to race, so he installed a set of Inglewood slicks and hit the 1/4-mile drags at Santa Ana, Lions (near Long Beach), Orange County, and the 1/2-mile drags at Riverside and Minden, Nevada. "My best time at Lions was 107-108-mph in 12 seconds," he remembers. "Then we ran at Riverside, never changed gears, buzzed the motor to seven grand, and hit 124 mph " When Chet ran the car at the drags, he didn't need the streamlining, so he used a Model A nose and a sheet of aluminum for the hood – and no hood sides. It wasn't as pretty as the Clayton nose, but it was fast. Osgood was a member of the famed *SCTA Dolphins* hot rod club whose members included Norm Lean and the Daigh brothers, Chuck and Harold.

I asked Osgood why he never painted the car. "I never had the funds," he replied. Now, with its faded primer and unfinished aluminum, it looks very period, and somehow especially correct.

In the mid to late 1950s, Osgood built a full roll cage and planned to go sports car racing, but that never transpired. After storing the roadster for years in his shop, he sold the car to John Koehnke a few years back; John sold it to Jim Busby, and then bought it back in 2004.

John Koehnke is the perfect caretaker for Chet Osgood's old roadster. He insists he'll never sell it again, and he doesn't intend to finish painting it. He'll keep it just as it is – saying, "I'm just going to leave it alone. I can't really drive it on the street, but I'll take it to a few events, like *LA Roadsters*, where people can see it. It's fun to play with, and fun to own, and the Ardun sounds just plain nasty."

Chester Osgood's roadster is an exceptionally sophisticated, well-engineered car that used the best parts available in its day, and it benefited from the talented hand of a legendary craftsman. That low silhouette, racecar nose, big Ardun powerplant, and all those competition-flavored elements, like the Bell wheel, flip-up filler cap, and knock-off wires, point the way for a few contemporary builders to use it as a worthy example – what are *you* waiting for?

The Ardun's ignition needs are handled by a Kong distributor; the handsome, side-by-side four-carb log manifold was handmade from the original Ardun setup by milling off the original carb risers and making new ones, and the quartet of Stromberg 97s face outwards. Years ago, the engine had an Addis oil pump and a dry-sump oiling system, but Chet decided to save them for another engine he's building.

12

Pete Henderson built this highboy deuce roadster before World War II ended. It has all the elements that roadster jockeys have imitated for decades: great stance, a chopped windshield, a hot flathead, big-and-little tires on Kelsey-Hayes wires, and an Auburn dash panel. Note the straight '32 axle; dropped axles were a postwar trend, and Pete had sold this car by that time. (Tom Shaw)

It's the hot rod that raced (and beat) the horse! One of my favorite hot rod photos of all time is the one of Pete Henderson's '32 roadster at a gas station in Pasadena, California, around 1947. With its highboy stance, raked windscreen, chopped top, and big-and-little tires on Kelsey-Hayes wire wheels, with a hopped-up Mercury stroker under the hood, this deuce epitomized what a hot rod was all about – then and now.

If you think it's a coincidence that my own '32 roadster borrows a lot from Pete's old car, you're wrong. I spotted several photos of Pete's car in Don Montgomery's books, and that was it. There's no way to improve upon it if you want an authentic late-1940s California highboy. Pete got it right, over half a century ago, and I tip my cap to him.

Henderson's roadster's fascinating history was extensively researched by its restorer, Chuck Longley, and by the late Gray Baskerville. Gray wrote a definitive feature on the car in *Rod & Custom* in June 2001, just after the restoration was completed. The fact that this highboy, originally built by Henderson in 1943, has survived to the present day, despite a succession of owners, is nothing short of remarkable.

Even more remarkable, is the fact that Akton "Ak" Miller (builder of the famous El Caballo de Hierro, the La Carrera Panamericana road racing T roadster) and Baskerville both believed they could trace the concept of quarter-mile drag racing to the Henderson '32 and a now-famous match race against a quarter horse that took place back in 1944. Here's how Gray recounted that story:

Ak Miller told Baskerville that a "stranger" walked into the garage where he was working in 1944, and asked if he had a fast car. It seems this man made a living touring the country, looking for guys who thought they had fast cars, who would race him for 50 yards. The trick, of course, was that the challenger was riding a champion quarter horse. Known for explosive acceleration, a fast quarter horse could cover 50 yards in just a few strides, and do it in something like four seconds.

Pete Henderson's '32 Roadster

This fellow's clever MO was to cruise bar parking lots, pick out what looked like a hopped-up car, usually a late 1930s Ford, then go inside, find the owner, and challenge him to a race. Egged on by his fellow drinkers (and perhaps a few drunks) the patsy would agree to the contest, and soon find himself looking at the horse's rear end. The victorious challenger would then run off into the sunset in search of his next victim.

Ak Miller supposedly didn't think his own flathead-powered '32 was up to the task, but he'd heard about a local kid from Pasadena with a 3/8ths stroker in a '32 roadster "…that was supposed to be the quickest thing in the San Gabriel Valley."

Then-18-year-old Pete Henderson's torquey '40 Mercury flathead engine had been built by noted Pasadena speed shop proprietor and lakes racer, Don Blair. It was ported, relieved, bored, and stroked to 296 ci, and it ran a hot Pierre "Pete" Bertrand cam, a Spaulding ignition system, milled aluminum "Denver" heads, and twin 97s on a Weiand hi-rise manifold. At the time, Henderson was a student at Pasadena Junior College "…waiting for his draft notice."

In June 1944, Pete's roadster had turned a creditable 120.9 mph at Harpers' Dry Lake and he had a coveted Russetta timing tag to prove it. Alternatively a member of the *Roadrunners* and the *Excellerators*, Henderson was game for any challenge. He knew he had a pretty hot setup.

Ak Miller and his friend Connie Weidell (who owned a very quick Cad flathead-powered '27 T that had been clocked at 127 mph) apparently did a little research first. They checked to see just how fast a thoroughbred racehorse could accelerate, and found that the legendary Seabiscuit, at the time, one of the fastest horses at Santa Anita racetrack, could cover 50 yards in 4.3 seconds.

Pete Henderson told Baskerville that he met Miller and Weidell through a mutual friend. "They had driven Weidell's T over from Whittier to see if my roadster was faster than his. We marked off 60 yards, on Foothill Boulevard, or about two telephone poles apart. After a couple of practice races, we found that I could out-accelerate Weidell's T for about 200 yards

before he would come by me with that big Cadillac engine he had. It was then that I learned about the race with the horse."

As Pete told Gray Baskerville, "I can still remember it was one of those gloomy June days when we met at the agreed spot on Highway 39 near the city of La Habra. Miller and his pals had already marked off the course. (It was) the distance between two telephone poles with a line of dirt spread across the street to indicate the end of the race."

A big crowd had gathered. "Ak had really talked it up," Henderson told me. "Over 100 roadster guys were there, too," Pete recalled, "including Phil Weiand, Ed Winfield, and Vic Edelbrock, (Sr.). The race had become a big deal, with a lot of money on the line. My mom loaned me $20 and the rest of the guys had chipped in as well."

Pete Henderson's '32 Ford will always be famous as the car that raced (and beat) the quarter horse. In a match race in 1944, Henderson's deuce caught and passed a swift horse to win a specially staged race in Pomona. The horse's owner had a nice little side business going, until Pete's '32 saw him off, while hundreds of hot rodders watched and cheered. "I was too young to be nervous," Henderson told me. "Today I'd probably be scared." (Pete Henderson/Gail Longley)

Young (18-year-old) Pete Henderson's torquey '40 Mercury flathead engine was built by noted Pasadena speed shop proprietor and lakes racer, Don Blair. It was ported, relieved, bored, and stroked to 296 ci, and it ran a hot Pierre "Pete" Bertrand cam, a Spalding dual-point, dual-coil ignition system, milled aluminum "Denver" heads, and twin 97s on a Weiand hi-rise manifold. In 1944, Henderson was a student at Pasadena Junior College "…waiting for his draft notice." (Pete Henderson/Gail Longley)

Here's one of my favorite hot rod photos of all time. It's Pete Henderson's '32 roadster, in a shot taken in a gas station in Pasadena, California, around 1947. With its classic highboy stance, raked windscreen, chopped top, and big-and-little tires on Kelsey-Hayes wire wheels, with a hopped-up Mercury stroker under the hood, this deuce epitomized what a hot rod was all about – then and now. (Pete Henderson/Gail Longley)

Simple interior was par for the course in the 1940s. These roadsters were essentially stripped-down stockers, with everything removed that wasn't essential, including, in this case, even the door panels. A pressure pump in dash, to the left of the steering wheel, was a popular add-on, usually purchased from Bell Auto Parts. The onyx-swirl shift knob is another classic roadster touch. (Tom Shaw)

Twin 97s on a Weiand hi-rise were state-of-the-art induction in 1944. Phil Weiand developed this manifold before the war; Barney Navarro machined early examples, before he began developing his own manifolds. Tall manifolds allowed the generator to be retained in the stock location. Although rodders didn't know this, the "stacks" actually provided a ram effect that was superior to many popular "low-rise" super manifolds. (Tom Shaw)

The bet was on – and hot rodding's honor was at stake.

Apparently, the horse owner showed up with the animal well rested and in a trailer, and he had a jockey as well. The '32 and the quarter horse were to race alongside each other – the roadster on the pavement and the horse on the adjacent shoulder. The horse had become accustomed to the sound of a car; the animal's owner, who also acted as a starter, had trained the horse to take off as soon as he reached for his cap, probably gaining a half second in the process.

"I was too young to be nervous," Henderson told me. "Today I'd probably be scared."

Pete Henderson was ready to rumble, with his gas tank full of avgas and full advance on the twin-coil Spaulding distributor. As he said to Baskerville, "we lined up, but I was still winding up my engine, when the horse took off. I tried to feather the throttle," he remembered, "because the rear tires were breaking loose. All I could hear were my friends yelling, 'Stay on it; keep staying on it!' I did, catching the horse at the top of low gear (fortunately Pete's '39 toploader had a long-winding Lincoln-Zephyr first and second gear cluster), and I won the race by barely a hood length. It was right after the race that we found out that this was the first time the horse had ever been beaten."

Fortunately, Ernie McAfee photographed the contest, just as Henderson's hard-charging '32 passed the horse, so we have visual proof that the race occurred. But that was just the beginning on that fateful day. There was another race scheduled, too.

The horse's owner had also challenged Chuck Basney, owner of an 80-ci Indian V-twin that had been tuned by the famous Clay Smith. After a few minutes' rest, the protagonists lined up again. But this time it was no contest. When Basney twisted the throttle, his big Indian, crackling through straight pipes, scared the horse. The startled animal bolted across a field, with its jockey "holding on for dear life." No one ever saw the man or the horse after that.

Pete Henderson headed home to return the $20 bill to his mother. Ak Miller claims that the race, run over a quarter mile, set the precedent for the quarter-mile drags that followed. As Gray Baskerville said, "…it's hard to believe the guy who adheres to the old adage, 'old age and treachery will always overcome youth and enthusiasm', can ever be wrong."

Pete Henderson had purchased his roadster in 1943, from Don Casselman, and he rebuilt and raced the roadster at the dry lakes until 1946. As was true for many early hot rodders, Pete's '32 was both his street and racing car. Unfortunately, the '32 was stolen in 1946, and some parts were removed. "I had driven down to Pasadena from Oregon, where my folks had moved," Pete recalled, "and I left the car parked on the street. When I came back, it was gone, and all my clothes were in it, too. It was a disaster for a 20-year-old with no money."

Three days later, Pete got his car back. The Weiand hi-rise was missing, so Pete replaced it with an Edelbrock two-carb manifold. The milled Denver heads were gone too. Not long afterward, Pete had Don Blair build him a new '46 Mercury 24-stud block, but he wasn't destined to keep the car much longer.

Henderson sold the roadster to one L. K. Chappelow of Monrovia, California, in 1946. The following year, it was purchased by lakes and track racer Manny Ayulo who ran

Nothing fancy here: carbs, stacks, milled and polished Denver aluminum heads, but in a lightweight roadster, a stroker motor like this was good for 0-60 times in the 6 to 7 second bracket and, depending upon gearing, the car could top 120 mph. The Longleys restored this engine very close to the way it looked in 1944; just look at the original photo. (Tom Shaw)

it in circle track events at speedways in the greater LA basin. Some time in 1950, Ayulo sold the roadster to another talented racer, Jack McGrath. Both Ayulo and McGrath worked at Eddie Meyer's shop in West Hollywood. We know that Ayulo was considered a talented man with a grinder. He expertly ported and relieved Ford and Mercury blocks for many early rodders, including Jim Khougaz, of Van Nuys.

George Rowland bought the roadster from McGrath in 1952. At the time, California law enforcement officers were cracking down on hot rodders, strictly enforcing an annoying set of rules that specified fender requirements, headlamp height, muffler loudness, etc. Rowland had Art Chrisman install a pair of bobbed rear fenders. Henderson's hot flathead was still under the hood. In 1954, Rowland reportedly sold the car to finance the purchase of a 1954 Mercury that had been mildly customized by Art Chrisman.

A clean rear view shows practices that became hot rod basics: exhaust pipes running alongside the frame horns, small motorcycle taillights, accessory license plate light, a club plaque mounted below the state tag, and tall fenderless rear tires. (Tom Shaw)

A year or so later, in 1955 or '56, Ralph Guldahl, Jr. bought the roadster. He saw an ad for the car at Joe Rose and Carl Weeks' R&W Automotive. R&W brokered the sale so Guldahl doesn't recall the owners' name. Guldahl's father, Ralph Guldahl, Sr., was a well-known professional golfer, and he won the US Open twice. Apparently Vic Edelbrock, Sr. was a member of the Country Club where Guldahl, Sr. was a pro. Ralph, Jr. told Gray Baskerville he occasionally gave Vic a ride in his roadster, so he would have a lift back to his parked car. By this time, the '32 had been fitted with a '40 Ford steering wheel and column shifter. The now-tired flathead developed a rear main oil leak. Keeping up with the times, Guldahl swapped a '55 265-ci Chevy V-8 for the worn-out flatty. Apparently, he also replaced a dented gas tank (which through a weird circle of happenstances eventually ended up in Gray Baskerville's '32 roadster!).

Steve Lydecker, Jr. bought the roadster when Guldahl received his draft notice in 1957. We know the '32 appeared in a number of period hot rod B movies, including *Hot Rod Gang* and *The Spider*. It's believed the roadster also had a cameo appearance on the *Ozzie and Harriet* show. Unfortunately, Lydecker had a bad accident in the roadster. He flipped it, reportedly while street racing in Burbank. In 1959, the old roadster changed hands once again, when it was sold to Art Vitteraly. Modified extensively in the early 1960s, it was slightly channeled, fitted with a nailhead Buick V-8, and '50 Pontiac taillights, and it was raced at the drags.

Robert Takahashi bought the car in 1972 and kept it for five years, before selling it to Chuck Longley in June 1977. Longley beat out none other than Tom McMullen to this prize. As Longley says, "I wanted a '32 and I had been scanning the classifieds looking for one. This car came up, so I called the guy. Tom McMullen was after it too, but he didn't want to pay the asking price of $2,500." Luckily, Longley did. And Pete Henderson's old '32 was his. Trouble was, he didn't know anything about who'd owned it previously or anything about its history.

Chuck Longley advertised in many places, including *Hemmings Motor News*, trying to see if anyone recognized his car from the old days. Chuck was sure he had an old hot rod, but of course, he was looking at old photographs to find a car that was channeled, and had Pontiac taillights. As luck would have it, Pete Henderson, who was looking for a '32 himself, answered one of Chuck's ads. They spoke by phone. After listening to a description of the modifications, Henderson told Longley "...it sounded kinda like my car." Then, when some of the elements checked out, like the Auburn dash, and a few of the holes that had been filled – such as the ones for the starter button and the pressure pump, Chuck asked Pete if he'd kept the car's serial number. Of course he had. And it was the same car!

Chuck Longley had kept the roadster for a long time before deciding to restore it. "I wasn't sure what to do with it, or how to restore it," he says today. "But after I spoke with Pete, I knew exactly what to do." Longley says he ran into Tom McMullen one time, and Tom told him his plan, if he had bought the roadster, was to turn it into a clone of his Moser-Chevy-powered deuce. Luckily, that didn't happen, or Pete Henderson's car would have been gone forever.

The body and frame, some suspension pieces, and the windshield were still on the car as Henderson had built it. But when Chuck and his son Mike began the restoration in 1995, they had to find a lot of other pieces, including a proper flathead, with the right speed equipment, the Auburn dash, a pre-World War I Cadillac fuel pressure pump, a pair of '39 teardrop taillights, a '32 straight axle, and the car's unusual aftermarket rimless steering wheel. They didn't need the retrofitted Buick engine, the accompanying La Salle transmission, and the dash panel filled with individual Stewart-Warner gauges. When they stripped the body, it was obvious that the car had sustained a lot of damage when it had flipped end for end under Lydecker's ownership.

The Longleys studied old photographs and carefully restored the '32 to look as it did in the late 1940s. Pete Henderson, then 75 years old, retired from Sears, and living in Temple City, California, helped with photographs and advice. The Longleys eschewed plating for paint and were very careful not to over-restore the car, nor to add anything Pete hadn't put on it in the first place.

Chuck offset ground an 8BA crank to get a 4-1/8-inch stroke. The original Bertrand camshaft was impossible to find, so he used a period-correct Winfield SU-1A bumpstick. When the car was finished, they wanted to bring it to California and show it to Pete Henderson. Using a handy loading dock, they simply backed the roadster into a big Ryder box truck and drove cross-country to Los Angeles.

It was June 1999, just before the big *LA Roadsters'* Father's Day meet at the Pomona Fairplex. I was in my office on a sunny afternoon, as director of the Petersen Automotive

Museum in Los Angeles. My assistant told me there were "…a couple of guys who wanted to see me." The Longleys and I had spoken previously on the phone about the restoration, so I knew they were coming. But I wasn't quite prepared for what happened next…

Chuck and Mike had parked their rented Ryder truck on Wilshire Boulevard, since it was too tall to fit under the Petersen Museum portico. When they opened the truck's rear doors, I thought I was looking at a time warp. There was Pete's old blue roadster, jammed into the truck, with inches to spare on either side, looking just like it did in those faded old photos.

"Could you get us a space at Pete Chapouris' open house at the So-Cal Speed Shop?" Chuck asked. My response was, "Sure, but how are you going to get the car out of the truck without ramps?"

"Oh, we'll just cruise around until we find the right height loading dock," Chuck said. And they did.

Of course, I happily made the requisite call to Pete, and on the following Friday night, the ex-Henderson, now Longley, freshly restored '32 roadster was proudly parked right in the front row at So-Cal, for everyone to admire. The Longleys then took the roadster to Pomona where they reunited Pete Henderson with his old car.

I wasn't there until later, but I understand there were a few tears shed, on all sides, when Pete first saw his old '32. Pete later told me, "It was thrilling to see the car. I'd love to have it back again." The roadster was a big hit at the *LA Roadsters* Father's Day meet, and since then, the Longleys have shown it at several events, including the Amelia Island Concours d'Élegance, where it won an award for the best historic hot rod.

Pete Henderson has a Model T racecar now, and he just bought a '29 roadster to redo – he's never lost the hot rod bug. When he speaks about his old car, you can still hear the 20-year-old in his voice. Pete is blessed with a terrific memory, and he recalls the famous race against the quarter horse as though it happened yesterday.

The Longleys deserve a great deal of credit for retaining this historic hot rod's neat original proportions, and meticulously rebuilding it almost exactly the way it was. It's an important lesson where historic cars are concerned. It would have been tempting to fit a dropped axle, and perhaps put on steel wheels, etc., but they carefully perused those old photos and did the job right, maintaining this car's intrinsic value and ensuring it will be long remembered. As a result, we can appreciate what Pete Henderson's landmark '32 really looked like, and understand why it's still an inspiration to anyone who ever wants to build a classic deuce roadster, "the way they were."

Henderson's unusual steering wheel looked cool, but it must have been hard to grip. The red tag to the left of the Auburn panel is a Russetta Timing Association (RTA) tag. The car hit 120.9 mph at an RTA meet at Harper's Dry Lake in 1944. (Tom Shaw)

Gary Hubback of Los Altos, California, put the Pacific Gunsight Special's frame back in shape. The '32 rails have a Model A front crossmember, and the '32 K-member and the '32 Ford rear crossmember were modified. There's a Model A center section and arched spring to clear the Halibrand quick-change rear (with a 3.27:1 ratio) that's mounted in a '42 Ford setup and framed with '37 Ford radius rods. A '40 Ford donated the column-shift setup, the transmission, the torque tube, and the hydraulic brakes.

From Bonneville racer to Stroker McGurk-trophy winner, this deuce is a highboy classic. Here's a handsome '32 Ford highboy with everything going for it. This roadster was a bona fide competition car back in the day; it's been a major magazine feature car; it saw street duty as a hot rod; it was updated, as so many cars were, with a small-block Chevrolet; and it's been restored back to its original guise, with a flathead, and subsequently shown at Pebble Beach. It doesn't get much better than that for a historic hot rod. Now, for the rest of the story...

When Roy "Mack" MacKinney returned to Palo Alto, California, after World War II, he worked in a Union 76 filling station. Like many returning servicemen, "Mack" wanted a hot rod, and it had to be a '32 Ford roadster. MacKinney soon found a suitable car owned by a Chinese gardener in nearby Menlo Park. It was being used as a work vehicle. MacKinney purchased the car, then stripped off the fenders and converted it to a highboy. Fortified with a modified engine, it was raced (we don't know how well) at

Salinas and Redwood City, California, by Eldon Lange and Tommy Cheek. Later on, MacKinney's marriage ended in divorce, and the roadster was sold in 1951.

Enter Leo Juri of Palo Alto, California, who planned to race his 1947 Ford coupe at the 1952 Bonneville Speed Trials. When Juri acquired MacKinney's roadster, he installed the highly modified flathead that he'd previously intended to use in his coupe. Juri's hot, bored and stroked 296-ci racing engine ran top-drawer speed equipment: a Harman and Collins Super T cam, an 8R-101 magneto, Offenhauser high-compression heads (for 10:1 compression), and a four-carburetor Edelbrock intake. Internally, it had the era's customary porting, polishing, and relieving, along with a set of solid-skirt J.E. pistons and Grant rings.

Juri worked for the Pacific Gunsight Company, and resourcefully convinced his employers to sponsor his racecar. They did, and Juri had the company name stenciled on the car's upper rear panels. In 1952, running in the B Non-Fendered Roadster

The Pacific Gunsight Special '32 Roadster

class at Bonneville, and, wearing the number 533, the roadster hit 124.82 mph. The requisite SCTA timing tag was awarded – and it's still on the dash panel. After he returned from the salt flats, Juri used the roadster as his daily transportation to work, as well as at several Bay Area racetracks where Leo worked as a machinist on roadsters, Midgets, and sprint cars.

In 1961, Juri sold his roadster to the father and son team of Al Reynal, Sr., and his son Al Jr. Assisted by Leo Juri, they redid the roadster into a handsome street machine. According to an article called "Father/Son Combo," in *Rod & Custom*, in the July 1963 issue, the Reynals retained Leo's race engine. R&C quoted the bore as 3-3/8 inch and the stroke (incorrectly) as 4 inches. Of course, it would have to have been a 4-1/8-inch stroke to make the 296 ci displacement.

According to *Hot Rod*, a '40 Ford gearbox with Zephyr gears received the power from a Weber flywheel and a Hinds clutch. Interestingly, a close look at the interior shot shows a floor shifter, not the column shift you'd expect from a '40. The rear end was quoted as a 4.33:1, which must have been a custom ratio. Ford supplied a special 4.44:1 rear end to V-8/60s sold west of the Mississippi, so that 4.33:1 may have been a typo.

The Reynals chopped the '32's windshield four inches. The doors and deck were shaved and the cowl was filled. They repainted the car with 22 coats of maroon lacquer. Chromed 15-inch Mercury wheels were shod with 6.70s in front, 8.00s in back, and bobbed stock fenders were installed. The platers had a field day with those handsome external headers built by Al Sr. and Juri. The steering column, the front suspension, the dropped axle, and a myriad of other small pieces also felt the plater's dip. A '40 Ford donated the brakes, while the shock absorbers were Monroe tubular 50/50s on all four corners. Warren Thatcher of San Mateo was credited with the smart-looking white Naugahyde tuck-and-roll interior.

Interestingly, although you can see the coveted SCTA timing tag in the center of the dash panel, the *Hot Rod* article never mentions this car's Bonneville history.

Steve Lawson, of Los Altos, California, bought the roadster in 1966. He showed it at the Palo Alto Concours that year, the Oakland Roadster Show the following year, and several other Northern California shows later on. Lawson used the '32 extensively for several more years. He reportedly said it was the "… nicest-driving hot rod he'd ever owned."

In 1968 or 1969 (records vary), the roadster changed hands once again. This time, the buyer was Jim Ladley in Santa Rosa. Ladley, who passed away in 2003, drove the Pacific Gunsight '32 to many local events. He also owned the ex-Vic Edelbrock, Sr./Eddie Bosio '32 for years.

Jim Harvey, another Palo Alto dweller, bought the car from Ladley in 1971. He installed a small-block Chevy, but after a year, he decided he preferred a closed car. That's when Jim Palmer, the roadster's present owner, and dedicated keeper of the flame, was able to buy it.

Jim grew up in East Oakland, California, in the late 1940s and early 1950s when hot rods were rampant. When he was 10, he saw his first roadster, a black '29 highboy with a three-carb flathead, outside headers, and welded doors. Little Jim was impressed with the chromed undercarriage and the chromed five-gallon jerry can that was mounted in the trunk. "Hop in kid," the roadster's owner said. Palmer went for a fast blast around the block and underwent an immediate religious conversion. "I knew I had to have one of these machines," he said. Interestingly, that influential roadster survived and now belongs to Palmer's friend, Brian Hill, of San Ramon.

Bonneville or bust! Leo Juri displayed his company's name on the car's upper rear panels. In 1952, running in the B Non-Fendered Roadster Class at Bonneville, and wearing the number 533, the roadster hit 124.82 mph. The requisite SCTA timing tag was awarded – and it's still on the dash panel. After he returned from the salt flats, Juri used the roadster as his daily transportation as well as on trips to several Bay Area racetracks, where he worked as a machinist on roadsters, Midgets, and sprint cars. (Jim Palmer Collection)

In 1961, Juri sold his roadster to Al Reynal, Sr. and his son Al, Jr. Assisted by Leo Juri, they redid the roadster into a handsome street machine. According to an article called "Father/Son Combo," in Rod & Custom, in the July 1963 issue, the Reynal's retained Leo's race engine. R&C quoted the bore as 3-3/8 and the stroke (incorrectly) as 4 inches – it would have to be 4-1/8 for that displacement. (Jim Palmer Collection)

Jim Palmer finally got his roadster. He first saw the Pacific Gunsight '32 at Andy's Picnic, in Castro Valley, California, in 1972. Then-owner Jim Harvey decided to keep the Chevy engine he'd installed, and that propelled Palmer, who is more of a traditionalist, to reinstall the car's old flathead, a Champion Speed Shop-built engine supplied by former owner Jim Ladley.

Palmer later installed a Cub Barnett-built 284 ci (3-3/8 x 4) flathead. Not satisfied, Jim replaced that engine with a similarly bored and stroked Paul Gommi-built flathead, this one running Elco twin-plug heads and an S.Co.T. blower. Gommi repainted the car for Jim Palmer, and several chassis and running gear pieces were replated. The vestigial rear fenders were removed. Externally, the car began to look more like the way Leo Juri raced it at Bonneville in 1952.

Palmer drove the roadster for two years, averaging 10,000 miles annually, and then decided to restore it. His efforts paid off. Jim Palmer took his roadster to San Jose for the

Leo Juri built a wild flathead for his '47 Ford coupe, intending to run it at Bonneville. Then he decided to run the motor in a deuce highboy. Leo worked for the Pacific Gunsight Company, and he convinced his employers to sponsor his car, hence the name, Pacific Gunsight Special.

1984 Goodguys' Western Nationals, and drove home with the coveted Stroker McGurk award. "I have put many miles on the car," he says, "including several trips to Los Angeles for various car events. It has even been used as a push-car for me and my partner Neil O'Kane's Jr. Fuel dragster at nostalgia drag races. It was also the last 1932 roadster to make a pass down Fremont Drag Strip before the track closed."

In 1998, Palmer, along with Dave Wilkerson and several other friends, elected to return the car as accurately as they could to its "classic" 1952-53, Leo Juri, Bonneville racing configuration. This time, the car's restoration was very extensive.

Gary Hubback of Los Altos, California, put the frame back in shape. The '32 rails have a Model A front crossmember; the '32 K-member and the '32 Ford rear crossmember were modified. A Model A center section and an arched spring clear the Halibrand quick-change rear (with a 3.27:1 ratio), which is mounted in a '42 Ford banjo and framed with '37 Ford radius rods. A '40 Ford donated the column shift setup, the transmission, the torque tube, and the hydraulic brakes. The gearbox has a 26-tooth Lincoln-Zephyr first and second gear cluster. The flywheel was chopped, and the clutch is an 11-inch Ford truck unit. In front, a 3-inch dropped axle and a de-arched spring with reversed eyes further lowers the car. The original '32 Ford wishbone setup was retained but not split. The steering box is also '32 Ford, and the dropped

steering arm was handmade. Up front, the Ford tubular shocks were affixed with 1940-era Dodge shock mounts.

Brian Hill, of San Ramon, California, refinished and repainted the frame and sprayed the car in Ford Cabernet, a close approximation of the original hue. Herbie Martinez was responsible for the discrete white pinstriping that accents the car's reveals.

Hubbard's Machine Shop in Hayward, California, did the requisite machining before the rebuilt flathead was reassembled by Neil O'Kane. Palmer duplicated all the speed equipment components except for one item. "I just couldn't find a Harman and Collins Super T camshaft, so we used a re-profiled Howard M8 instead." The revised engine is a bit milder than the old stroker. It's bored .040 over with a stock 3-3/4-inch crank for about 244 ci. The flathead was balanced and fitted with oversized valves, Johnson adjustable lifters, and a Melling high-pressure oil pump. Jere Jobes rebuilt the smaller Stromberg 81 carburetors, and they've been topped with Stellings & Hellings bonnet-style air cleaners. The Offy heads are a more street-suitable 9.5:1 compression ratio.

Gary Hubback replicated the old 16-inch chromed steel wheels that the car had when it was first built. He used 16 x 4-inch '40 Fords in front and 16 x 5-inch '41 Lincoln wheels in the rear, along with pointed "baldy" caps. The result is very pleasing to the eye and infinitely better than the usual red-painted Ford steelies. There's a fine rubber rake, thanks to 5.50 front bias-plies and 7.50 rears. High Luster Metal Finishing in Hayward did the chrome. Mike Pauselius, of Tri-Valley Interiors in Pleasanton, copied the original upholstery pattern, this time in white leather.

Looking at the roadster in more detail, the grille shell was filled and the windshield was chopped two inches. Those snazzy headers required hood side panels and subtle frame rail modifications to fit. They're as neat a set of outside pipes as you'll ever find on a '32 Ford, and they connect, with an under-the-frame extension piece, to a set of Smithy 22-inch mufflers under the car and twin tailpipes that parallel the frame rails. The headers were actually made from '36 Ford driveshafts. The new system was built on jigs taken from the originals, by Kent Walton of RPM Mufflers.

The Autolamp accessory headlights are perched on Tornado brackets originally sold by Lee's Speed Shop. Popular '39 Ford teardrops round out the rear. The deck lid is opened via a remote, cable-operated latch, and the wide seatbelt is USAF surplus. The '32 dash was modified with a 1/2-inch-thick solid mahogany insert panel that's filled with six curved glass, smooth bezel period Stewart-Warner instruments – including the obligatory 160-mph speedometer and an 8,000-rpm tach. There were two fuel tanks, so the car could run on alcohol or other potent fuels. A dash-mounted Stewart-Warner pressure pump pressurizes the second

That row of fasteners across the cowl is for the roadster's tight-fitting black tonneau cover. The instruments are period 2-5/8-inch Stewart-Warner gauges with flat bezels. The speedometer is mounted at the far left; the fuel pressure pump is mounted in the '32 Ford dash panel. An 8,000-rpm tach is at the right, but unless your head is pretty low, it's tough to see when the tonneau is fastened for racing.

Hubbard's Machine Shop in Hayward, California, did the requisite machining before the present rebuilt flathead was reassembled by Neil O'Kane. Palmer duplicated all the speed equipment components except one item. "I just couldn't find a Harman and Collins Super T camshaft, so we used a re-profiled Howard M8, instead." The revised engine is a bit milder than the old stroker. It's a .040 over stock with a stock 3-3/4-inch crank for about 244 ci. The flathead was balanced and fitted with oversized valves, Johnson adjustable lifters, and a Melling high-pressure oil pump. Jere Jobes rebuilt the smaller-sized Stromberg 81 carburetors, and they've been topped with Stellings & Hellings bonnet-style air cleaners. The Offy heads make for a more street-suitable 9.5:1 compression ratio.

Classic elements on a classic '32: '39 teardrop tail-lights, twin exhaust pipes that parallel the frame rails, Halibrand quick-change, and Hayward Rod Benders club plaque...check, check, check. Ford Cabernet Red is the color, a close approximation of the original hue.

The racing tonneau fits snugly, keeping with the character and the reputation of this car. Palmer's '32 raced at the salt flats, and it has won the Bruce Meyer Preservation Award and the Stroker McGurk Award; along with many show trophies – it's like an old racehorse that still gathers accolades.

The hood sides were neatly and uniquely modified with openings and flared reveals for the external headers. The headers are this roadster's signature modification.

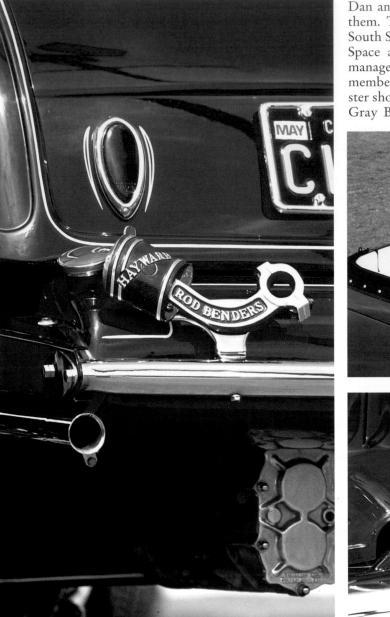

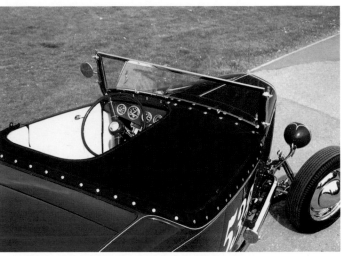

Dan and Charlene Cyr, Rick Perry was still working with them. The historic event was held at the Cow Palace in South San Francisco, and there was no shortage of entrants. Space availability was further complicated by the show management's wish to present many Bay Area Roadsters' member cars, and there was a fairly large display from roadster show stalwart Roy Brizio. It was tough. They even told Gray Baskerville he couldn't display his well-traveled '32

tank; it's located in the trunk and its fuel is filtered by an in-line C-2A fuel filter. A hidden S-W electric fuel pump ensures that the regular tank works without vapor lock.

Jim Palmer astutely restored this historic hot rod in the best possible way. He selected a point in time in its long history, and then, using photographic records, carefully redid his car to match.

My first look at the freshly restored Pacific Gunsight Special '32 was at the Oakland Roadster Show in 1999. Jim Palmer wanted to enter the show and had been told there was "no room at the inn." You may recall that was the 50th anniversary, and although the show was then managed by

roadster because it had primer on the fenders.

I was exhibiting my newly completed '32 Ford roadster for the first time, and when I saw Palmer's beautifully restored old deuce, I flipped. A number of us pleaded with the show management to accept Jim and his very worthy roadster. Fortunately, at the eleventh hour, they found room for the car. Even better, when the awards were handed out, the Pacific Gunsight Special won first place in the Vintage Racecar Class and the trophy for the Outstanding Overall Restored Antique Vehicle.

That summer, Jim's roadster was invited to be part of the second hot rod class at the Pebble Beach Concours d'Elegance. There was very intense competition, in the form of the ex-Dick Flint '29, owned by Don Orosco, the ex-Bob McGee '32 roadster, owned by Bruce Meyer and restored by So-Cal Speed Shop, Blackie Gejeian's '26 T Lakes Modified that he built and restored himself, and four other very worthy entrants besides the Pacific Gunsight Special. Jim Palmer's friends added to the allure of the occasion by smartly turning out in Pacific Gunsight logoed maroon

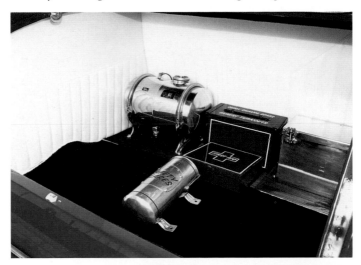

shirts. Although the '32 didn't win an award, it was very close, and it was wonderful to see the car on the show field.

Blackie Gejeian wasted no time inviting Jim to bring the roadster to his 41st Fresno Autorama. And when Jim returned to the Grand National Roadster Show in 2001, his car received the Bruce Meyer Hot Rod Preservation perpetual trophy. The following year, Jim and the Pacific Gunsight Special joined over 300 1932 Fords for the Petersen Automotive Museum's gala 70th birthday celebration. After that, it was displayed in the Bruce Meyer Gallery for a few months.

Jim swapped the four-carb manifold for a more street-tractable Eddie Meyer dual intake, and a modern electronic ignition setup has replaced the H&C mag. He let me take the roadster for a short spin around the Pleasanton Fairgrounds in the summer of 2003. The flathead starts immediately, thanks to a 12-volt conversion, and idles with a pleasant rumble. Although we didn't set any records, I've driven enough flathead-powered '32's to sense this car was tight, quick, and ready for many more miles. The unique Hayward Rod Benders twisted con rod plaque on its rear spreader bar tops off a fantastic restoration. Leo Juri would be proud. Thanks to Jim Palmer and his friends, the venerable *Pacific Gunsight Special* '32 highboy still looks ready to rumble.

Period trunk mods include matching carpet, racing fuel tank, battery box, and first aid kit, all painted to match. Astutely, Jim Palmer restored this historic hot rod in the best possible way. He selected a point in time in its long history, and then, using photographic records, carefully redid his car to match.

Jim Palmer loves to reunite his roadster with its former owners. Here's the car, with Leo Juri and Al Reynal flanking famous Northern California rodder, Art Gray. (Jim Palmer)

Blackie's T was meant to signal "hot rod" from any angle. In front, a sectioned and molded '32 grille, protected by a boldly initialed nerf bar, gives way to a polished flathead topped by four chromed Strombergs with curved racing stacks. The look Blackie achieved is consistent, purposeful, aggressive, and functional. There's a lot of chrome, but there's no pinstriping or really any superfluous items.

Another hot rod that's still in the hands of the man who built it, Blackie's "Shish-Kebab T" has a fascinating story. In hot rod circles, there are a few first names that everybody knows. They're unmistakable. Just say Roy, or Boyd, or Vic, Jr., and you know that's Brizio, Coddington, and Edelbrock. In the same vein, there's only one "Blackie."

His hair is all gray now, and a handsome beard frames his chiseled, tanned features. He's likely to be wearing an Oakland black and gold, Hall of Fame 50th Anniversary jacket. And he always has a wide smile on his face. Never alone at a car show, he's usually surrounded by an entourage of friends and admirers. Age 78, as this is written, grape farmer, ex-racer, hot rod restorer, and Fresno Autorama promoter, the indefatigable Blackie Gejeian is a living legend.

Pick the story you like best about Gejeian – they're all true. Like the time in 1953 when he took the fluids out of his roadster, removed the right-side hubcaps, and turned the T

on its side, every hour on the hour, (hence its nickname, the "Shish Kebab" Special) so spectators could walk completely around his car and dig the details.

I especially like the one about Blackie taking the mirror out of the ladies room at Oakland in 1958, to promoter Al Slonaker's horror, and putting it under the *Ala Kart*, so show goers could better see the chrome undercarriage – a show feature he pioneered. Blackie claims to have attended every day of every single Oakland Grand National Roadster Show. Why would you ever doubt him?

Michael "Blackie" Gejeian grew up as part of a large Armenian immigrant community in the Fresno area. He'd spent the war years in the Navy, returning in 1945, like so many other lucky vets, anxious to build a hot rod. He was a street racer in the late 1940s, and by all accounts he was a wild but skilled driver. Period photos show Gejeian's black '26 T modified, with the word "Blackie" painted on the driver's side cowl. He says that whenever he drove around,

Blackie Gejeian's '26 T Roadster

people would wave and yell, "Hi Blackie!" The nickname stuck. And no one calls him by his first name.

Blackie took his abbreviated roadster to the lakes in 1948 where it was promptly T-boned and badly damaged by an errant racer. That helped him decide to make a full-on show car out of it, and he began building it up, but also using it a lot. Blackie says that no less a personage than Doane Spencer came through Fresno in 1951 in his roadster, and he out-dragged and outran "Mr. Bracket" in an extended street race. Makes a great yarn and I'd guess, up against Doane's small-displacement 248-ci engine in his heavier '32, Blackie's big stroker, pulling a lighter T configuration, would definitely be quicker. I wish we had a photo of that historic encounter.

Gejeian completed the rebuild and repaint in time for the 1953 Oakland Show, and although he didn't win the top prize, (which went to Dick Williams' '27 T that year) he wasn't discouraged. And he'd caught the attention of every-one with his Shish Kebab car-on-its-side routine. He was back in 1954 (the year Frank Rose's T took the top prize), again a bridesmaid, but he kept improving his car, working on details, and running up big bills at the chrome plater's.

Blackie's turn finally came in 1955. He won the AMBR trophy, but for the first time, the finish was a tie. The co-winner was Ray Anderegg from Merced, California, with a yellow, channeled '27 T that coincidentally also had filled doors and a smoothly finished body. Anderegg's car has since disap-peared, although Franco (Von Franco) Costanza cloned it. Blackie, naturally, still owns his T modified, along with sev-eral other Oakland winners including the Dick Williams '27 T and the Barris-built '29, better known as "The Emperor."

Model T's seemed to be all the rage in the early years of the Oakland Show. Although Bill Niekamp's winning car in 1950, the first year, was a '29 A on Essex rails, the winners for 1951 through 1955 were all T-based. Blackie's was the

Blackie wanted to keep his roadster as original as pos-sible. As he told Michael Dobrin in an article in Street Rodder in November 1999, "the car had been 44 years in stor-age. Nobody had seen it. I had to make it authentic, so I took it apart and pho-tographed each piece. I looked everywhere for original parts, when I could get them. For instance," he says, "it still had the original battery cases."

Michael "Blackie" Gejeian grew up as part of a large Armenian immigrant com-munity in the Fresno area. He was a street racer in the late 1940s, when this shot was taken. By all accounts he was a wild but skilled driver. Earlier pho-tos show Gejeian's black '26 T modified, with the word "Blackie," painted on the driver's-side cowl. He says wherever he drove, people would wave and yell, "Hi Blackie!" The nick-name stuck. No one ever calls him by his first name. (Blackie Gejeian)

The small King Bee head-
lights and car trailer taillights are functional but
unobtrusive. Although
Blackie once drove this
car extensively, there
never was a top.

first car to win in true lakes modified style, although the
platform he used was hardly that of a lakes racer. Typically,
modifieds had narrowed bodies, and even Model T or low-
slung Essex rails, to better reduce wind resistance. Blackie
used a boxed and shortened '34 Ford frame, which despite a
wheelbase change from 112 down to 103 inches, lends the
tight little T body with its chopped windshield and slight
rake, a wider, more stalwart appearance.

This car was meant to signal "hot rod" from any angle. In
front, a sectioned and molded '32 grille, protected by a
boldly initialed nerf bar, gives way to a polished flathead
with a four-carb intake manifold and four chromed
Strombergs topped with curved racing stacks. The look
Blackie achieved is consistent, purposeful, aggressive, and
functional – and there's a lot of chrome, but there's no pinstriping or really any superfluous items.

Pick the Blackie story you
like best – they're all true.
Like the time in 1953 when
he took the fluids out of
his roadster, removed the
right side hubcaps, and
turned the T on its side,
every hour on the hour
(hence its nickname, the
"Shish Kebab" Special) so
spectators could walk
around his T and dig the
details. In 1958, Blackie
took the mirror out of the
ladies room at Oakland
and slid it under Ala Kart,
so show goers could see
the chrome undercarriage.
Gejeian claims to have
attended every day of
every single Oakland
Grand National Roadster
Show. Who'd doubt him?

Blackie once told me that he closely watched the cars that
won at Oakland, and incorporated details each year, for
three years running, that he thought made a winning difference. His T's running gear is boldly out in the open. Nearly
everything's plated, of course. Stock wishbones in front
team up with a '37 Ford tubular axle. In the rear, there are
radius rods and chromed tube shocks. The license plate is
pinned to a vestigial, authentic-looking 20-gallon gas tank
that looks like an extension of the body. The doors are filled
for a smooth look, and the body was channeled and molded
seamlessly onto the frame for a smooth appearance. The
engine block is painted white, and everything else that isn't
black lacquer is chromed – right down to the reversed
wheels (front and rear) with their '50 Mercury flat caps.
Tires are 5.60 x 15s in front and 8.20 x 15s in back. The small
King Bee headlights and car trailer taillights are functional
but unobtrusive. Although Blackie once drove this car
extensively, it never had a top.

Checking out the snug cockpit, this T's pleated white tuck-
and-roll upholstery is typical of the mid 1950s, and the white
trim theme is continued around the beltline of the body. The
seat squab was sectioned to accommodate the body channel.
There are depressions in the floor for shoe heels so the driver wouldn't poke his toes up under the dash. A Bell four-

spoke steering wheel (the steering box is '34 Ford) and traditional 2-5/8-inch Stewart-Warner convex lens gauges line the
painted panel. A shortened chrome floor shift rises from the
'34 Ford toploader. If it weren't for all the chrome, Blackie's
car would closely resemble a serious dry lakes racer, albeit
sitting a little wider than most. You could argue that some of
the finest racecars of the 1950s were equally minimalist, polished, and well prepared. Certainly the 1955 Oakland
National Roadster Show judging team, led by that year's
chief judge, Wally Parks, thought it was a winner.

The '48 Ford 59AB flathead lights up and idles with a powerful lope. It has all the approved period modifications: it was
bored and stroked to 296 ci (3-3/8 x 4-1/8), ported, and
relieved; and it runs an Edelbrock four-carb manifold and
Edelbrock heads. A Harman & Collins 8R101 mag handles the
spark detail. Inside, an Isky 404 full-race cam, Jahns pistons,
and Johnson adjustable lifters are found – only the best would
do for Blackie. There's no fan, but there's no hood either, so the
flatty probably runs cool enough unless it's really hot.
Attractive headers exit to lakes pipes that run alongside the
smoothed frame rails. Under them, the plated exhaust pipes
(even the twin Smithy glasspacks are chromed) run under the
frame and reappear just under the rear crossmember.

While the styling of this roadster was different from many,
more conventional cars, its proportions work very well.
Although they're not connected by a hood, the grille shell and

Stewart-Warner instru-
ments abound – and they
all function. A tip for
restorers: Stewart-Warners
were so well made origi-
nally that they could be
refurbished by skilled
instrument rebuilders and
reused with confidence.

the cowl height match perfectly. If there's anything to question, it's that two feet of empty space between the gas tank and the rearmost crossmember. On more conventional lakes modifieds, the wheelbase might have been shortened more and the frame bobbed in back, so that the fuel tank would be even with the rear of the car. Of course, you'd sacrifice ride and handling with that abbreviated setup. And Blackie had already chopped nine inches out of the original '34 frame's wheelbase. Still, the combination of the (relatively) longer wheelbase and reversed wheels in all four corners gives the car a squat, bulldog-like stance that exudes power, and it's very visible thanks to that uncovered engine that almost looks too big for its bay, since the carb stacks are higher than the cowl. This roadster is decidedly different – that's what makes it fascinating, even to this day.

Blackie had built a backyard shop in 1948. Sadly, it burned up completely in 1956, along with a lot of important records and photos. People assumed the T was lost in that blaze, but fortunately, it was stored somewhere else. In 1979, Blackie moved

This T's pleated white tuck-and-roll upholstery is very typical of the mid 1950s. The white trim theme is continued around the beltline of the body. The seat squab was sectioned to accommodate the body channel. There are depressions in the floor for shoe heels so Blackie wouldn't poke his toes up under the dash.

When he re-restored his car, Blackie refurbished all the individual pieces – he did almost no replacing. He smoothed out dented headlight buckets, carefully resurrected all the little bits, and made countless trips over to Western Chrome in Fresno, bird-dogging the plating and polishing process.

There's no engine fan, but there's no hood, so the flatty runs cool unless it's really hot. Attractive headers exit to lakes pipes that run alongside the smoothed frame rails. Plated exhaust pipes (even the Smithy glasspacks are chromed) run under the frame, reappearing just under the rear crossmember.

it to a new storage area, and it just sat there, covered up for nearly 20 more years. The Oakland Grand National Roadster Show was celebrating its 50th anniversary in 1999, and many cars from the early days had been invited. Blackie decided to restore his old car and bring it to the show, which was to be held that year at the Cow Palace in South San Francisco.

It was the fall of 1998, and having made that decision, Blackie only had four months to do the actual job. While his car was relatively complete, the chrome (and there was a lot of it) had deteriorated. Adding to the complications, Blackie wanted to keep the roadster as original as possible. As he told Michael Dobrin, in an article in *Street Rodder* in November 1999, "the car had been 44 years in storage. Nobody had seen it. I had to make it authentic, so I took it apart and photographed each piece. I looked everywhere for original parts, when I could get them. For instance, it still had the original battery cases."

Blackie knew that there were a few small flaws in the car originally. And he insisted that they be included in the restoration. For example, there were a few crooked seams in the upholstery. Blackie insisted that Howdy Ledbetter redo the interior exactly the same way, crooked seams and all, with the same materials. And he did.

At 73, when this work was undertaken, Blackie was no youngster; but then he's always had the energy of guys half his age. Predictably, Blackie Gejeian was tireless in his meticulous devotion to this cause. As he told Michael Dobrin: "We had a cold, early winter here and snow was coming in. I never had a meal outside of this shop for four months. Sixteen hours a day, I lived in this sucker."

Blackie restored individual pieces; he did almost no replacing. He smoothed out dented headlight buckets, carefully resurrected all the little bits, and made countless trips over to Western Chrome in Fresno, bird-dogging the plating and polishing process. Chuck Krikorian (former owner of *the Emperor*, a car that is now one of Blackie's proud possessions) did the bodywork and repainting, and as noted, expert trimmer, Howdy Ledbetter, used the old interior pieces for patterns, and redid the white leatherette to perfection.

The four-month process ended with a running car. Blackie's son Charlie proudly drove it into the Cow Palace, completing Blackie's four-car display of *the Emperor*, the Dick Williams '53 AMBR T, the *Mod Rod*, and an early T-bucket by Dan Woods. It was a great hit at the 50th anniversary show, and the timing was perfect, as many former winners were on display as well.

It's hard to beat the great looks of a show flathead. Four carbs, high-compression heads with plated acorn nuts, red ignition wires contrasting with a white-painted block – this is a fine-looking engine, and it goes as well as it looks.

In August 1999, Blackie's T was invited to the second iteration of the hot rod class at the Pebble Beach Concours d'Elegance, where it won a creditable third place against the Dick Flint '29 roadster (which won first place and the Dean

Out of respect, entrants come from all over the country, because it's Blackie's show. Loud, fast, and minimalist in design, Blackie's "Shish Kebab Special," like its owner, has never been duplicated, and my guess is, it never will be.

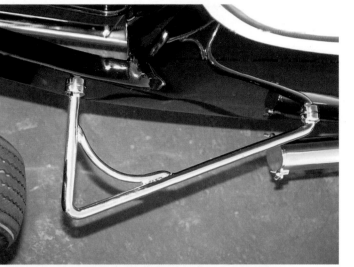

A chromed '37 tube axle, '48 Ford front brakes, plated drums, and a bull-dogged front end...they all spell classic hot rod.

A triangular nerf bar protects the rear tires, a feature borrowed from sprint car practice. T builders: take note.

Batchelor Award), and the Bob McGee '32 highboy (second place) – no small accomplishment given the quality and historical significance of the cars that year. I think Blackie may have been a bit disappointed, as his car probably had the highest percentage of original parts on it. All three winners were virtually perfect, meaning the judges had to rank the entrants according to style, historical significance, and technical achievement. You can imagine – the voting was very, very close for the first three places. As far as this Chief Class Judge was concerned, they were all winners.

Blackie Gejeian's '26 T is a rare example of a unique hot rod that was built by, and still remains in the hands of, one very talented individual. Blackie could do it all, and he still does. His energy is contagious. He personally picks and arranges each entrant's car for his invitation-only Fresno Autorama.

While the styling of this roadster differs from conventional cars, its proportions work well. Although a hood does not connect them, the grille shell and the cowl height match perfectly. If there's anything to question, it's that two feet of empty space between the gas tank and the rearmost crossmember. On conventional lakes Modifieds, the wheelbase might have been shorter and the frame bobbed, so the fuel tank would align with the car's rear. You'd sacrifice ride and handling with that abbreviated setup, and Blackie had already chopped nine inches out of the original '34 frame's wheelbase, so he probably didn't want it any shorter.

15

The ex-Bob Schaeneman '32 Ford highboy is a great example of a dual-purpose street and racing rod. It's still very true to the period in which it was built. The two most distinctive features are a '29 Chrysler split windshield, which was sectioned and chopped to fit the '32 cowl, and a low-chromed roll bar – both are visible in an old Hot Rod magazine photo. This is the only '32 Ford we've ever seen with a Chrysler windshield.

Over time, the car went one way, and the engine went another. Miraculously, they've been reunited in this fine historic hot rod. Restoring historic hot rods became a popular pastime as the twentieth century ended. The practice accelerated because significant Concours d'Elegance, namely Meadow Brook Hall, Louis Vuitton in New York City, Pebble Beach, and Amelia Island, welcomed them. And you can credit an interest in these old hot rods on the part of enthusiasts who grew up in the 1950s, remembered them, sought them out, and wanted to bring them back.

Several people deserve praise for helping to jump-start this interest. Arguably one of the first was Jim "Jake" Jacobs, who restored the first Oakland AMBR winner, the ex-Bill Niekamp '29 roadster, back in 1969-70. But at that time, few people noted this as the start of a trend.

A few years later, the precedent was followed by Bruce Meyer (Pierson Bros.' coupe, So-Cal Speed Shop belly tanker, and the

Doane Spencer and Bob McGee roadsters), Don Orosco (the Tony La Masa and Dick Flint roadsters), Gordon Apker (the McGowan Bros.' '31 A), Mitchell Rasansky (the Ralph Cooper '32 roadster), Jim Palmer (the Pacific Gunsight Special '32), and Ron San Giovanni (*Cam Carriers* '23 T altered). All these individuals should be credited with helping to start and maintain this important rodding trend.

Bruce Meyer went a step further, contacting the people who had built the historic hot rods he owned, and involving them in the restorations. Ron San Giovanni deserves special mention, too. In 1991, Ron entered the Hartford, Connecticut, *Cam Carriers* '23 T altered roadster at the Hershey Fall National Meet to compete for an AACA Junior award. In doing so, he proved that if you had a genuine hot rod, with legitimate racing history, you could qualify under AACA rules for consideration in Class 24-A.

Following Ron's example, in 1992, Kirk F. White, then living in Wayne, Pennsylvania, brought the first street and lakes

Bob Schaeneman's '32 Roadster

roadsters to display at Hershey (see Chapter 7 on the Ray Brown '32). After their winning appearances were noted in several magazines, interest in historic rods really took off.

The ex-Ray Brown roadster's Hershey appearance was a hit, but AACA Fall National Meet attendees that year will remember that Kirk White wasn't taking any chances. He actually entered two '32 highboys. The second one is the subject of this chapter. And like all of these old hot rods, there's an interesting tale of discovery behind it. It starts with an engine – a flathead, to be precise.

In 1990, when he was at Hershey, Kirk spotted a black '32 highboy with a full-race, three-carb flathead. A talented Massachusetts rodder and restorer named Jim Lowrey, Sr., and his son, Jim, Jr., had built it. A fiberglass-bodied car on a genuine '32 frame, the roadster was very well built, had some period parts, and it looked and sounded great. Kirk was hooked; he bought the roadster and drove it quite a bit. I saw it at a Ferrari meet in Philadelphia where it attracted more attention than most of the V-12s.

The Lowreys had built their highboy around a modified engine that reportedly had come out of an early hot rod that had run a very respectable speed at El Mirage in 1952. The engine block had been stenciled with the details of the actual top speed run. Kirk felt that added value to his purchase, but he didn't know the whereabouts of the car that had once contained that engine.

The following year, Kirk ran several advertisements in *Hemmings Motor News*. He was looking for vintage historic hot rods to buy and resell, but despite his beautifully written appeals, he didn't get many responses that panned out. One that did was from a Massachusetts man named Bob Magane.

Magane owned an historic '32 Ford highboy, which he said had been built in Stockton, California, by a man named John Erracalde back in 1938-39. Magane knew quite a bit of the history of his roadster. He told Kirk that after the war, the roadster was sold to Gordon Ingram, who raced it up through 1951. The April 1951 *Hot Rod* magazine ran a piece on the Valley Timing Association, and the article noted that

Ingram ran an impressive 122.86 mph in his '32, winning the C Roadster division at a Valley Timing Association Meet at El Mirage in late 1950. That was a 350-mile trip from the VTA's Northern California base. Ingram then sold the car to Bob Schaeneman, also of Stockton.

Schaeneman eventually set a record in it, turning 128.57 mph at El Mirage dry lake in 1952. He later exhibited the '32 at the Oakland Roadster Show in 1954. A photo of the roadster appeared in the January 1954 issue of *Hot Rod* magazine in a report on a Northern California VTA drag racing event at Kingdon airstrip, near Stockton, California.

The *Hot Rod* magazine text read, "Robert Schaeneman's '32 Ford roadster, a jet black '32 Ford street machine that showed unmistakable signs of having been lavished with much meticulous care, won the award for the meet's Best Constructed Street Roadster." The photo of the car shows it with a raised front end (presumably for better traction) and the headlight bar is somewhat higher than it appears today – possibly as a response to strictly enforced headlamp height restrictions in the 1950s.

Late in the 1950s, Schaeneman sold the roadster to a Stockton policeman named Bob Cress. Not long afterward, the roadster was put in storage, and it literally dropped out of sight until 1977, when it appeared in a for sale ad in

This early photo shows the Schaeneman roadster with a young Bob Schaeneman. The era is probably the very early 1950s. Note the high-mounted Guide headlights, in an era before dropped headlight bars became fashionable. The car also appears to have 16-inch wire wheels with spoke covers. The '29 Chrysler split windshield is already in place, along with a top for those cool Northern California nights. The later cycle front/bobbed rear fenders aren't yet evident. (Photo courtesy of Mark Mountanos)

Inside, the dash was modified extensively. It contains 10 early Stewart-Warner gauges, including a coveted Auburn panel insert, a Valley Timing Association timing tag, the 1954 Oakland Roadster Show commemorative plaque, and two popular early Bell Auto Parts accessories – a fuel pressure pump and a four-spoke, racing style steering wheel.

Rare "block letter" Edelbrock finned high-compression aluminum heads are a highly sought-after early hot-rod item. Authentic black ignition wiring uses Rajah spark plug terminals, just as rodders did back in the day.

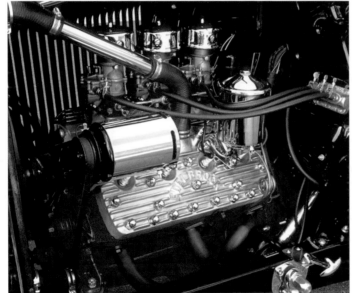

The engine is a Canadian 59L flathead of 1946-48 vintage. Its odd 291-ci displacement comes from a .030 over 3-5/16 bore and has a 4-inch stroke. Jahns pistons with Grant rings, plus Edelbrock "block letter" heads, yield a 9:1 compression ratio. The camshaft is a Winfield full-race SU-1A; the ignition is a '42 Ford "crab cap" distributor.

Three Stromberg 97s, on an Edelbrock intake manifold, fitted with Stellings air cleaners, top the dynamically and statically balanced Jim Lowrey, Sr.-built engine. A 10-inch Ford clutch and chopped flywheel are paired with a '39 toploader with a Lincoln-Zephyr 26-tooth first- and second-gear cluster and a chromed shift handle. When you think classic hot rod, you have to have this car in mind.

paper clippings and the pertinent articles in *Hot Rod* magazine. Kirk White drove the roadster as he found it with the Chevrolet engine for a while, and then sent it to the Lowreys for a full restoration. It was time to set things right. The restorers yanked the historic flathead from Kirk's glass-bodied '32, and reinstalled it in the Schaeneman '32 where it belonged.

In September 1992, the Lowreys and Kirk F. White showed the freshly restored Bob Schaeneman and Ray Brown '32 roadsters at the *Ty-Rods* annual post-Labor Day meet in Massachusetts, where both cars were big hits. A few weeks later, they exhibited the historic roadsters at the AACA Meet at Hershey. Each car was certified by the AACA as a competition race vehicle. Even better, both '32s won First Junior awards.

The ex-Bob Schaeneman '32 Ford highboy is a great example of a dual-purpose street and racing rod, and it remains very true to the period in which it was built. Basically a

Hemmings Motor News. Bob Magane flew to California, bought the car, and drove it home to Massachusetts. In 1978, Neal East wrote a piece about the '32 in *Rod Action*, called "An Oldtimer Gone East." He did a follow-up piece in the same magazine the following year. Before long, Bob Magane decided to replace the record winning, but now old flathead with something he considered more reliable – a small-block Chevy. He sold the flathead engine to Jim Lowrey, who rebuilt it and used it for the glass-bodied roadster he was building – which was the car, of course, that Kirk White eventually bought. If you're guessing where this is going, you're probably right. It's a remarkable coincidence.

Meanwhile, Kirk White bought the ex-Schaeneman '32 roadster from Bob Magane. In his methodical style, White researched the car and located former owner, Bob Cress, who showed him a collection of references that included local news-

stock-bodied roadster on '32 rails, the car rides on a dropped axle in front (probably a MorDrop) under a Model A crossmember with a stock, un-split Ford wishbone and tubular shocks. The rear end was taken from a '40 Ford; the steering from a '49 Ford. Front spindles are '40 Ford, with 15-inch '48 Mercury rims running big-and-little 6.00 x 15 and 8.20 x 15-inch blackwall tires.

The car's two most distinctive features are its Schaeneman built '29 Chrysler split windshield, which was sectioned and chopped to fit the '32 cowl, and a low chromed roll bar – both of which are visible in the old *Hot Rod* magazine photo. This is the only '32 Ford we've ever seen with a Chrysler windshield. When he built the car, Schaeneman filled the cowl, filled and peaked the grille shell, shaved the door handles, and fabricated the front and rear fenders and the rear bumper. The trunk handle was retained, and an accessory license plate light is mounted under the historic black California plate.

The low-mounted headlamps, painted black with chromed rims, are Dietz accessory items; the taillights are the popular '39 Ford teardrops. Inside, the dash was modified extensively. It contains 10 early Stewart-Warner gauges, including an Auburn panel insert, a Valley Timing Association timing tag, the 1954 Oakland Roadster Show commemorative

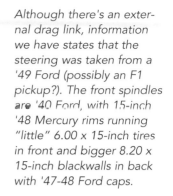

Although there's an external drag link, information we have states that the steering was taken from a '49 Ford (possibly an F1 pickup?). The front spindles are '40 Ford, with 15-inch '48 Mercury rims running "little" 6.00 x 15-inch tires in front and bigger 8.20 x 15-inch blackwalls in back with '47-48 Ford caps.

A '34 Auburn panel is stuffed with convex-lensed vintage Stewart-Warner gauges. A Bell fuel pump is mounted in the center, and the panel inserts are engine turned. The stock '32 panel was extended and reshaped, so the Auburn component fits as though it was designed that way.

A Valley Timing Association timing tag indicates Bob Schaeneman drove his '32 at El Mirage in 1952. His top speed was a very creditable 128.57 mph. The small tag (above) between the pressure and oil temperature gauges certifies the car was entered in the Exhibit d'Elegance at Oakland's National Roadster Show in 1954.

plaque, and two early Bell Auto Parts accessories – a pressure pump and a four-spoke racing-style steering wheel.

The engine is a Canadian "59L" flathead of 1946-'48 vintage. It was bored .030 over 3-5/16 and has a 4-inch stroke, for a 291-ci displacement. Jahns pistons with Grant rings, along with coveted Edelbrock "block letter" high-compression heads, yield a 9:1 compression ratio. The camshaft is a Winfield full-race SU-1A, and the ignition is a '42 Ford "crab cap" distributor. Three Stromberg 97s on an Edelbrock intake manifold, with Stellings air cleaners, top the modified engine, which was dynamically and statically balanced by Jim Lowrey. A 10-inch Ford clutch and chopped flywheel are paired with a '39 toploader with a Lincoln-Zephyr 26-tooth first and second gear cluster and a chromed shift handle. When you think classic hot rod, you have to have this car in mind.

During the restoration, Dave Emory of LeBaron Bonney in Amesbury, Massachusetts, upholstered the car in the correct early Ford-style red leatherette. The finish is deep Black Centari paint, expertly applied by Jim Lowrey, Jr. Larry Hook of Cumberland, Rhode Island, redid the pinstriping in bright red.

The result is a stunning, go-anywhere roadster that Kirk likes to say, "drives like a bear." It certainly was a lucky coincidence that Kirk was able to find the record-setting engine, and then locate the actual car it came from, and reunite them.

After keeping the ex-Schaeneman roadster a few more years, Kirk sold it to Mark Mountanos, who also owns the ex-Joe Nitti '32 (see Chapter 4). Mike says he has enjoyed driving the abbreviated-fendered, historic black roadster, and it certainly makes a fine stablemate for the purple Nitti '32. Kirk White and the Lowreys must be credited for showing restorers and historians the way with these two accurately restored period racing deuce roadsters. Their research and careful restoration ensures future rodders can see these great cars, just as they were built.

During the restoration, Dave Emory of LeBaron-Bonney, in Amesbury, Massachusetts, upholstered the car in the correct early Ford-style red leatherette. The finish is deep Black Centari paint, expertly applied by Jim Lowrey, Jr. Larry Hook, of Cumberland, Rhode Island, redid the pinstriping in bright red. Throw in the '39 toploader, Stewart-Warner-stuffed Auburn panel and extra gauges, Bell pressure pump, and an authentic VTA timing tag – did somebody say historic hot rod?

Bob Schaeneman filled the '32 cowl, filled and peaked the grille shell, shaved the door handles, and fabricated the front and rear fenders, as well as the custom rear nerf bar bumper. The trunk handle was retained and an accessory license plate light is mounted under the historic black California plate. The trunk is fully upholstered.

Essentially a stock-bodied Ford roadster on '32 rails, the Schaeneman car rides on a dropped axle in front (probably a MorDrop) that's been tucked under a Model A crossmember, with stock, un-split Ford wishbones and tubular shocks. The rear end was taken from a '40 Ford; the fenders are slightly bobbed, stock '32s; the taillights are the ever-popular '39 teardrops. This rod also has many individual touches, like the chromed roll bar and the unique rear nerf bar.

"Comin' at ya." The So-Cal coupe's unmistakable profile, sleek track nose, and distinctive red and white livery marked a car that terrorized Bonneville and Southland drag strips in 1953-54. When this car showed up, there was always a good chance records would fall.

Billed as the "Double Threat Coupe," this hammered hurricane, with its blown Ardun, is still a hot rod hero. Alex Xydias opened his now-legendary So-Cal Speed Shop in Burbank, California, in March 1946; virtually on the day he received his honorable discharge from the US Army Air Corps. "I trained as a flight mechanic, but I never went overseas," he likes to say with a chuckle. "I think the Germans heard I was coming and surrendered."

Alex's shop wasn't fancy. He started with a storefront on Olive Blvd., in Burbank, "but I realized I wanted a place where we could work on cars." He then built a single-story Sears prefab building, slightly bigger than a two-car garage, on Victory Blvd., but it had room for a limited inventory of speed equipment. Soon it was a popular spot for Los Angeles-based hot rodders. Alex reminisces, "if someone came in wanting a set of Edelbrock heads with a particular compression ratio, we'd stall him while my assistant drove down to Vic's garage on Highland Avenue and returned with the right set."

16

When Alex and his good friend, Dean Batchelor, conjured up the record-setting So-Cal Streamliner, they learned a few unscheduled lessons about aerodynamics after the 'liner got airborne and crashed with Dean at the wheel. The undaunted duo were soon back in the game with a sleeker, faster 'liner that soon set several acknowledged FIA records. Their efforts forced the vaunted international racing world to accept the fact that just because America's hot rodders worked in a so-called "backyard" atmosphere, they weren't to be taken lightly.

The So-Cal coupe effort grew out of Alex's continued efforts to publicize his business. Along with Keith Baldwin, who joined him in 1949, Alex correctly reasoned that if he had a record-setting car, one that was neat enough to win "Best-Appearing Car and Crew" awards as it captured its class at events from the drags to Bonneville, the right people would notice. He was right – they did.

Hot rod competition wasn't confined to racing in the immediate postwar period. The Southern California Timing

The So-Cal '34 Coupe

Association (SCTA) and the Russetta Timing Association (RTA) were intense rivals. Both were loosely knit groups of active hot rod clubs, and lakes racing was their main focus. Wally Parks ran the SCTA; Lou Baney headed up the RTA. There were other timing associations, but none were as large and as well organized. One of the principal differences between the two groups was their differing viewpoint on just what constituted a proper dry lakes racer. The SCTA had been founded back in 1937; they only sanctioned agreed-upon racing cars and modified production roadsters. Starting in 1940, and modeled closely after the SCTA, Russetta (the name loosely translates as a red chariot) was more ecumenical, welcoming hot-rodded coupes, sedans, and other closed vehicles.

SCTA stalwart Alex Xydias told me, "we didn't think coupes were real racing cars. A coupe or sedan was something you drove on the street. It seems crazy now, but we looked down on guys who raced them." Other SCTA members looked askance at the RTA, but began reconsidering when some RTA record speeds, especially in the more aerodynamic coupes, exceeded theirs. The desire to race overcame a lot of objections. During the Lakes season, each timing association held at least one monthly meet. Club competition was intense, with long waits between runs. Quite a few enthusiasts joined both timing groups, so they'd have more opportunities to run.

Trophies were awarded for individual efforts as well as for aggregate club scores. Your competition numeral denoted where you had finished in the points race, so everyone knew where you stood. Low numbers were highly coveted, as were the dash-mounted timing tags – SCTA's tags were black and gold, and Russetta's were red and silver. The Pierson Brothers' '34 Ford coupe, a well-known and beautifully turned-out Russetta record-holder, proudly wearing the number 2D, attracted SCTA attention and starred on the cover of *Hot Rod* magazine when it began turning close to 150-mph speeds.

Bob and Dick Pierson and their friend and Edelbrock engine wizard Bobby Meeks were members of the hot rod club of Inglewood. Invited by the SCTA to compete, they jumped at the chance. The Piersons were certain the rival association wanted to see if their coupe's speeds were real. After Bob Pierson blasted off a 151-mph trap speed, the SCTA grudgingly set up two closed-car classes. Coupes were unchopped or channeled, stock-bodied cars; Modified Coupes were chopped and/or channeled cars, with the overall height reduction being the determinant. At Bonneville in 1950, the only year they competed on the salt in their '34, the Piersons handily won the B and C Modified Classes with two-way averages of 146.365 mph and 149.005 mph, respectively. Bob Pierson's experience at Douglas Aircraft had helped him improve the car's aerodynamics, thanks to a severely chopped roof and a full belly pan that vented trapped air to the rear of the car.

Other racers rushed to copy the Piersons' success. Jim Gray and Russell Lanthorne built a not-as-radically chopped, racecar nosed '34 Ford with a GMC six-cylinder powerplant. In 1951 at Bonneville, running in a new third coupe class called Competition Coupes (which had been established for hardtops with more wind-cheating bodywork), and still in primer, the barely finished three-window turned an impressive 153.061 mph, good enough for fourth in class. Interestingly, the class-winning coupe for that meet, with a clocking of 164.233 mph, was the former Pierson '34, by then owned by Dawson Hadley. This was the only time these cars competed against one another, until they went head-to-head, over half a century later, at Pebble Beach.

Alex Xydias and the Pierson Brothers both benefited from Edelbrock sponsorship. The Piersons had become Edelbrock employees; Alex was selling enough Edelbrock equipment to merit some support. Gray and Lanthorne retired their coupe after its maiden racing season. It was a good-looking car; Frank Kurtis in nearby Glendale had crafted one of his distinctive, streamlined racecar noses for it. Xydias bought the car, brought it to Burbank, and planned to campaign it in a hot new form of competition – organized drag racing. Alex says he liked the fact that the car was already substantially built, and he "…didn't have to start from scratch." Now he had a platform for a series of hot engines. "I wanted a car that we could run at Bonneville, but also one that we could race more than once a year." The drags were the answer.

The So-Cal coupe gets a running start on its way to a record-setting performance. Running a blown 258-ci Buddy Fox-built flathead, the car was bumped up from Class B (under 260 ci) to Class C. Wearing Tom Cobbs' coveted number 1, the chopped '34 set a new two-way record average of 172.749 mph. Completed just a few days previously, with Cobbs' clever crank-driven supercharger setup, the gleaming red and white speedster ran with its engine set back 22 inches. Crank driving the 4-71 avoided the belt slippage common with a conventional supercharger mounting above the engine and permitting a low hoodline with no protrusions. (Alex Xydias)

A year later, here's the 1954 edition of the So-Cal coupe, receiving some attention in the parking lot of the Wendover Motel. The engine now sports Ardun OHV heads, and the car has been chopped again for better streamlining, for a look that's similar to the Pierson Bros. coupe. Sadly, 1954 was not a good year. The So-Cal coupe suffered from ignition and blower-drive problems and failed to set a record. The Wendover Motel parking lot was always a busy place during Speed Week. Guys worked on their cars there, often late into the night, and some fellows rebuilt engines right in their motel rooms. (Alex Xydias)

Tom Cobbs was responsible for the 4-71 GMC blower and its complex intake, comprised of shapely sheetmetal ducting and a pop-off valve. In this second edition of the coupe, the Mercury V-8 was fitted with an Ardun OHV conversion. Four Stromberg 48s slurped the alcohol mix, while the ignition was a Scintilla-Vertex magneto. (Alex Xydias)

This rear shot of the coupe in 1953 shows the triangular "shark fin" push bar needed to get the ultra-high-geared coupe up to proper starting velocity. The chopped and channeled three-window was low, but an additional whack at the roof for 1954 would make it even sleeker. A full belly pan helped manage airflow. (Alex Xydias)

Enter Alex's friends, Buddy Fox and Tom Cobb. Cobb was one of the first competitors to run a supercharger – for his first try, in a roadster, he used a smaller GMC Roots-type unit adapted from a 3-71 diesel engine, mounted atop the flathead, with a quartet of Stromberg 97s. In 1952, Fox and Cobb devised a chain and sprocket-driven setup that allowed them to locate a bigger 4-71 GMC blower in front of the engine for a lower silhouette and better streamlining. The coupe had languished for over a year in Alex's garage, and now there was a flurry of activity to prepare it for the 1953 SCTA Bonneville meet. Alex was pleased to provide his car as the Fox and Cobb engine platform, just so long as it competed under the So-Cal banner, wore the shop's vivid red and white livery, and featured Tom Cobb's coveted number 1 on its doors.

Ready for action, Alex's coupe ran a Buddy Fox-built 258-ci Mercury flathead, set back 22 inches, spinning a crankshaft-driven, GMC 4-71 blower fired by a Vertex magneto. It was fed by a quartet of Stromberg 48 carbs. Blower wizard Tom Cobb perfected the slick direct-drive setup. The last nut was torqued on Monday night of the 1953 Bonneville Salt Flats opening. Three days later, the So-Cal team nailed a 172.749-mph Class "C" record for the flying mile, beating the Chrisman Brothers and Duncan Model A in the process.

Back in the "Southland," sans blower, the '34 turned 121-mph in B Modified at the Pomona drags. Finished in red and white So-Cal Speed Shop colors, it graced the cover of *Hot Rod* magazine in 1954 as the "Double Threat" coupe. Looking for more speed, and basically copying the Piersons' effort, the coupe's top was re-chopped to narrow, gun-slit proportions. Unfortunately, the radically reshaped So-Cal coupe suffered ignition setup and blower drive problems, so the 1954 Bonneville meet was a bust.

The coupe's drag-strip prowess that year was a different story. Thoroughly sorted, and running an Ardun OHV conversion, the So-Cal coupe developed upwards of 400 hp, and managed a 132-mph run. Alex told me, "I was such a flathead loyalist, I didn't want to go with the overheads. But when I had a chance to buy a new Ardun setup, and then a front-driven blower, I figured that was the best of both worlds."

Then tragedy struck. Although he'd never driven the coupe, Dave DeLangton (Alex's brother-in-law) thought he could better its already impressive performance. "Alex had moved the record up some 8 mph." Bonneville racer and crack wrench, Jim Travis, who was there that day, remembers it well. With Dave at the wheel, and the mighty Ardun turning sky-high revs, its unshielded clutch exploded, setting the fuel tank on fire. DeLangton bailed out while it was still rolling, but he had inhaled the flames and he suffered mortal burns and lung injuries. "The unoccupied car coasted the length of the fairgrounds," Travis recalls, "and right across the highway before it stopped." Sadly, DeLangton died in a

Los Angeles hospital a month after the explosion. A grieving Alex Xydias retired the '34 and never raced again.

The So-Cal coupe was sold to John Moxley, who repainted it blue and white, and ran it at Bonneville, with a 400-ci Chrysler Hemi, setting additional records. In 1956, it was sold to Rich Stricker and was driven by Jerry Eisert. They raced the coupe for four years before Moxley retired the car and put it up on blocks. Jim Travis bought the '34 from Eisert in 1970. Travis is perhaps best known for his work on Mickey Thompson's quad Pontiac-engined streamliner. "I'd always wanted that car," Travis said. "So I put my roadster up for collateral when it became available for sale."

"I installed the record-setting flathead out of my roadster, updated the car with a roll cage and the other SCTA requirements, then ran the lakes with it in '71 and Bonneville in '71- 72," Travis recalls. In 1973, running a stout 3/8-by-3/8 296-ci flathead with three Stromberg 48s on alcohol, Travis turned 142.999-mph, a Bonneville class record.

Alex Xydias gets ready for a fast blast in the coupe at Pomona. He broke the class record by eight mph. Sadly, Alex's brother-in-law, Dave DeLangton, wanted a try. Dave over-revved the Ardun, running this time without the blower. The clutch exploded – there was no scatter shield – and the ensuing fire badly burned DeLangton, who died soon afterward. In this photo Alex is wearing an open face helmet, a t-shirt, and no gloves or any fire-proof gear. Note the deep channel and the holes cut into the frame. Alex recalls that the steel rails were very tough, and cutting the holes was "the hardest thing we had to do."
(Alex Xydias)

Salty Jim Travis campaigned the coupe for years at Bonneville. He began with a 296-ci flathead and set a class record of 142.999 mph. Later, running a 300-ci blown Chevy V-8, Travis worked the car's speed up to 236 mph, an astonishing velocity for a car basically unchanged (save for aerodynamic improvements) since it was chopped the second time. Travis owned the coupe for 28 years, longer than anyone, and its distinctive blue and white livery helped make him and the coupe a fixture on the salt.
(Alex Xydias)

Travis skipped racing the coupe in 1974 and 1975. Seeking more speed, he installed a 300-ci small-block Chevrolet with a front-mounted Potvin-style blower. Over the years, and with a continual series of modifications, he heroically worked the old car's top speed up to an incredible 236 mph. But it was not without a few problems. Travis found that as his trap speeds topped 200 mph, aerodynamic forces compressed the car on its rear springs, forced the rear wheels to rub on the body, made the front end light, and on several occasions sucked part of the belly pan right off the car. "It would just spin the back tires at 221 to 225 mph (!)," Travis recalls, "and I couldn't figure out why."

Ever inventive, Jim used a series of 1 to 1-1/2 blocks to raise the rear, and he continually modified the belly pans. After seeking advice from experts like Dan Gurney, Don Ferguson, Jr., Bill Burke, and Art Chrisman, Travis eventually determined the optimum suspension settings and pan design. "I always Magnafluxed everything to make sure the

car was safe," he says today, "but aerodynamically, it was like pushing a barn door into the wind." At the same time, Tom Bryant was increasing his speeds to well over 200 mph in the former Pierson Bros. coupe, "but we were in different classes, with different-sized engines," Travis says, "so we didn't compete against each other. Bryant and I were the first guys to get a '34 over 200 mph."

Travis decided to pass on further top-speed efforts when Don Stringfellow set a 256-mph class record. "I made up my mind there was no way I was gonna beat that 256 in a 60-year-old car," he declared. Earlier, Art Chrisman had told Travis, "203 mph is a pretty respectable speed in that car," and Jim soon bettered that mark by over 33 mph. "If I'd listened to Art's suggestions for modifying the belly pan the first time around," he admits cheerfully, "I could have saved a couple of years of experiments."

"At Bonneville, we always drew a crowd. I remember some guys tellin' me one time, 'Do you realize, you don't own this car? We've been watching it for so many years, we feel like it's our car, and we came here to see it run.' One time, I took it out and photographed it alongside the ex-Pierson Bros., then Bryant, coupe. That '34 was skinny and tall; my

Viewed from the side, the ultra-low chopped and channeled So-Cal coupe displays its wind-cheating form. The windshield extends back into the roofline, conforming to the SCTA seven-inch vertical height mandate. Over the years, culminating with Jim Travis' subtle modifications to its underside and belly pan, the coupe's Bonneville speeds rose from 172.749 mph (when Dawson Hadley owned it) to over 236 mph with Travis behind the wheel.

Frank Kurtis' racecar shop in Glendale was responsible for the car's wind-cheating track nose. It was hand-formed from aluminum sheet stock, and it matched the '34's hood contours perfectly. That small grille opening is reminiscent of those on Kurtis noses for Champ cars and Midgets. Other race shops like those of Whitey Clayton and Emil Diedt also supplied hand-built noses to the hot-rod fraternity. Lakes racers quickly realized these sleek snouts were far more aerodynamic than a typical upright Ford grille – and they looked good, too.

Alex and his crew drilled lightening holes wherever possible. The front axle was perforated with one-inch holes in the center and smaller holes at each axle's stub end. Reed Engineering supplied the handsome sand-cast aluminum friction shocks. The hairpin radius rods were Kurtis units, originally made for Championship racecars. Cadmium plating made for a handsome, well-protected finish.

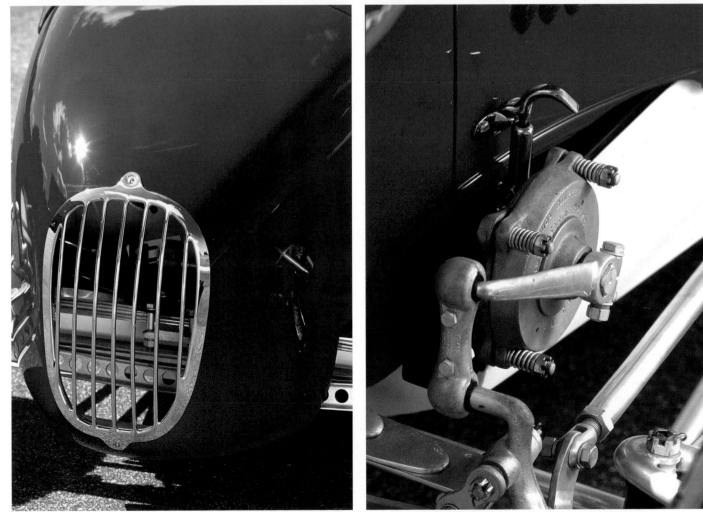

The open door reveals the car's body was channeled the full width of the frame. Xydias told Hot Rod magazine that drilling Ford's rugged steel rails was "...the toughest single job" in building the coupe. The yellow five-gallon fuel tank, a war surplus find, was originally used in a P-51 Mustang fighter aircraft. Fire extinguisher is clamped securely atop the frame. Behind it is a Bell hand-operated pump used to pressurize the fuel system.

The coupe has no radiator. Instead, a water transfer tube (center) runs from the engine through the firewall, and then into a 20-gallon aluminum tank in the trunk that was originally part of a DC-3 transport de-icing system. The detail-oriented Orosco crew even found an original float gauge for the tank – not an easy task some 50 years later.

Five Stewart-Warner gauges are mounted on an aluminum firewall. The steering column is finished with a mount for a mechanical tachometer and topped with a drilled Bell four-spoke wheel. Xydias and company bored holes everywhere they could to help keep the coupe's weight down.

talented crew at DBO Developments, led by Ole Erickson and Brad Hand, took the car down to the last nut and bolt, in their well-equipped shop in Monterey, California, and returned it to mid 1950s guise. The Ardun engine and crank-driven, chain-and-sprocket blower setup, with its lengthy aluminum tubular intake plumbing and neat four-carburetor plenum, were long gone, so Brad Hand had to re-create it all, and he did so, beautifully. The powerful engine starts with a hoarse cough from the Ford starter and bursts into life with a cacophony of basso profundo rumbles through the straight flex pipes that make your skin tingle.

Just before the Concours, I was in Don's shop, as the pinstriper was carefully lettering the So-Cal name on the doors. Alex Xydias and his wife Helen walked in. Alex just stood looking at the car as tears welled up in his eyes – nobody could say a word for a few minutes. Then Alex shook everyone's hands and told them how proud he was of what they'd accomplished. "That was the first time I saw the car finished," Alex recalls, "and it was an unbelievable thrill. It was perfect, they did a marvelous job."

car was short and fat. When I ran my '34," Travis says, "it always barked loud, pulled hard, and never missed a beat."

Shortly before he retired the coupe, Travis reinstalled a flathead "and my son Randy ran 138 mph in it at El Mirage." Under Travis' long stewardship, the coupe accompanied Mickey Thompson's *Challenger* and the Summers Brothers' Goldenrod on a multi-city European tour through 10 cities in four countries. The coupe was displayed at the Toronto Automobile Show in 1993, and at the Petersen Automotive Museum in 1997. "I had that car for 28 years," Travis declares with undisguised pride. "I made it more famous than it ever was when it was red and white."

In 1996, Travis sold the coupe to Don Orosco. Don decided to restore the coupe back to the way it was at the Pomona drags. After decades of corrosion from salt and sand, the old warhorse needed a painstaking restoration. Orosco and his

As restored, the So-Cal coupe ran a set of Orosco's reproduction Ardun heads, a Scintilla-Vertex magneto (back in the day, Alex had used the highly efficient mag instead of his usual Kong distributor and twin-coil ignition setup). The driveline was a '39 Ford gearbox linked via torque tube to a Halibrand quick-change rear. The drilled front axle, Kurtis Champ car hairpin radius rods, and Reed friction shocks were all done as original, and liberally cadmium plated. The 20-gallon water tank had originally been a de-icer tank for a DC-3. It's mounted under the deck lid and connected to the engine via a long transfer tube that runs through the cockpit. Like so many cars in the early postwar period, the So-Cal coupe uses a war surplus 5-gallon fuel tank – adapted from a P-51 Mustang de-icing tank, a Bell Auto Parts pressure pump setup, and a four-spoke, liberally drilled Bell wheel. The frame rails on the car were originally drilled for lightness – a task Alex Xydias remembers was very difficult due to the strength of the Ford frame steel. The expertly crafted belly pan runs the entire length under the car, with a vent to clear the quick-change. Bonneville tires on Divco milk truck 18-inch rims in the rear and ribbed Firestones on 16-inch rims in the front round out the running gear. The engine-turned wheel discs are an exquisite touch, as is the distinctive triangular push bar. The finished car resembles a crouching lion.

Competing at the 2001 Pebble Beach Concours d'Elegance, against the Pierson Brothers' '34 and Art Chrisman's '30 Model A, the So-Cal coupe notched a tightly contested class win. Orosco and his team appeared in So-Cal Speed Shop vintage-style red jackets with white pith helmets, just as the So-Cal crew had done in the old days, when the boys from Burbank frequently won Best-Appearing Car and Crew awards. The Pierson car, owned by Bruce Meyer, and restored by Pete Chapouris and his team in Pomona at the born-again So-Cal Speed Shop, was awarded the Dean Batchelor Trophy and second place; the Chrisman and Duncan Model A coupe, restored by Art and Mike Chrisman, came in third –- prevailing over an incredibly competitive field that included the ex-Chili Catallo "Little Deuce Coupe," and the Andy Kassa '32 three-window.

I was Chief Class Judge that day for the competition coupes, and it was a very tough decision. The three class-winning cars were equally and very accurately restored, but we concluded that the So-Cal '34 held a slight edge on aesthetics, technical accomplishment, and overall fame. It was very, very close.

I have to admit that I was choked up a bit when the three coupes assembled in front of the judging stand at Pebble Beach and waited for the signal to cross the ramp. Considering the effort it took to get all of them there, and very relieved after the tension of intently judging these fabulous restoration efforts, I shed a happy tear. As I was wiping my eyes, Jacques Nasser, then-CEO of Ford Motor Company, who sponsored the coveted Dean Batchelor Award for the most significant hot rod, was standing alongside. "Nice job, Ken," he said. For me, that was the frosting on the cake.

Not long after its Pebble Beach appearance, Don Orosco brought the So-Cal coupe back east to the Lime Rock Vintage Fall Festival, where it was inspected and admired by many enthusiasts who had never seen it in the metal. In 2003, Orosco sold the coupe to Bruce Canepa. "I'd done everything I wanted to do with the car," he said, "and now it's like a very expensive bookend. It was time for someone else to enjoy it."

In hindsight, and while Jim Travis certainly has a point concerning his lengthy ownership of the coupe, I believe it was imperative to restore the So-Cal car (and the Pierson coupe) back to the way they both were at their initial peak of hot rodding fame – the early 1950s. Both teams of restorers went the extra mile to recover or redo the wonderful historic elements that give each car its essential character. All credit to Tom Bryant and Jim Travis, for their courageous Bonneville drives in the ex-Pierson and ex-So-Cal coupes, but for my vote, I love both these cars the way they were, and I'm glad that's how they'll remain for all time.

Tom Cobbs originally designed a log-type blower manifold for this engine, and he built a beautiful aluminum collector plenum that runs forward and attaches to the 4-71 GMC supercharger. On the blower's opposite side, another smaller plenum supports a quartet of Stromberg 48 carburetors that were originally jetted for alcohol fuel.

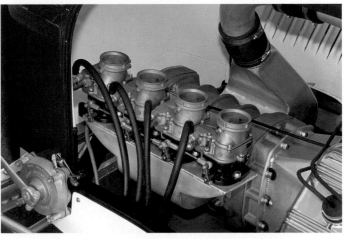

The born-again blown Ardun fires easily, idles with a healthy lope, and shakes the ground when it revs. Output is estimated at around 400 hp. Cad plating, neat fittings, and vintage-type hoses are all period correct.

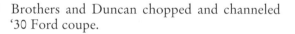

The body of an abandoned '31 Model A coupe provided the basis for the Chrisman machine. Thanks to extreme height-reduction efforts, it could run in the competition coupe class. The body was severely chopped, and a cowl from a '35 Ford, complete with its slanted A-pillar section, was grafted to the front of the coupe above the firewall. This gave the much-modified coupe the rather severe windshield rake Art wanted to achieve.

This is the most fantastic coupe, and Art Chrisman is a living legend who's just about done it all. In the late 1940s, Art was racing at the dry lakes. He competed and won in some of the earliest dragsters, and went on to record-setting exploits at Bonneville. He's still a skilled mechanic and engine builder – and he's always been a talented racer. Art is an integral member of a historic hot rod family, which included his late father, Everett, his brother Lloyd, and his cousin Jack. The Chrisman family advanced the sport, and set records, wherever they competed.

Truth be told, Art is crusty, laconic, and hard-nosed, especially with anyone he feels is wasting his time. That's simply who he is. We could discuss the ex-Lewis/Harvey/Lehman/Caruthers/Neumayer/Chrisman lakester, one of the oldest known competitive hot rods, that Art and his brother Lloyd turned into one of the country's first winning dragsters, or the Chrisman-built '29 A roadster of Ed Losinski that set fast e.t.'s whenever it ran. But for the purpose of this book, we'll focus on the radical Chrisman

Brothers and Duncan chopped and channeled '30 Ford coupe.

First, a little background: Art Chrisman first ran at Bonneville in 1951 with a '34 Ford highboy three-window coupe, and it shouldn't surprise you to learn that he set a class record. In 1952, his second year, moving up several speed notches, Art drove Chet Herbert's Chrysler-powered streamliner, setting a record in the D Streamliner Class at 232.35 mph. With that accomplishment, Art and five others became charter members in the coveted 200-mph club. For Art's third try at the salt in 1953, he brought the sleek, copper-colored coupe that you see on these pages.

In the early days of the Bonneville Speed Trials, there weren't many cars in competition, but there were a lot of classes. Art and Lloyd Chrisman and their dad, Everett, decided to build a competition coupe that would incorporate a simple but effective way of changing engines – not just for quick repairs, but to facilitate the use of engines of different sizes, so as to compete for records in several classes. The Chrismans

The Chrisman Brothers & Duncan '30 Coupe

intended to bring several engines to the salt, and to try for as many records as they could, in as many classes.

But before we get into how well the '30 A ran, and which engines it used, let's examine the construction of this "Fantastic Coupe"– as named in a cover story, in the February 1954 issue of *Hot Rod* magazine. Chosen as Hot Rod of the Month, the Chrisman coupe was featured in one of those famous Rex Burnett cutaway pen-and-ink drawings. These precise cutaways peeked beneath a car's bodywork and showed *Hot Rod* magazine readers just how the car was built. In its day, the coupe was cutting edge in conception. The Chrisman brothers already had a fine reputation for building and driving fast cars at the dry lakes and the drags. It was arguably a slam-dunk for *Hot Rod* magazine's editors to predict great things from the latest Chrisman's Garage effort.

Burnett's clever cutaway showed the Chrismans had built a 3-1/2-inch-diameter tube frame, shaped and welded with crossmembers in key locations to provide the framework for the mid/rear (behind the driver) engine location. The chassis had no rear suspension; the frame rails were instead bolted directly to the early Ford rear end. It featured a Halibrand quick-change center section, containing a 3.78:1 ring and pinion. With tall 18-inch tires, the resulting final drive ratio was 3.05:1.

The body of an abandoned 1931 Model A coupe provided the basis for the machine, and with extreme height reduction efforts, it would run in the competition coupe class. The body was severely chopped, and the cowl from a '35 Ford, complete with its slanted A-pillar section, was grafted to the front of the coupe above the firewall. This gave the coupe the rather severe windshield rake that Art was seeking.

Chrisman then went to the Alameda wrecking yard, just down the street from his shop, to find suitable sheetmetal to fill the roof section. He discovered the hulk of a '40 Ford Tudor, and torched the roof out to provide a large enough panel. As he was cutting, he pushed over the hood that was leaning up against the side of the sedan. It fell forward and landed atop another hood that was already lying upside down on the ground. After removing the roof panel and setting it aside, Art noticed the two hoods lying there together on the ground.

"There's my nose," he muttered to himself, as he envisioned the two hood panels, one atop the other, forming the pointed, wind-cheating front of the racecar to come. Chrisman loaded the roof panel section and the two '40 Ford hoods he'd found into the back of the truck, and returned to the shop. He and Lloyd spent the better part of the following weekend cutting and tack-welding together what was to become the Chrisman's Garage (Compton, California) competition coupe.

Streaking across the Bonneville Salt Flats, the Chrisman Brothers and Duncan '30 Model A competition coupe was a record setter and a tough competitor in several classes, due to the relative ease in which its skilled crew could change engines.

Leaping off the cover of the February 1954 issue of Hot Rod *magazine was a car the editors called, "The Most Fantastic Coupe!" Chosen as Hot Rod of the Month, the copper Chrisman Model A was featured in a Rex Burnett cutaway pen-and-ink drawing that peeked beneath the car's bodywork and showed* Hot Rod *magazine readers how it was built. Back in its day, this cool coupe was cutting edge in conception.*

Eight exhausts, made of flex pipe, facilitated quick engine changes. In the early 1950s, there weren't a lot of competition coupes at Bonneville, but there were a lot of records. The Chrisman's reasoned that if they could change engines relatively quickly, they could compete (and win) in several classes.

The 331-ci Chrysler Hemi turned 196-mph in 1955 on five percent nitro. They felt they'd break 200 mph on a 20-percent load, but the unfortunate death of a teammate, John Donaldson, in the Reed Brothers belly tank, precluded their making a record run. Sadly, they took the coupe home and never ran it in competition again.

A surplus aircraft seat and seat belts were installed in the scant space left in front of the firewall that separated and isolated the driver from whatever engine was installed. Art was the designated driver. He sat very close to the front of the cab with his nose just inches from the windshield. Getting in and out was quite a chore: "You grab the roll bar and pull your body in the air, like a chin-up, and then you swing your feet into the front well. Then you swing your rear end into the cab. Getting out is much simpler," says Art, "you just turn your shoulders to the right, roll over onto all fours, and crawl out." I've seen him perform this remarkable maneuver. It would be a challenge for a man half Art's age, but he makes it look easy.

On Monday, when Art's dad, Everett, came into the shop, a cobbled-together pile of tin that resembled a racer, but was still pretty raggedy, greeted him. Looking at the huge gaps in the fit of the hoods, cowl, and roof panel he commented in passing: "Looks like you two have a lotta welding to do!" Without looking up, both brothers nodded in agreement and moved closer to the task at hand.

As the body progressed through stages of build up, each change was carefully test-fitted to the tube chassis. The goal was to have the engine, transmission, and rear end fashioned together with a splined coupling, so they could be unbolted as a unit. Then, the body and front half of the chassis could be readily lifted up and rolled forward for complete access to the running gear. This would make it easy to change engines to run other classes or to repair any damage that may have resulted from too big a dose of volatile and sometimes unpredictable nitromethane – the coupe's intended fuel of choice.

The straight front beam axle was taken from a '38 Ford, the shocks were Houdaille lever-action 50/50 units, and the center steering, with a 6:1 ratio, was adapted from a Franklin. In its present, restored guise, the front axle is a '37 Ford tubular unit.

A seven-gallon fuel tank (some sources say 3 gallons, but it's obviously much bigger) was mounted behind the engine, just above the '40 Ford side-shift transmission. Two war-surplus five-gallon "jerry" cans were mounted on the chassis alongside the engine, carrying the necessary coolant to pull the heat from whatever engine sat in the bay. Easily removable, flex-pipe exhaust headers ran under the car, above the belly pan, and exited through the tail pan.

A surplus aircraft seat and seat belts were installed in the scant space left in front of the firewall that separated and isolated the driver from whatever engine was installed. Art, of course, was the designated driver, and he sat very close to the front of the cab, with his nose just inches from the windshield. Getting in and out was quite a chore.

The car's initial set of 18-inch Halibrand wheels were owned by the Chrismans' engine partner, Harry Duncan. This tall tire and wheel combination was used on the coupe for the first year. Art and Lloyd thought they were too big, so they changed to a set of 6.00x16 Indy tires on red steel wheels with aluminum discs.

"You grab the roll bar and pull your body in the air, like a chin-up, and then you swing your feet into the front well," says Art, making it sound easy, "then you swing your rear end into the cab. You then press up and squeeze in between the seat and the dash, and you're in. Getting out is much simpler," says Art, "you just turn your shoulders to the right, roll over onto all fours, and crawl out." I've seen him perform this remarkable maneuver. It would be a challenge for a man half Art's age. He makes it look easy, as only a man who's performed this maneuver many times can.

The business-like cockpit was painted white for better visibility. Right at the driver's fingertips were the brake handle (operating the rear wheel brakes only), a fire extinguisher, a hand-operated fuel pressure pump, and a magneto on-off switch. The shift lever was a single push-pull device for a modified '40 gearbox that contained a 28-tooth cluster running only second and high gear. A hefty roll cage and a hoop where the original firewall would have been helped stiffen the chassis and provided a measure of protection – just in case.

Above the driver's head, a little air scoop ducted intake air to the engine. Shortly after running the car for the first time, a small air inlet was fabricated to direct air to the driver – that was a detail the Chrisman brothers somehow overlooked in the initial construction. The sleek little coupe was finished in distinctive bronze lacquer, a Chrisman trademark color, accented with red trim, and outfitted with a set of 18-inch Bonneville Firestone tires on Halibrand magnesium wheels. The Chrisman's engine partner, Harry Duncan, owned the Halibrands. This tall tire-and-wheel combination was used on the coupe for the first year, but afterwards, Art and Lloyd thought they were too big. They changed to a set of 6.00 x 16-inch Indy tires on steel wheels. "This got the car down lower, and it looked much better," Art recalled.

The low, fully belly-panned coupe, with its smartly V'd front end, was finished in time for the 1953 salt meet. It was taken to Bonneville for Speed Week, and the team was prepared to run for class records with three engines – each a different-sized flathead. One 304-ci example was equipped with a set of Ardun OHV cylinder heads.

The initial engine was a Class C 304-ci Merc stroker that the boys had taken out of Art and Lloyd's dragster. It ran 163.63-mph one way, but vented the pan on the return run. "It had a little too much nitro," Art allowed sheepishly, "so we put Duncan's smaller 258-ci Ardun in."

"With that engine," Art recalled, "we qualified at 156.52-mph and set the B competition coupe class record at 160.178 mph. Then we pulled the engine and installed the motor from Ed Losinski's roadster, a 304-ci, Sharp-equipped Mercury flathead that was a consistent winner at the drags. The intent was for another shot at the C record… We didn't get the record," Art recalls, "because we couldn't get it to run right and we ran out of time." The winning Class C record-setter that year, at 172.749 mph, was the So-Cal '34 Ford coupe of Alex Xydias and his crew.

That notwithstanding, the Chrisman Brothers and Duncan '30 Model A coupe was an unqualified success, and was one of three finalists for the Maremont award, which judged cars on performance, appearance, design, and safety. The Chrisman's planned a triumphant return the following year.

"We came back in 1954," said Art, "with two new Hemis that Tony Capana built for Harry Duncan; a 243-ci Dodge "Little Red Ram" for Class B, and a 276-ci DeSoto for Class

C. We got both records this time – 180.87 mph in Class B and 180.08 mph in Class C... we were feeling pretty good."

Unfortunately, the Chrisman luck was about to change. "The last time we ran the coupe was a very sad time for us," says Art. "We went to Bonneville in '55 with a fresh 331-ci Chrysler Hemi for Class D, with the hopes of getting a record to add to our B and C titles. Two other cars that ran out of our shop were pitted with us – the Reed Brothers belly tanker and the Losinski roadster, a record holder in Class C."

Although the Chrisman coupe was not designed or perfected in a wind tunnel, its shape was obviously very effective. "We qualified the coupe for the record run in Class D at over 190 mph. We then set the record with the fastest run, an impressive 196 mph with the Chrysler, running five percent nitro," said Art, proving that what looks good, often is good. "We were prepared to up that to 20 percent and try to go 200 mph, but unfortunately we never got the chance."

"The Reed Brothers belly tank, with Leroy Neumayer's Ardun, set the C Class Lakester record the previous year at 205.71," Art recalled, "and that got Leroy into the 200-mph Club. For 1955, John Donaldson drove it (because Leroy had been drafted into the Army) and on one run, early in the week, the radiator cap blew off and John's back was badly burned. They flew him to the hospital in Salt Lake City for treatment. We fixed the radiator and I got in it and drove it fast enough to qualify the car – I don't remember the exact speed – but it was over 200 mph and faster than the existing record. When John returned he got back in the car for the record attempt."

"We were ahead of him in line in the coupe for our record run. We ran and set the record as I said at 196 mph. We were on the return road when he left the line. We weren't paying much attention until we heard the engine quit and we looked up to see the car slowly turning off the course. We figured he broke something and was pulling off to wait for the push truck. We later learned that the car had spun and flipped, and what we thought we saw as a car turning slowly off the course was in fact a car upside down, and since there was no roll bar...well, you know the rest."

"We were all pretty upset over the incident," Chrisman recalls sadly, "and we decided to take the coupe home. We never ran the car again."

But that's not the end of this story. "I sold the car to Harry Duncan," says Art, "and he painted it purple and continued to run it. Then I lost track of it. I know it passed through John Geraghty's hands in Glendale, and after that it wound up in George Barris' shop where it was butchered into a show car, and fitted with gull wing door openings, a blown Olds engine, and antennas sticking out of fake scoops placed above the windshield. They painted it white pearl with red accents...it

The severe chop on Chrisman's competition coupe helped the car achieve more streamlined proportions. Cleverly, Art and Lloyd grafted a chopped '35 Ford coupe windshield section to get the aerodynamic slant they needed.

was awful." The front wheels were replaced with motorcycle wires, and the car appeared in a TV show, *The Many Loves of Dobie Gillis*, starring teen heartthrob Dwayne Hickman.

After many years of languishing on the show circuit in its "Hollywood guise," custom car show promoter Bob Larivee acquired the coupe, and soon commissioned Chrisman to "put it back exactly like it was" when it was raced at Bonneville. After Art did the restoration work, Larivee returned the car to the show circuit, but this time it was presented as the Historic Chrisman Brothers Coupe, in its original copper livery, complete with a 331-ci Chrysler Hemi.

Several years later, Joe MacPherson (a Southern California auto dealer and a Chrisman benefactor) bought the car from Larivee and added it to his "Joe's Garage" collection, located in the Tustin Auto Center in Orange County, California.

In 2001, when the promoters of the Pebble Beach Concours d'Elegance decided to include Historic Hot Rod Coupes, one of the nine cars selected for competition "on the lawn" was the Chrisman Brothers Model A. Owner Joe MacPherson was contacted. He wasn't too enthusiastic, and he did not attend the event, but he agreed to enter the car if Art and his son Mike would participate. After some arm-twisting, Art agreed to prepare the car to run (on 50-percent nitro!). He planned to polish and detail the coupe for display at the Lodge.

"I knew going in we weren't going to win...I just knew it," says Art, who is still nothing if not competitive. "When we were picked, along with the Pierson Brothers' '34 Ford Coupe and the So-Cal '34 Coupe as finalists, I thought maybe we had a chance. Then they called me up first, which meant we got third place."

"I thought about tossing the ribbon back to them, but that would be showing no class," he said. "Instead I fired up the engine, and ripped the throttle several times, and smoked the tires off of the platform. I know the nitro made all those stuffy folks' eyes water and the ladies' mascara run."

The coupe's initial engine was a Class C 304-ci Merc stroker that the boys had taken out of Art and Lloyd's dragster. It ran 163.63 mph one way, but vented the pan on the return run. "It had a little too much nitro," Art admitted, "so we put Duncan's smaller 258-ci Ardun in. With that engine," he recalled, "we qualified at 156.52 mph and set the B Coupe class record at 160.178 mph. Then, we pulled the engine and installed Ed Losinski's roadster motor, a 304-inch, Sharp-equipped Merc flathead that was a consistent winner at the drags." The intent was for another shot at the C record. "We didn't get the record," Art recalls, "because we couldn't get it to run right, and we ran out of time." The winning Class C record-setter, that year, at 172.749 mph, was Alex Xydias' So-Cal '34 Ford coupe. No matter – with its mail-slot rear window, louvered deck lid, shapely push bars, and Sharp logo – this copper coupe always meant business.

Now here's the rest of the story: The Pebble Beach Concours d'Elegance is, among other things, a beauty contest. The Chrisman coupe, while purposeful, functional, accurately restored, and a former record-holder, was simply not scored aesthetically, in the opinion of the judges, as high as the other two cars. The level of finish on the Pierson and So-Cal coupes edged the Chrisman car, as well, although I'd be the first to suggest all these cars were restored better than they were ever built. My recollection, and I was the Chief Class Judge, is that we did not penalize Art significantly, if at all, for the stainless bolts, reasoning that they could have been authentic war surplus parts, given the era when the car was constructed.

It took a great deal of cajoling to convince Joe MacPherson and Art Chrisman to bring the coupe to Pebble Beach. We thought it was so important that the Chrisman and Duncan car be represented, that two anonymous donors chipped in to pay their preparation and transportation expenses. That rarely happens at Pebble Beach. And it was not done for the other entrants in the coupe class, with this one exception: transportation costs and insurance fees were paid for the Mooneyham & Sharp '34 Ford 5-window coupe, which was generously loaned to us by Don Garlits on behalf of the Don Garlits Museum of Drag Racing in Ocala, Florida.

Art Chrisman's skill and racing courage can't be denied here, but at Pebble Beach, the car is judged, not the owner, or builder/restorer, or the presenter. Nine cars were entered in the historic coupe class; eight were eligible for awards (the Mooneyham & Sharp coupe wasn't running, and a car has to operate and be run across the ramp to receive a trophy), and just three cars – one of which was the Chrisman coupe – went home with the honors.

Art was surrounded with appreciative fans all day, and he seemed to be enjoying the attention. I'm sorry he was disap-

Chrisman, to say the least, was disappointed. He expressed as much to Don Prieto, who helped with this chapter. In Art's words: "Here we had the original builder: me, the original restorer: me, and the original driver: me, and we lose to a couple of rich politically connected guys who bought and spent huge sums of money to restore cars that they never had anything to do with in the first place. That sure beats me all to hell."

"Don't get me wrong," Chrisman added. "It was fun and I enjoyed myself – but I won't ever do it again."

"It's really funny," Art concluded. "I learned later from one of the judges that the reason we lost points was because we had stainless steel Allen (head) bolts in the rear end housing. Truth is: Those are the same bolts we put in the car when we built it originally. In fact they are the exact ones that my dad pilfered when he worked for Todd Shipyard during the war. So much for authenticity…I'd rather race."

The straight front beam axle was taken from a '38 Ford, the shocks were Houdaille lever-action 50/50 units, and the center steering (with a 6:1 ratio) was adapted from a Franklin. In its present restored guise, the front axle is a '37 Ford tubular unit.

pointed with the results, but as Pete Chapouris likes to say about Pebble Beach, "…you get one happy guy (the winner), two sort of happy guys (second and third place), and six pissed off guys (the folks who didn't win). As far as I'm concerned, just being there with a car is great. Everyone's a winner."

That said, watching Art Chrisman nimbly swing into his coupe's snug cockpit, with the agility of a man half his age, and then running the old 196-mph coupe over the ramp on nitro (a first!) was a thrill for everyone.

The Chrisman and Duncan coupe is a great example of a car that was a racing winner, had a successful movie career, performed on the International Championship Auto Show circuit, and was then restored to look the way it appeared in its heyday. I'd call that a full-circle success, wouldn't you?

Located above the driver's head, there's a little air scoop that ducted intake air to the engine. Shortly after running the car for the first time, a small air inlet was fabricated to direct air to the driver – a detail the Chrisman brothers somehow overlooked initially.

The Chrisman coupe had no springs in the rear. The rear axle housings bolted directly to the frame tubes. Raising the body permitted quick and easy engine changes.

"After we ran it a few times and realized there was a lot of frame flex," Bob Pierson recalls, "Vic Edelbrock himself boxed the center section of the frame rails, and we added a roll bar for protection and even more stiffness." What was the coupe like to drive? "It hunkered down and went where you put it," Bob Pierson recalls. "I used to be considered a hot dog, because I'd pitch the car from side to side, outside the cones, trying to break the tires loose, so the revs would get up even higher. Then when the tires bit, I'd really get on it."

This is the competition coupe that started it all. Check out this famous chopped '34 Ford coupe. That hammered top is the first thing you see – and it's the feature you can't forget. Severely flattened, with armored car slits for windows, it looks as though a building fell on the car. There is quite a story behind this 142-mph Russetta Timing Association record-holding racer.

Over half a century ago, this largely home-built hot rod copped an attitude long before that expression was applied to anything on four wheels. For a brief time, it was the fastest closed car in America. Its wide exposure at the lakes, and in rodding magazines of the period, served to define the postwar American youthful obsession with power and speed. It also helped put Edelbrock Equipment on the high-performance map. Stated simply, it's the coupe that beat the roadsters.

The Pierson Brothers' coupe was a sensation when it topped 140, and soon afterward, it ran over 150 mph. Back then, for many people, hot roadsters defined hot rod. The quickest top-of-the-heap roadsters in 1949-50, with big 296-ci flathead strokers, stripped of everything nonessential (probably 250 pounds lighter than a hardtop), were hard pressed to top the 130-mph mark. Coupes were déclassé.

For a long while, the SCTA didn't even consider them to be racecars, an in-your-face gesture to pioneer era rodders like Lou Baney, Lynn Yakel, and Bob Rounthwaite, not to mention two brothers from Inglewood, Dick and Bob Pierson and their friend (and crack engine builder), Bobby Meeks. All three were members of the *Coupes* club of Inglewood and the RTA, of course, because the SCTA wouldn't let them run.

"We didn't think coupes were real hot rods," says Alex Xydias, an SCTA board member at the time. "We were very conservative guys, and these cars didn't fit our pattern. At first, we didn't even believe the numbers. Of course, when Baney and the Piersons started going fast, we had to give in. I actually recruited Bob to run under the (Glendale) *Sidewinders* banner so we could win the points Championship one year."

The Pierson Brothers' '34 Coupe

It's hard today to understand what the coupe-versus-roadster fuss was all about. "Lakes cars were roadsters, modifieds, lakesters, and streamliners," Bobby Meeks explained. "But a lot of guys owned coupes and sedans, and they needed a place to run too. The old Western Timing Association (WTA) would take anything. And then there was Russetta. We were equal to the SCTA in many ways, especially after the SCTA guys saw the light."

Coupes were heavier than open roadsters, and until the Piersons and Bobby Meeks began setting records, it was generally thought the closed cars couldn't possibly run as fast. The last thing many roadster jockeys probably saw was this hardtop's deck-mounted *Coupes* plaque as it sped out of sight.

A half-century ago, the stalwarts of early hot rod competition were the guys who drove or towed their cars to the dry lakes for a weekend of racing. Faded photos from that era show long lines of scruffy Ford roadsters, their owners patiently waiting for a chance to run the course and storm through the time traps. In the midst of these dust-covered warriors, is an obviously beautifully built, painted, and plated '34 Ford coupe. "You could walk down the line and only find one or two cars that were even painted," Bob Pierson recalls.

Why was this particular coupe turned out so well? "Some of the sports car guys had been sneering at our hot rods," Pierson recalls, "so we decided to finish this car like the Midgets and Indy racers, with shiny paint and chromed suspension parts. Dan Gurney, himself a lakes racer remembers, "When the Piersons showed up with this car, compared to our roadsters, it looked as though it had come from another planet."

And there was a meteor behind the wheel. "I was a bombshell, looking for a place to explode," Bob Pierson exclaims today. "Vic Edelbrock (Senior) knew we were using his equipment. We were one of Vic's guinea pigs," he recalls. "What we'd learn test-

Bob Pierson shows Hot Rod magazine editor Wally Parks the Bobby Meeks-built 265-ci '46 59A Ford flathead. This engine powered the Pierson Brothers coupe to a 142.98-mph Russetta Timing Association record at the lakes in 1949. Not long afterward, the streamlined coupe topped 150 mph. Now the disbelieving SCTA boys had to take Russetta and its coupes seriously. (So-Cal Speed Shop)

Although Hot Rod readers couldn't see it, in an issue that was still all black and white, the Pierson Brothers arguably claimed the first "candy" paint on a hot rod. Bob Pierson convincingly claims to have invented candy paint. Trying to match the effect of "pre-war German Christmas tree ornament balls," he was "thrown out of his local paint store many, many times" before he was able to successfully mix the iridescent, blood-red shade he wanted. The Piersons followed it up with the deep cobalt blue that appears on the car's roof and deck. "It was shown at the LA Exposition in November 1949," he says proudly. "Nobody had it earlier." (So-Cal Speed Shop)

Besides the severe nine-inch chop, the gutted body was channeled three inches. A stock hood was mated to Harry Jones' beautifully crafted racecar nose. The frame horns were snipped front and rear, and new tubular crossmembers were fabricated. A World War II surplus bucket seat (probably from a tank) and a webbed khaki seat belt comprised the principal safety touches. The top of the steering wheel was cut off so the driver's already limited vision wasn't further impaired. A flat panel held a row of curved glass Stewart-Warner instruments, but it's doubtful they could be read as the stiffly sprung coupe bounced along the dusty course. (So-Cal Speed Shop)

ing on Sepulveda or Lincoln Boulevards (often topping three figures) on a Thursday night, we'd use at El Mirage on Saturday." Was he worried about hitting someone at those illegal speeds? "There wasn't much traffic in those days," he shrugs. "We'd run till the cops showed up, then scatter."

Bob Pierson convincingly claims to have invented candy paint. Trying to match the effect of "pre-war German Christmas-tree

Going to the lakes in 1949-50, the Piersons towed their racecar with Bob's chopped and customized '36 three-window. The '36 was no slouch in its own right. Running on alcohol, it turned over 120 mph at several Russetta Timing Association meets. Note the '38 DeSoto bumpers, twin Appleton spotlights, and fender skirts. (Don Cox)

and the chop," he chuckles, remembering the trio's history-making night's effort decades earlier. "The rules said the windshield had to be seven inches high, but they didn't specify the angle. So I laid the posts back until you almost lost vision (about 50 degrees), then raised 'em up a bit, and that was it. Those thin Plexiglas side and rear windows helped too."

When he first stood back to look at the car, he realized immediately what he had done. "We didn't even paint the racing class letters on at first," Meeks recalls, "because we knew the officials would take one look at it and raise us a class."

Besides the severe nine-inch chop, the gutted body was channeled three inches. A stock hood was mated to Harry Jones' beautifully crafted racecar nose. The frame horns were snipped front and rear and new tubular crossmembers were fabricated. A World War II surplus bucket seat (probably from a tank) and a webbed khaki seat belt comprised the principal safety touches. The top of the steering wheel was cut off, so that the driver's already limited vision wasn't further impaired. A flat panel held a row of curved-glass Stewart-Warner instruments, but it's doubtful they could be read as the stiffly sprung coupe bounced along the dusty course.

"After we ran it a few times and realized there was a lot of frame flex," Bob Pierson recalls, "Vic Edelbrock himself boxed the center section of the frame rails, and we added a roll bar for protection and even more stiffness." A '37 Ford V-8/60 tube axle was used with precise '39 Ford cross-steering, beautifully fabricated hairpin wishbones, and reworked Ford Houdaille lever-action shocks. In the rear was a high-priced piece of technology for the era, made in nearby Culver City. One of Ted Halibrand's alloy quick-change center sections, supported by a modified Model A crossmember and buggy spring, permitted a choice of high speed gears. The first records were set with a 2.94:1 rear end ratio. The front tires were ribbed 5.00 x 16-inch Firestones, while the rears were 7.00 x 16s on stock Ford steel rims, still wearing '48 Ford beauty rings and hubcaps.

Bobby Meeks was (and still is) a natural mechanic who used much of the same fine speed equipment on this car as many rivals, but his high-level preparation, skilled machining, and careful assembly preceded what later became known as "blueprinting." The Meeks-built engine included Edelbrock high-compression heads and triple manifold, Stromberg 48 carburetors with 20 cfm each more than the popular Stromberg 97s, a Winfield Super H cam, a Kong dual-point, dual-coil distributor, and Belond W-2 headers.

In his wonderful book, *The American Hot Rod*, the late Dean Batchelor, himself a successful lakes racer, extolled Meeks' virtues. "Some engine builders became legends in their own time... one of the most prominent, and arguably the best, is Bob Meeks. What Bobby did to these engines is basically the same thing other builders did, but Meeks gave

Tom Cobbs' engine of choice was a small-block Chevy with a Potvin-style front-mounted GMC blower equipped with a two-port Hilborn fuel-injection system. The engine was set back in the frame nearly two feet for better weight distribution. Nothing fancy here: painted valve covers, tubular headers (Siamesed in the center), and virtually no plating. The coupe was not too different-looking from the era when the Piersons scorched the lakes in it some 40 years earlier. Talk about a great design. (So-Cal Speed Shop)

ornament balls," he was "thrown out of his local paint store many, many times" before he was able to successfully mix the iridescent, blood-red shade he wanted. Pierson followed it up with the deep cobalt blue that appears on the car's roof and deck. "It was shown at the LA Exposition in November 1949," he says proudly. "Nobody had it earlier."

Working at Douglas Aircraft, Bob Pierson learned the rudiments of streamlining and aerodynamics. He conceived the car's airfoil-like, flat under-tail section with its narrow opening that allowed rushing wind to exit across a flat panel and probably helped hold the light rear end down. The stock gas tank was axed, and a small racing tank was located alongside the driver, right next to the battery. Pierson's kid brother Dick did much of the preparation. Modest Bobby Meeks, an Edelbrock employee for 50 years, was responsible for the coupe's high-performance flathead – and the car's unique look as well.

"One of my jobs at Edelbrock was to find guys who could be successful racers," says Meeks. "So I recruited them and we helped with the latest equipment." Edelbrock devotees included Bill Likes, Fran Hernandez, Don Waite, Alex Xydias, and, of course, the Piersons. "That's why Edelbrock cars had so many records," Meeks says.

After the Piersons agreed to prepare their coupe for the lakes, it was Meeks who decided on the excessive roof chop. "Naturally, we were looking for high speed," he says. "That dictated the narrow shape of the front end, the full belly pan,

Dawson Hadley, a dry lakes racing pioneer, bought the coupe from the Piersons. His best time was 165.23 mph. Then Tom Cobbs, who owned the car when it was photograph at Bonneville, coaxed it up to 198.86 mph with one of his favorite setups, a Chevy V-8 with a crank-driven GMC 4-71 blower. The grille opening has been covered for improved wind resistance. The radiator had been removed, and a water tank was used for cooling. (So-Cal Speed Shop)

The Pierson Brothers coupe disappeared for a while in the 1960s. Reportedly, it was sold off a side street in Santa Barbara. Tom Bryant acquired the coupe in the late 1970s. At first he didn't know what he had, so he quickly prepared the coupe for Bonneville in 1980. Racers there recognized it and told Bryant its history. (So-Cal Speed Shop)

Hot rods are known by the name(s) of their original builders, so this '34 will always be called the Pierson Brothers' coupe. But it was destined to pass through several hands over the years. Seldom away from racing, it continued to run faster and faster. After a long hiatus, Tom Bryant (shown here) took it over and set more records in the car than anyone else. In 1991, he achieved the coupe's best speed – 227.33 mph, albeit with blown Chevrolet V-8 power. (So-Cal Speed Shop)

them his own special touch; partly the result of many years of building engines, and partly from many hours of experimentation on the Edelbrock dynamometer. If any 'speed secret' was in these engines," Batchelor confided, "it was one of extreme care in assembly."

This example from Batchelor proves his point. "Bobby developed a jig to hold a slightly tapered core-drill, which was run into each of the intake ports a predetermined distance, thus guaranteeing all eight ports were exactly the same size." Meeks would install intake valves so oversized they had to be

seated on the flathead block itself. He fabricated a metal divider to separate the Siamesed center exhaust ports on each side. "The 4-inch Mercury crankshaft didn't come along until 1949," Meeks told me, "so we stroked the stock shaft 0.125-inches, bored the block out the same 0.125-inches, and the engine would still rev reliably to about 5,800 rpm."

The meticulous Mr. Meeks just did everything just a little better. He experimented with fuels before SCTA authorities realized just how much advantage that practice was. "But we ran that coupe on alcohol in 1949," he insists today. The infamous Edelbrock nitromethane experiments began a few years later,

in the summer of 1951, first with Midget racers at Gilmore Stadium, later with many of the hottest cars in racing.

What was the coupe like to drive? "It hunkered down and went where you put it," Bob Pierson recalls. "I used to be considered a hot dog, because I'd pitch the car from side to side, outside the cones, trying to break the tires loose, so the revs would get up even higher. Then when the tires bit, I'd really get on it."

Hot rods are known by the name(s) of their original builders, so this '34 will always be called the Pierson Brothers' coupe. But it was destined to pass through several hands over the years. Seldom away from racing, under new management, it continued to run faster and faster. In 1953, then-owner Dawson Hadley achieved 165.23 mph. In 1956, supercharger wizard, Tom Cobb, turned 198.86 mph. Tom Bryant actually set more records in the car than anyone else. In 1991, he achieved the coupe's best speed – 227.33 mph, albeit with blown Chevrolet V-8 power.

Present owner and noted historic hot rod collector, Bruce Meyer, of Beverly Hills, California, bought the coupe from Bryant and commissioned Pete Chapouris (back when his shop was called PC3g) to restore it to 1950 specifications.

Bob Pierson gets a push start at the lakes, probably in 1949 or 1950. The high-geared coupe needed a running start to get going. Once underway, on alcohol, it could top 150 mph. Note the single red taillight and license plate below the deck lid, for towing from Inglewood, or for the occasional late night blast. The Coupes club plaque above the California tag was displayed proudly. The coupe originally ran Russetta Timing Association meets only, because the SCTA would not recognize coupes as competition cars. When Wally Parks heard about this car's prowess, the Piersons were invited to El Mirage and an SCTA meet, to see if they were for real. They were. Even with hubcaps, this coupe ran rings around the roadsters. (So-Cal Speed Shop)

Bob Pierson's experience at Douglas Aircraft inspired the coupe's full-length belly pan and the air vent below the tail panel. Air flowed smoothly under the car and any trapped air exited through the vents. Note the Halibrand quick-change rear. Although relatively expensive in that era, it was a very necessary accessory for serious racers like the Piersons.

A '37 Ford V-8/60 tube axle was used with precise '39 Ford cross-steering, beautifully fabricated hairpin wishbones, and reworked Ford lever-action shocks. In the rear was a high-priced piece of technology for the era, made in nearby Culver City. One of Ted Halibrand's alloy quick-change center sections, supported by a modified Model A crossmember and buggy spring, permitted a choice of high-speed gears. The first records were set with a 2.94:1 rear-end ratio. Front tires were ribbed 5.00 x 16 Firestones, while 7.00 x 16s were used in back on stock Ford steel rims, still wearing '48 Ford beauty rings and hubcaps.

The coupe's track nose was beautifully hand-formed by Harry Jones. Why was this particular coupe turned out so well? "Some of the sports car guys had been sneering at our hot rods," Pierson recalls, "so we decided to finish this car like the Midgets and Indy racers, with shiny paint and chromed suspension parts." Dan Gurney, himself a lakes racer, remembers, "When the Piersons showed up with this car, compared to our roadsters, it looked as though it had come from another planet."

The battery and the fuel tank share limited floor space alongside the driver. The SCTA and RTA allowed that practice on comp cars half a century ago. It would be considered unsafe and illegal today.

Red, white, and blue candy paint with bold scallops was a very distinctive treatment. With an engine by Edelbrock's crack builder, Bobby Meeks, and Edelbrock heads and triple manifold, this car had to look sharp. And it did.

Meeks would install intake valves so oversized they had to be seated on the flathead block itself. He also fabricated a metal divider to separate the Siamesed center exhaust ports on each side. "The 4-inch Mercury crankshaft didn't come along until 1949," Meeks told me, "so we stroked the stock shaft 0.125 inches, bored the block out the same 0.125 inches, for a modest 267 ci, and the engine would still rev reliably to about 5,800 rpm." Bobby Meeks was (and still is) a natural mechanic who used much of the same fine speed equipment as many of his rivals, but his high level of preparation, skilled machining, and careful assembly preceded what later became known as "blueprinting."

Bob and Dick Pierson's signatures adorn the coupe's aluminum abbreviated dash panel. In 1949, it took skill and courage to drive this car at 150 mph on skinny bias-ply tires. Bob Pierson had plenty of both.

"I've always loved that car," Meyer explains. "It's the quintessential hot rod coupe. When I bought it, Tom Bryant was still racing it. He wasn't anxious to sell, but thankfully he did. This car just had to be restored to its original configuration. What's remarkable is that it ran well over 200 mph, and the body and running gear were still substantially the way the Piersons and Meeks had built it. Talk about right the first time."

Pete Chapouris took what hc called "an archaeologist's approach" to the Pierson coupe's restoration. "Most of the sheetmetal was intact, but over the years, extensive frame bracing had been added," he explains. "I peeled away the layers until it looked exactly like the Rex Burnett cutaway drawing and Tom Medley's photos in *Hot Rod* magazine." A perfectionist, Chapouris saved as much of the original steel as he could, and metal master Steve Davis massaged the old panels back into shape.

Although they took a few fit liberties and lowered the nose a tad, the restorers left the car's characteristically ragged door gaps. Thankfully, there was enough of the original paint below many accumulated layers so they could duplicate the original candy red and blue hues. "The front A-pillars were shot, so we replaced those," Chapouris explained, "and the roll cage was welded to the body panels, so we had to separate them. But now most of the car is exactly the way it was built." Both Piersons and Bobby Meeks (who also built the car's present engine) helped oversee the restoration.

In November 1992, Bruce Meyer held a gala coming-out party for the finished car with a "Who's Who in Hot Rodding?" cast of characters present. Boyd Coddington, one of many hot rod luminaries on hand that evening, was philosophical about the return of the Pierson Brothers' coupe. "This is one of our ancestors," he noted. "It's important to understand cars like this one, to know where we've been and where we're going."

Since its restoration, the Pierson Brothers' coupe has made countless public appearances. It was the first car inducted into the Dry Lakes Hall of Fame. When it's not traveling to shows, it's often on exhibit at the Petersen Automotive Museum in Los Angeles. But Meyer doesn't hesitate to take it out. He raced it up the hill several times at the Goodwood Festival of Speed in England, in 2000. "It was awesome," he says, "a real challenge, particularly because you can't see out of it. Of all the cars I have, it's the one people find the most interesting. And it's amazing how many people over there knew what it was. Besides saving an important piece of hot rod history," Meyer says, "the fact that so many people can share its significance makes me warm all over."

In August 2001, the Pierson Brothers' coupe was one of nine 1940s to 1950s era competition coupes (including Alex Xydias' So-Cal coupe, the Chrisman Brothers Model A, and the Mooneyham & Sharp '34) on display at the Pebble Beach Concours d'Elegance. So-Cal Speed Shop's Pete Chapouris and his crew had freshened the coupe up for a different kind of competition: the lawn at the 18th green. "When we did that car, nine years ago," he said, "hardly anyone had restored a hot rod before. To get the car up to Pebble Beach standards today, with correct cotter pins, castle nuts, instruments, etc.," he says, "we had a lot of work to do."

They did a fine job. Although the Pierson Brothers' coupe finished second in class behind the So-Cal '34, it won the Dean Batchelor award for the most significant car in the class. After all, it was the first hot rod coupe to top 150 mph, and its racing career spanned half a century.

I've long been a big fan of the Pierson Brothers' coupe, so when I was director of the Petersen Automotive Museum and the opportunity came, while setting up an exhibit, to drive it on the roof and around the parking structure, I didn't hesitate. The small displacement flathead fires after a few spins and, thanks to its lusty Winfield cam, it "idles" at 1,200 rpm. Blip the throttle and the Meeks-prepared flathead responds instantly, with a crackle from the straight pipes that sends a chill up your spine.

There are no frills in the cramped office – just an unlined tank seat, tapered shifter, and cutoff steering wheel. The exhaust notes echo loudly off the walls. Within seconds, we'd set off many car alarms in the parking garage. Inside, it's deafening – like driving a motorized snare drum. Nail the gas and the little coupe leaps ahead, obviously eager to run. Peering through the slit of a windshield, I can't imagine the courage it took practicing speed runs in this car late at night on Lincoln Boulevard, let alone pointing it towards the far horizon at the lakes or Bonneville and hammering the pedal.

The Pierson Brothers' '34 remains a key link in the legend of early hot rodding – a raucous fast coupe speeding in harm's way. Dean Batchelor graciously told his readers, "I wish you could have been there; it was great." Surely cars like this were the reason.

Dick and Bob Pierson celebrate the coupe's renaissance together. Bob (left) was the driver, Dick (right) was the mechanic, and Bobby Meeks built the engine. Bruce Meyer had a "coming out" party to celebrate the just-completed restoration of the Pierson Brothers' coupe in November 1992. The attendees were a "Who's Who in Hot Rodding." The cast of great hot rodders present included Robert E. Petersen, Wally Parks, Carroll Shelby, Dan Gurney, Pete Chapouris, Jim Jacobs, Alex Xydias, Ray Brown, Tom Sparks, Bobby Meeks, and Bud Meyer. Boyd Coddington, one of many hot rod luminaries on hand that evening, was philosophical about the return of the Pierson Brothers' coupe. "This is one of our ancestors," he noted. "It's important to understand cars like this one, to know where we've been and where we're going." (Bruce Meyer Collection)

HOT ROD MILESTONES

The Pierson Brothers' Coupe: Fantasy and Fact

It's well after midnight on a warm summer night in 1949. A low, white, fenderless hot rod coupe noses its way out of a suburban Inglewood, California, garage and quickly gathers speed on deserted, arrow-straight North Sepulveda Boulevard. Bob Pierson gives his dash-mounted fuel pressure pump a few more hard strokes, floors the teaspoon-shaped gas pedal, and runs his car's powerful engine up tightly to 5,800 rpm in first. The high-winding Lincoln Zephyr gear-set streaks to well over 60 mph before he snap-shifts up and across to second. Flames crackle as the coupe's straight exhaust pipes drum rhythmically over the pavement. Inside the stripped and lightened car, the wind whirls dust around; the engine's noise is deafening…

Seconds later, over 90 mph, he shifts to third. Peering through the coupe's impossibly low windshield, Pierson sees the ever-narrowing street ahead is clear and decides to go for it – hard on the gas… past 100, 110, 120, 130… the lamp posts flash by. His engine still pulls cleanly; oil pressure is holding; acrid fumes from a home-brew alcohol fuel mix are blown rearward out of the snug cockpit. Everything's fine, but a flickering traffic light far ahead signals it's time to begin slowing. Turning around, a charged-up Bob Pierson notes with satisfaction that there were revs to spare on top. "140 won't be a problem," he thinks, "maybe even 150."

Fast forward to the present. It looks a bit odd by today's standards, this vintage, candy red, white, and blue '34 Ford coupe, with its severely altered roofline, pinched track nose, and skinny tires, but nearly a half-century ago, this was the fastest closed car in America – bar none. In late 1949, driven by Bob Pierson, the sleek rod hit 142.98 mph, later topping 153 mph at the Bonneville Salt Flats. Featured on the cover of Hot Rod magazine in April 1950, this largely home-built car had wide exposure at shows, at the lakes, and in rodding magazines of the period. Along with the roadsters of Bill Likes and Don Waite, this car helped put Edelbrock Equipment squarely on the high-performance map.

Let's put it in perspective. Barely one year after a modified factory-built XK120 Jaguar (with a 3.0-liter DOHC six) hit a then-impressive 132 mph on a closed section of Belgium's Jabbeke highway, a trio of young California hot rodders, brothers Dick and Bob Pierson and their friend (and crack engine builder) Bobby Meeks, went considerably faster in amateur competition. And they did it with a normally aspirated but highly modified 267-ci Mercury flathead that they tested, late at night, on the streets of their hometown.

We probably don't need to remind most of you, but just in case, it helps to understand that from 1932 to 1953, Ford's gutsy "valve-in-block" V-8 was the powerplant to beat. Light, cheap, and capable of over three times its stock output, this remarkable three-main-bearing engine was long the darling of the hot rod set. Take one stock 239-ci flathead, refashion its ports, pop in bigger valves, boost displacement with over-sized light-weight pistons and a stroked crankshaft, add a set of high-compression aluminum heads, a racing camshaft, and multiple carburetion, goose up the ignition, improve exhaust flow with a curvy set of headers, and drop it in the lightest roadster you could find. That was a recipe for speed that was cooked and served all over Southern California.

The times were right. Young vets had returned from the war with plenty of money saved up. As soon as Detroit caught its production breath, pre-war cars became cheap. Especially out West, these guys wanted fast, expressive transportation. And the quickest *American* way to go fast, beating all but the most exotic cars, was to do it yourself. As soon as hot rodders discovered the knack of standing start acceleration, they began breaking those records. But top speed was the lure for a long time, and these speeds were attained not by factory-backed pros, but by canny backyard experimenters. Stuart Hilborn's single-seater ran 150 mph as early as 1947; three years later, Alex Xydias' So-Cal Speed Shop streamliner topped 210 mph. And there was more to come.

Although John Bond, *Road & Track*'s talented editor, was listed on the masthead of fledgling *Hop Up* magazine in 1951, there was really a wide gap between sports car enthusiasts and hot rodders. Purists revered those few high-performance imports that managed to cross the ocean; the backyard guys didn't know much about Talbots, Bugattis, Jags, and Porsches, and couldn't afford them anyway. But they were determined, using ingenuity and available domestic equipment, to prove they could run just as fast, and probably even faster. Import car fans probably hated them, but guys like Duffy Livingston, Chuck Manning, and Max Balchowsky competed in home-built sports cars that often outran and out-handled far more expensive imports.

Shortly before he died, Dean Batchelor, a lakes racer himself, who'd started at *Hop Up* magazine and later progressed to the editorship of *Road & Track*, produced the definitive book on this subject: *The American Hot Rod*. Summing up the period, Dean wrote: "The US economy was good, everybody who wanted to was working, the interest in rodding was high, and the availability of both parts and the knowledge to assemble them was there. It was no longer, as it had been in the 1920s, '30s, and most of the '40s, a mysterious pastime, a black art, so to speak. Hot rodding was maturing and the rodders were ready for it."

Arguably, the essence of this early competition was the guys who drove or towed their cars to the dry lakes for a weekend of racing. Faded photographs from that era show long lines of scruffy Ford roadsters, their owners patiently waiting for a chance to run the course and storm through the time traps. In the midst of these dust-covered warriors is an obviously beautifully built, painted, and plated '34 Ford coupe. "You could walk down the line and only find one or two cars that were even painted," Bob Pierson recalls. Taunted by the circle-track buddies, the Piersons elected to build their car to rival anything it raced against.

Then and now, the Pierson Brothers' coupe set the highest of standards. Today, although it spends most of its time in the dry lakes exhibit at the Petersen Automotive Museum in Los Angeles, owner Bruce Meyer takes it out occasionally, and it's been shown at The Louis Vuitton Concours d'Elegance in New York City, Eyes on Classic Design near Detroit, and very fittingly at the SEMA show in Las Vegas. It will always be hot rodding's definitive dry lakes/Bonneville coupe.

19

When you think of award-winning show rods from the 1960s, like the Barris Twister T, and Andy Kassa's wicked channeled '32, you can appreciate how Catallo's cool coupe cornered the extreme visual impact that all the top-ranked show entrants sought. This car's combination of contemporary modifications on a somewhat traditional, although chopped and sectioned, shape, was very well executed. In the genre of its day, the coupe was a spectacular home run.

"*Little Deuce Coupe, you don't know, you don't know what I got.*" Even if you weren't a hot rodder in the 1960s, you'd recognize this snazzy, scalloped '32 coupe. It first appeared on the July 1961 cover of Hot Rod. Not long afterward, Eric Rickman's lead photo in that story, sans the car owner's head and shoulders, became a best-selling Beach Boys' record album cover. Little matter that the "actual" '32 in the catchy tune boasted "...a flathead mill and four on the floor," and the album cover car was powered by a blown Olds – this radical three-window was, and always will be, the quintessential, "Little Deuce Coupe."

Clarence Catallo, of Dearborn, Michigan, purchased this car for just $75 in 1956 when he was just 15 years old. It was sitting in a gas station across from his parents' small grocery store in Allen Park, a working-class suburb of Detroit. A friend had to drive it home for him because young Catallo didn't yet have his drivers' license. But that technicality didn't stop him from getting right to work on a car that was to become one of the most famous deuce coupes of all time.

He started by channeling the car a full six inches, then he painted it dark blue and dropped in a carbureted OHV Olds V-8. By the time Catallo was licensed to drive, he had built quite a ride. Early photos of this car show it out at Detroit Dragway in 1958. A McCulloch supercharger hunkers on top of the Olds engine, making the power plant and accessories look as though they were forced into the abbreviated engine compartment with a whip and a chair. Flex-pipe headers and chromed, reversed wheels, with slicks on the rear, showed this coupe meant business. Catallo apparently drag-raced the wheels off this car, continuously perfecting the bored-out, 344-ci Olds, originally built by Bill Wanderer. The coupe ran sub-13-second quarter miles, turning a best trap speed of 112 mph.

The grille in those early days was a full-sized, filled '32 item. The front frame horns were bobbed, there was no front spreader bar, and a pair of tiny headlights was perched atop accessory aluminum brackets. Catallo's car epitomized a minimalist look that soon appeared all across the country,

"Chili" Catallo's "Little Deuce Coupe"

especially from the East Coast to the Midwest. Although it was a complex modification, channeling was often the first thing done to make a deuce a hot rod, particularly back East. But Catallo went even further. He modified the coupe's rear fender wells to closely follow the outline of its big rear 8.20 x 15-inch Inglewood slicks, accenting the car's lowness and making it look even racier.

By now, Catallo had become known as "Chili," a euphemism for "cool." His car was becoming even cooler. Silver scallops were one of the coupe's next major modifications. And in 1959, Chili upped the ante even more. He took his '32 to Detroit's reigning customizers, "The A Brothers," Mike and Larry Alexander. They sectioned the body six inches, fabricated a distinctive, hand-formed grille shell with a mesh insert and eight horizontal grille bars, and added then-fashionable quad headlights with flamethrower lamps. On each side of the car, a trio of sweeping wings accented the frame rails and flowed from the engine compartment toward the back of the car. The lower edges of the doors were raised to the top of the frame rails, leaving room for the flowing side strakes and permitting a flat floor inside the car. The sculpted aluminum exterior strakes simulated a modern running-board effect and made the exhaust pipes appear to be in use, even when the engine wasn't running.

Chromed reversed wheels (with Mercury centers and Chrysler rims), side exhausts, a fabric top insert, and a rolled rear pan that matched the grille were also on Catallo's extensive modifications list. For a while, Chili ran custom '57 Plymouth hubcaps that had been fitted with natty little plastic flippers, but reversed wheels with chrome bullets were essential to this car's signature, so they became the standard. So, too, were the small front tires, with whitewalls on both sides.

As a tribute to its drag racing days, the coupe's highly polished engine received a set of Jahns blower pistons, bigger intake valves from a Chrysler, and exhaust valves from a GMC truck, coupled with a hot Clay Smith cam. The *pièce de résistance* was a gleaming GMC 6-71 blower, on a custom-fabricated intake, topped with three Strombergs. An earlier intake setup with six two's on the big Jimmy eventually gave way to the three-carb arrangement, reportedly on

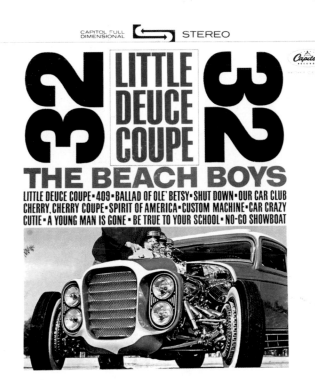

Recognize this chopped and sectioned electric blue '32 Ford? It's the cover car from The Beach Boys album, Little Deuce Coupe, and it's arguably one of the most famous '32 Fords of all time. The album photo editor cruelly lopped Catallo's head and shoulders out of the shot, but you can see the original Eric Rickman color photo, in its entirety, on the July 1961 cover of Hot Rod.

Here's the coupe at Detroit Dragway in 1958 with a McCulloch supercharger atop the Olds V-8. Flex-pipe headers and chromed, reversed wheels, with slicks on the rear, showed this coupe meant business. Catallo drag-raced the wheels off his car, continuously perfecting the bored-out, Bill Wanderer-built 344-ci Olds. At its peak, the "Little Deuce Coupe" ran impressive, sub-13-second quarter miles, turning a best trap speed of 112 mph.

Catallo's coupe starred in many major car shows. Here it is alongside Ed Roth's legendary *Beatnik Bandit*. Show promoters paid transportation and appearance money to the major players, then advertised that their hit cars would appear. Righteous rods like the Catallo '32 were a big draw. Most hot rodders had hitherto only seen major custom rods like this one in magazines. (Curt Catallo)

Tight fit: Clarence Catallo demonstrates the suicide door opening on his coupe. Stock '32 3-window doors opened rearward, of course. But these were shortened to clear the side strakes. (Curt Catallo)

Wouldn't it be interesting to learn what the late Ed Roth thought of this car? It was arguably far too conventional for Big Daddy, whose stylized creations were influenced by early Fords, but after *Tweedy Pie*, they shared nary a panel with anything Henry built. (Curt Catallo)

the advice of Ed Roth. Offenhauser finned valve covers added to the engine's visual appeal. Cragar provided the abbreviated blower drive, and that setup meant the stock water pump had to be replaced with a remote Jabsco electric unit, affixed to the front crossmember. The firewall was polished, so from the right angle, the engine looked even longer and more impressive.

When the coupe was featured in *Hot Rod*, Catallo was running a stock Olds clutch, and that backed up to a hefty three-speed La Salle floor shift. The open driveline ran to a narrowed and plated '55 Olds rear end. Nearly everything up front was chromed: the '37 Ford tubular front axle, Monroe tube shocks, the leaf spring (which was mounted in front of the axle), split wishbones, even a sexy, highly polished pair of chromed front Kinmont disc brakes (by then, long out of production). This coupe had it all.

The Alexander brothers installed their trademark twin antennas, in a frenched housing, and those became the switches for the coupe's electric solenoids to open the filled doors. Those purposeful rear slicks, the wild blue metallic paint, and lots of chrome were all popular period modifications. Chili wowed 'em at the '59 Detroit Autorama. When you think of award-winning show rods from that era, like the Barris *Twister T*, and Andy Kassa's wicked channeled '32, you can appreciate that Catallo's coupe had the extreme visual impact that all the big show entrants sought. This car's combination of modern (for the period) updates on a traditional shape was very well executed, and it all worked. In the genre of the day, Catallo's coupe was a spectacular home run.

In his book, *The American Custom Car*, author Pat Ganahl referred to cars like this as "custom hot rods," citing examples like the Eddie Dye/Gil and Al Ayala '29 A roadster (as two of the earliest), the Dick Peters/George Barris *Ala Kart*, Chuck Krikorian's *Emperor*, and Ed Roth's *Outlaw*. "Hot rods and custom cars are related by culture," Ganahl explained, "but they are very distinct species. But during the 1970s, as builders competed for show trophies and magazine covers, the line began to blur." The resulting phenomenon consisted of cars that weren't really intended to be driven. And in many cases, they became subjects for scale models. Show promoters often underwrote the entrant fees and provided financial incentives to their owners, to attract bigger crowds.

In accordance with International Championship Auto Shows (ICAS) practice of that era, most major feature cars were given a "stage" name. Clarence Catallo's hard-working show coupe became the *Silver Sapphire*. That was cool, but Chili was just getting hot. He was about to cross the country to get some help from a team that was then considered the highest echelon of customizing.

Chili Catallo devised a great idea to push his coupe over the top. He convinced his parents that he had to go to college in California. But he had an ulterior motive when he left Detroit to tow his coupe out West. While Catallo attended classes at Long Beach Community College, beginning in 1960, he astutely exchanged his labor as a shop helper at Barris Kustom, in Lynwood, California, for a primo three-inch top chop. To hammer his coupe, "Chili" worked with Herschel "Junior" Conway, who was also responsible for the coupe's Pearl and translucent Oriental Blue finish, applied just before the car graced *Hot Rod* magazine's famous cover. After the chop, the car's rooftop was a full 15 inches lower than a stocker, with virtually perfect proportions. The Barris signature crest found its way on to both sides of the cowl, contributing to a little confusion over the years because some people thought the entire car had originated in the Barris shops. George himself did little to dispel that notion.

Interestingly, if you browse further through an old copy of the July 1961 issue of *Hot Rod* that featured Catallo's car on the cover, the same issue also contains a two-page feature on Andy Kassa's channeled '32 from Passaic, New Jersey. Inspired by the *Silver Sapphire*, Kassa took his coupe out to Barris' in 1964 for a unique custom grille that sported a Cyclopean single headlamp pod on the left-hand side. Although unusual, it was no weirder than many of the shocking show car modifications favored in the swinging Sixties.

Returning to the Catallo coupe, Larsen Upholstery was responsible for the tufted white Naugahyde interior with blue accent trim. Twin bucket seats (really padded backrests), were matched with two seat cushion pads that were attached to the flat floor. Color-coordinated seat belts were installed,

along with a roll bar behind the seats. Button-tufted white roof inserts, matching inside and out, were complemented with still more white Naugahyde trim under the dash and over the chopped windshield. In addition to the gauges in front of the driver, additional dials and switches were added in the overhead panel. A chromed shifter was readily reachable from the driver's seat. The steering wheel was a big, dished unit adapted from a '59 Lincoln Continental. There wasn't an untouched element on the car, because that's what it took to win the top awards 40 years ago – and that much is still true for Ridler award winners today.

Clarence Catallo sold the car for either $5,200 or $5,500, we're not sure, not long after its Beach Boys album cover appearance, reportedly because he had done everything he wanted to do to it. Owned at first by the Washington Timing Association, a Pennsylvania car club, the coupe appeared in several major shows, notably the 1962 ICAS Grand Finale at the National Guard Armory in Washington, D.C., and then it was sold again briefly to a buyer from Montreal, Canada. But another phase of its life was about to begin. Ray Woloszak, from Long Island, New York, was the car's next owner, around 1965. He converted the show car into a street rod and replaced the GMC blower and three-carb setup with a single four-barrel carburetor. Woloszak also removed the distinctive side strakes and installed exhaust headers that ran over the frame and along the sides.

Gerry Burger, in a fine historic piece on the Catallo coupe for *Street Rod Builder* magazine, recalls seeing the '32 at Northeast rod runs in 1970-71. "Like many rodders of the time," Burger wrote, "we assumed it was a West Coast car, when actually it was East Coast-built [*sic*] and driven for most of its life."

Ray Woloszak bought a '69 Mopar 440-ci engine, Torqueflite automatic transmission, and Dana 60 rear end for the car from John Lang. According to Burger, Bob Saputo, who

taught at the Freeport (New York) High School auto shop, supervised a group of students who installed the 440 engine, trans, and rear in the ex-Catallo coupe. Saputo told Gerry Burger that the bodywork on the Catallo car was "incredible – the top chop was so meticulous that little filler of any sort was used." Saputo recalled that the attention to detail on the car was equally meticulous. "Every single wire was blue, to match the Oriental Blue paint job. It sure looked nice, but the monochromatic wiring harness made it extremely difficult to troubleshoot any electrical problems."

In another wonderful detail about the car, Bob Saputo told Burger, "I remember the voltage regulator was mounted up under the cowl on the passenger side to keep the firewall clean. Now, all the workmanship on the body was really good, but I looked up at the voltage regulator, and it's mounted to a Michigan license plate that has been formed into a mounting pad, but that's just early hot rod stuff for you." Apparently, the chassis work, in Saputo's view, was not as well done as the bodywork – a practice that was typical in that era when show was everything for display cars, and go was less important. Bob Saputo and his student crew replaced the early Ford steering box (which had apparently worn out) with a later unit from a Chevrolet Corvair. Interestingly, the car's original Olds engine, transmission, and chrome-plated rear end were reportedly installed in a '47 Ford coupe, and it has not been seen since. Does anyone know where it is?

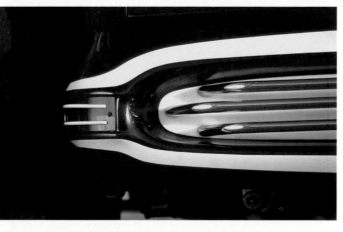

Chili took his '32 to Detroit's "A Brothers," Mike and Larry Alexander, in 1959. In this photo, the "A Bros." appeared with a youthful Catallo. The Alexanders sectioned the body six inches, built the flat floor, fabricated a hand-formed grille shell with a mesh insert and horizontal grille bars, and then added quad headlights with flamethrower lamps. On each side, a trio of sweeping wings accented the frame rails and ran from the headers toward the rear of the car, as if to simulate the flowing exhaust. The lower edges of the doors were raised to the top of the frame rails. (Curt Catallo)

After the chop, and as a result of the extensive section and channel work, the car's rooftop became a full 15 inches lower than a stocker's, with virtually perfect proportions.

The lighting details on this coupe are surreal. The bodywork by the Alexander Bros. was imaginative and exceptional. Chili Catallo had a knack for assembling great help for his project, from the "A Brothers" to Barris to Junior; and it shows.

Evoking its drag racing days, the coupe's engine received a set of Jahns blower pistons; along with Chrysler intakes and GMC truck exhausts, coupled with a torrid Clay Smith cam. A gleaming GMC 6-71 blower, on a custom-fabricated intake, is topped with three Strombergs. An earlier intake setup with six twos on the big Jimmy gave way to the present three-carb arrangement, reportedly on the advice of Ed Roth.

When the coupe was featured in Hot Rod, Catallo was running a stock Olds clutch backed up to a hefty 3-speed La Salle floor shift. The open drive-line ran to a narrowed and plated '55 Olds rear end. Nearly everything up front was chromed: the '37 Ford tubular front axle, Monroe tube shocks, the leaf spring (which was mounted in front of the axle), split wishbones, and even a sexy, highly polished pair of front Kinmont disc brakes (by then, long out of production). This cool coupe had it all.

New owner Ray Woloszak drove the Little Deuce Coupe everywhere, to events up and down the East Coast and to Midwest rod runs. And he did a great deal of work to make the car roadworthy. A new frame was installed, along with an early Ford spring arrangement that placed the spring on top of the tubular front axle. Interior updates included blue cloth inserts and billet door handles. Reportedly, at this time, a pair of foot wells was built into the flat floor to make driving easier. A third brake light was also added to the car, and it was repainted Oriental Blue, once again.

"I owned that car for 32 years," Woloszak told me. "We were just forming some of the New England rod groups like the *Long Island Street Rods*. I lived in New York, had friends in New Jersey, and once the chassis was sorted out, I drove the car everywhere. I'm a driver," Woloszak insists, "not an angel hair person." He's referring here to the whispy cotton candy-like decorations that were popular car show props in the 1950s and 1960s. "But once I was driving the coupe and a shock fell off," Ray told me. "That's when I knew I had to reconstruct the car. Someone told me about a new GTX that some kid had rolled in 1969. That was the going thing. So I got the 440-ci engine, transmission, and rear end."

Once the new driveline was installed, Woloszak hit the road as often as he could. "The biggest gratification I had," he says, "is that people would come up to me and thank me for bringing that car to events. They'd thank me for driving it. And we wanted guys to drive their cars. I was one of the

people who pushed for inspections at events to make absolutely sure these cars were safe."

Ray Woloszak bought a place in Palm Beach Shores, Florida, in the 1980s, and the coupe went south with him. "The car was in storage for eight years, while I raised a family. Then I actually drove it back and forth from the Northeast to Florida – twice! I rebuilt it three times, with a new frame, a lot of Chassis Engineering parts, Posies' springs, etc. I did it right. Here was one of the world's best-known cars, and there were parts of the frame where there was only an inch of metal holding it together. So I had to fix it." Woloszak says he never sought publicity with the car. "I took it to Lead East, because that's where I go. I took it to Syracuse. You'll never know how close I came to cutting the top off. I always loved roadsters, and that car was chopped so much I could hardly see out of it. But that's me."

Some time later, Woloszak rented the coupe to Bob Larivee, Sr., and his son Bob, Jr., for their ISCA shows. "The car had been damaged on the way to an NSRA event in Columbus. One of my buddies accidentally backed into it. There was a series of things. So I rented it out. They paid me $10,000 for six months. And they had to fix it (which they did). I told them, "don't bring the car back. Once you take that car, I won't miss it. But when I look at it, I love it.""

E. F. Hutton, but he had no pretensions whatsoever. Back when he initially owned the car, we rented it for our shows. Clarence was always a terrific person to deal with."

Shortly after they purchased the coupe, the Larivees' decided the car had been exposed sufficiently for the time being. They elected to sell it back to Clarence Catallo, who immediately started collecting the correct parts to restore it to its earlier *Hot Rod* cover car guise. "When my dad got the car back, and saw there was a Chrysler engine in it, he got fired up to do it right. We were in touch with the Alexander Brothers and George Barris. Dad wanted to preserve what they had done. Fortunately for us, Ray Woloszak had saved a lot of the parts he took off the car. That meant the world to me."

Today, Ray still regrets that he sold the Little Deuce Coupe. And, of course, he preferred the car the way he modified it. "Am I thinking it's a mistake now (that I sold it)? Yes," he says. "Absolutely. When I had it, it was a functional car. I think it's scary that they put it back the way it was." Ray still has his memories, though. "I loved all those years where I'd

In the late 1990s, Curt Catallo, Clarence's son, persuaded his father to find and purchase his old coupe. "As a kid," Curt says, "I knew the trophies before I knew the car. Many of them were my height. And it seemed like we had acres of them stored in an attic. Finally, most of them were thrown away, but we kept a few, probably because I had them in a tree house."

"I thought it was great that my dad had a cool car that won a lot of trophies. He sold it before he met my mother. A few years ago, I really got under my dad's skin about it. I thought of the coupe like a family heirloom that should be preserved. Fortunately, Bob Larivee, Jr. helped us find it. Without him, we never would have gotten it back."

Bob Larivee, Jr. actually bought the Catallo coupe from Ray Woloszak in 1999, for about $40,000, and he initially planned to continue to use it, as a feature attraction, in his family's car shows. His dad, Bob Larivee, Sr., recalls, "Clarence was the nicest guy. I knew him when he first built the car. He eventually became a top-ranked executive with

The Barris signature crest found its way onto both sides of the cowl, contributing to a little confusion over the years because some people thought the entire car had originated in the Barris shops, rather than just the chop job and the iridescent blue finish.

Over-and-under headlamps reflected what was happening on Detroit iron in the early 1960s. They work well alongside the chunky grille on this car.

The Alexander brothers installed their trademark parallel twin antennas in a frenched housing, and those became the switches for the coupe's electric solenoids that opened the filled doors. Fat rear slicks, wild blue metallic paint, and beaucoup chrome plating were popular period mods. This car was unmistakable, unconventional, and unforgettable – then and now.

At "Lead East," in Parsippany, New Jersey, Ray Woloszak (left) and his wife join George Barris in showing off The Beach Boys' album cover. Ray's wife is holding the Barris crest George gave the Woloszaks. the original crests were stolen. Ray drove the car up and down the East Coast. It was fired by a Chrysler 440 with twin 4-bbls, linked to a TorqueFlite transmission. Woloszak bought the car in 1965 and actually owned it for 32 years – much longer than Catallo. But in hot rod parlance, it will always be "Chili" Catallo's "Little Deuce Coupe."
(Ray Woloszak)

show up at events in that car, unannounced, and people would play Beach Boys music. That was enough. I didn't want my name in the paper. I'm not a guy who seeks publicity."

Sadly, Clarence Catallo died suddenly of a heart attack at age 58, before his objective to restore the car the way he built it could be completed. Curt Catallo took over the project, and he brought the car to Wheel to Wheel, in Troy, Michigan, for restoration. The coupe was invited to appear at the 2000 Meadow Brook Concours d'Elegance, and Curt wanted to make the date. The short timetable didn't permit a full and accurate rework, but a blown, 394-ci Olds engine with a three-deuce setup, built by Charlie Price of Vero Beach, Florida, was installed, along with a Hydra-Matic transmission. (Apparently the La Salle three-speed tranny was only in the car for a short time. Curt Catallo has the correct La Salle transmission, and he's debating whether to install it.)

During the restoration Mike Alexander dropped by Wheel to Wheel to help the restorers do the work correctly, drawing upon his accurate memories of the coupe. New taillights were made, new rear nerf bars were fabricated, and the original aluminum side panels were located and repaired. The later tilt steering column, that had been installed by Ray Woloszak, got the axe in favor of an original style column, and a '59 Lincoln Continental steering wheel was located to complete the interior. The initial restoration was completed just in time for an important debut for the freshly redone Little Deuce Coupe.

I was at the Meadow Brook Concours (in Oakland, Michigan) in August 2000 with the Ray Brown '32 roadster, representing the Petersen Museum. It was a drizzly Sunday, and a lot of people were hesitating to drive their detailed display cars onto the soaked field. Without hesitation, Curt Catallo fired up his dad's freshly restored coupe and rumbled onto the lawn, turning heads right and left. The blown Olds engine sounded great, and in the diffused light from the overcast skies, the *Silver Sapphire* glowed like its namesake. There were a few tears shed when people realized, here was Curt Catallo, driving his dad's old car. Fittingly, the Detroit-born Little Deuce Coupe won the coveted People's

Choice award, at the Midwest's leading concours for classic cars. It was everyone's sentimental favorite, as well. History had repeated itself. A winning car had won again.

"I underestimated the effect this car had," Curt Catallo says today. "The right guys touched this car and it touched a lot of people. Guys would come up to me and say they'd seen it back in the day, or that they'd built the Aurora model of it. It was great that it won the People's Choice award, because the people are the ones my dad built it for."

After Meadow Brook, Curt planned to further restore the car with the correct chromed Olds rear end, new diamond tufted door and seat inserts, and whatever else was needed to bring it back to its 1961 show configuration. "There were a few wrongs done to it over the years," Catallo said, "but nothing that was terminal. My dad had these gauges mounted up over the windshield and someone had upholstered over them; when we took off the upholstery, we found the holes he'd drilled were still there. Junior (Hershel Conway), who painted the car the first time, helped with paint advice, and Teddy Z from Barris' had saved an original paint chip, so we knew the right color."

Acknowledging the coupe's Olds heritage, Dave Hansen and John Moss of Chevrolet Special Vehicles helped with the work, in spite of the fact that the Little Deuce Coupe was a Ford. They wanted to use the car for several events celebrating Oldsmobile's Centennial. Their timing couldn't have been better. "My dad was a decent wrench," Catallo says, "but he also knew how to find and use someone else's talents. That's what I tried to do to get the car back together. There's a widespread hot rod cult at GM, and they were very helpful. We had all the pieces of the puzzle; Wheel to Wheel did the rest."

It was my pleasure to invite Curt to bring his '32 to the 2001 Pebble Beach Concours d'Elegance, where historic hot rods had been displayed in 1997 and 1999, and now hot rod coupes were being featured for the first time. When I explained to Curt over the phone that we wanted his car for the Concours, he was delighted.

"I've been waiting for your call since I heard about hot rods at Pebble Beach," Catallo told me. "We're gonna dress her up and take her to the prom. My dad retired the coupe because he thought he'd taken it everywhere it could go. He'd really be proud."

The competition at Pebble Beach that year was very tough. The hot rod class winner was the ex-Alex Xydias, So-Cal Special '34 Ford Coupe of Don Orosco. In second place, barely a point behind, and winner of the Dean Batchelor trophy, for the most historically significant car, was Bruce Meyer's ex-Pierson Brothers' '34. In third place was Art Chrisman's '31 Model A race coupe, edging out the Catallo '32 by the narrowest of margins.

On the lawn at Pebble Beach, the *Silver Sapphire* was reunited with the late Andy Kassa's *Cyclops Deuce*, and it was a fine addition to the field of nine coupes, attracting considerable attention the entire day. Later the coupe was displayed in the Bruce Meyer Gallery at the Petersen Automotive Museum, so Southern Californians could admire it too.

The Little Deuce Coupe is a remarkable restoration of a "custom hot rod" that perfectly personifies its era. Show rods and customs in the 1960s reached elaborate heights; and this coupe was a winner many, many times. The unusual grille was never duplicated. It is reminiscent of a highly stylized '32, and it's the signature element of this car. Rejuvenated in brilliant, almost electric blue, lathered in chrome and accenting scallops, with a gleaming blown motor and a pedigree that includes the talented Alexander Brothers, George Barris, and Junior Conway, this exceptional '32 is a proud part of hot rod history as well as an enduring tribute to Clarence "Chili" Catallo.

"I told my dad that he had to get this car back," Curt Catallo muses today, "and that it would be good for our communication. I used that angle, and I'll be damned if I wasn't right."

But there's one last issue, and we'd be remiss not to discuss it. We're speaking of the historical parallel with the Bob McGee '32 roadster (Chapter 3) which enjoyed a great deal of fame when Dick Scritchfield owned it, during which it set a Bonneville speed record for street roadsters and appeared in countless films. Restoring the McGee car as it was built erased all but the photos of its active second life. The same is true here, and we can't blame Ray Woloszak, who owned

and actively drove the "Little Deuce Coupe" for three decades in somewhat different guise, and Dick Scritchfield, who owned "his" roadster far longer than Bob McGee, for feeling somewhat bitter.

That said, I agree with both restoration decisions, difficult though they may have been. In each of these cases, functional or not, I prefer the originals. Picking a point in time to peg any hot rod restoration can be a tough decision. But it's hard to argue against using a car's first appearance on the cover of *Hot Rod* as the restoration standard, as was done in both these cases. Curt Catallo proudly owns his dad's car, and he occasionally brings it to major events like the SEMA show in Las Vegas where it was further memorialized in 2003 in an evocative Ken Eberts painting.

Back in the family again, the Little Deuce Coupe rests proudly in the carriage house behind their converted church home. Somewhere, I'd like to think that Clarence "Chili" Catallo is smiling.

In addition to the gauges in front of the driver, additional dials and switches were added in the overhead panel. A chromed shifter for the '37 La Salle box was readily reachable from the driver's seat.

We don't know what shape this T roadster body was in when Frank began his work. By the time he started, that already thin tin would have been over 25 years old. But it's in perfect shape today, just as straight as can be. Imitating period oval racing practice, Frank channeled the body three inches over his "new" frame, and hid the rails with a louvered aerodynamic aluminum belly pan. The hood and side panels were also fabricated from sheet aluminum. Compact, purposeful, and with perfect proportions, this iconic T still turns heads.

20

The first Detroit Autorama winner is still the definitive T roadster. Talk about a time warp. Frank Mack's beautifully proportioned '27 T track-style roadster still looks just the way it did when it won Best Hot Rod at the first Detroit Autorama, back in 1953. It's never been restored, and it never will be, as long as Bruce Meyer owns it. This is one of a few significant East Coast and Midwest hot rods that have always had West Coast guys scratching their heads in disbelief. Interestingly, there are a lot of parallels between this roadster and Bill Niekamp's '29 on Essex rails, the winner of the America's Most Beautiful Roadster trophy at the first Oakland Roadster Show.

Both Bill Niekamp and Frank Mack were somewhat older than their contemporaries; Bill was 42 when he showed his car at Oakland, and Frank was 26 when his T appeared in Detroit. Both cars were largely home-built by their owners (although the legendary Whitey Clayton helped Niekamp with the aluminum racecar nose and hood, and, very likely, the belly pan). Both of these roadsters were the inaugural

winners of two enduring hot rod shows: the Grand National Roadster Show (although its name has changed to the Oakland Rod and Custom Show) and the Detroit Autorama, and each car is perfectly proportioned, albeit quite differently. Just as importantly, although their owners/builders have passed on, both cars have survived. The Niekamp '29 (Chapter 2) is fully restored; the Mack '27 T is beautifully preserved. And they're both on permanent display in the Bruce Meyer Gallery at the Petersen Automotive Museum in Los Angeles.

So much for parallels, let's learn more about the Mack car. Reportedly, Frank Mack, a body and fender man (to use the terminology of his era) began this car in the late 1940s and completed it in 1950. As far as we know, Frank did virtually all the work on this car himself, from body to paint to suspension and steering – he also sewed the convertible top. The interior, that is to say door panels, seats, and kick pads, was done by Detroit's Jack Stanley in maroon leather. Frank's own work reportedly took some 3,000 hours. He

HOT ROD MILESTONES

Frank Mack's '27 T Roadster

drove the car a bit, and then it won the first Autorama in Detroit. But we're getting ahead of our story.

Rodders on both coasts first saw this perfect little T when *Hot Rod* magazine ran a four-page article featuring the Mack roadster in its November 1953 issue. Mack began with a set of '27 T rails that he reinforced by welding a strip of 2 x 3-inch angle iron along the lower edge of the frame rails. He fabricated a center crossmember from steel plate. The front crossmember was a cut-down '37 Ford unit and the rear was the stock unit from the donor '27 T frame.

The remainder of the running gear consisted of a '37 Ford tubular front axle, with the spring in front, and Houdaille 50/50 lever shocks. The radius rods, which were mounted to the side of the frame rails, were neatly split and chrome plat-ed to match the transverse leaf spring and the axle. In back, a narrowed '34 Ford rear end, fitted with 4.11:1 gears, is suspended with two sets of shocks, 50/50 Houdailles again, along with twin Hartford friction units. The rear radius rods were also split and frame-mounted with Ford tie-rod ends. Frank Mack nailed the track roadster look with this car and it spawned a host of imitators.

Typical of cars from this era, when aftermarket pieces were only sparsely available, Mack utilized '41 Ford hydraulic brakes, a master cylinder from a '37 Plymouth (along with its pedal assembly, modified of course), while the steering box came from a '36 Pontiac – probably from a wrecking yard. Many hot rodders, spoiled by today's remarkable custom parts availability, have forgotten that "back in the day," you planned your car, then went to a junkyard and cannibalized suitable pieces that were cheaply available and would fit your application. Today, we have specialists like Borgeson and Mullins for steering or ECI for brakes. Fifty years ago, you adapted what you could buy in a boneyard – and part of the fun was the search for the right pieces and the subsequent negotiation. Long before "Pick 'N Pay," hot rodders were combing yards for Auburn dash panels, tubular Ford front axles (like the one Frank used), and late 1930s V-8/60-powered Ford models with their highly desirable 4 x 16-inch rims.

History doesn't record what shape this T roadster body was in when Frank began his work. By the time he started, that already thin tin would have been over 25 years old. But it's in perfect shape today, just as straight as can be. Imitating period oval racing practice, Frank channeled the body three inches over his "new" frame and hid the rails with an aerodynamic belly pan that he liberally louvered for cool-

Then and now, Frank Mack's beautifully proportioned T roadster set a high standard. It won the first Detroit Autorama in 1953, and it was present at the event's 50th anniversary in 2003. Sadly, Frank Mack is gone, but his unrestored, remarkably well-preserved roadster is still with us.
(Greg Sharp Collection)

Low, mean looking, and ready to rumble, Frank Mack's T, shown with its convertible top up, is a great example of one talented man's efforts. Frank did virtually all the work on this car himself, from body to paint to suspension and steering – he also sewed the convertible top.
(Dain Gingerelli)

ing. He fabricated that beautiful racecar nose from two '41 Chevrolet fenders. I've looked at this car a lot, and I'll be damned if I can see where the two pieces are joined, nor can I relate their shape to the Chevy fenders. That's how good a job he did, of course. Next, Mack carefully fabricated the grille from steel strips, and made the neat top and hood sides that fit together with concealed '36 Dodge latches. Frank eschewed Dzus fasteners and lunch box latches and instead carefully fitted some hidden hardware, adding to this car's smooth appearance. Under the grille, there's an air scoop for the engine. The door and trunk fit are exemplary on this car, and the wheelbase is 102 inches.

The lozenge-shaped E&J accessory headlamps fit this roadster's profile perfectly. These exotic-looking lights reportedly came from a 1927 Jordan, though I've seen them on other defunct makes like late 1920s Rickenbackers. This may have been the first time they were used on a hot rod. Frank inset small '37 Chevrolet taillights into the rear of the T's turtle deck at an appropriate height. Again, this car's oval track racing influence is shown by the front, rear, and triangular nerf bars, which Frank fabricated from 7/8-inch seamless steel tubing, then plated. He hand-fashioned his car's rear roll pan from sheetmetal pieces he took from a '37 Ford. It's seamless and so well integrated, you could never tell from whence it came. Inside the trunk is a fuel tank of indeterminate origins (and size) and a Stewart-Warner electric fuel pump.

A word on nerf bars here: they were immensely popular in the early 1950s. Often they were personalized with the owner's initial on the front bar. They're perfect on this car, and seeing them, I can't help but wonder why more hot rodders, in search of a period look, don't consider these distinctive (and useful) protectors. You'll see that quite a few cars in this book, like the Gejeian T and the Dick Flint '29, were fitted with them.

The abbreviated windshield is the lower half of the stock '27, so it's appropriately low and proportional with the rest of the car's sleek silhouette. Speaking about low, the cockpit is so low; the cover over the center portion of the torque tube is used as the center armrest. The '39 toploader is partially exposed, as is the front U-joint that links the torque tube to the transmission. When you get into the car, you step over the frame rails and down into it, and there's a narrow well for your feet. It's cozy, and very functional in appearance. The overhead pedals and small '23 T three-spoke steering wheel help maximize space. But there's still very little room for tall people in this car, which explains why Craig Smith, who purchased the car from Frank, and Bruce Meyer, who bought the car from Craig, logged little time behind the T wheel – each is over six feet tall. The dash originated in a '37 Ford (some sources say '38 but it's a '37). Frank retained the stock dials, but he narrowed the panel five inches to fit.

The wheels on the Mack T are 15 x 5-inch steelies (they are

The front suspension used a '37 Ford crossmember and lightweight, smart-looking, V-8/60 tube axle. Split radius rods attach to the reinforced Model T frame rails. The brakes are '41 Ford, but Frank used the master cylinder from a '37 Plymouth. The shock absorbers are 50/50 lever-action.

Friction shocks, modified for 50/50 action, are found in all four corners. There's also a supplementary pair of Hartford shocks in the back. The rear nerf bar above the split radius rods is a sprint car touch. These look great on track Ts.

probably from a '48 Mercury, although some references say Lincoln), presently fitted with modern 5.00 x 15 front tires and G78 x 15 rears. Period pictures show the car with Firestone bias-plies. The hubcaps are modified '47 Hudson, each with a cast brass spin-on, knock-off nut that functions as a wheel bearing cover for the front wheels. Clever; but that's the case for many things on this trend-setting roadster.

The car was driven extensively in its first years. There are surviving photos of Frank flinging it sideways on dirt. No doubt the low center of gravity, short wheelbase, and stiff suspension made for great cornering capability. The late Gray Baskerville enthusiastically drove the T out to Pomona for the 1995 Father's Day event and reported in *R&C* that it rode and drove pretty well.

This car had a succession of three engines. Mack began with a V-8/60, but soon abandoned the little 135-incher because it was too weak. He replaced it with a stock 239-ci '48 Merc with Edelbrock heads. The present power plant, added some time after 1953, is a 255-ci 8CM (1949-53 Mercury) block, with heads and headers. Frank adapted a Chevy 409 water pump, much later than when the car was first shown at Detroit's Cobo Hall, of course. He may have been one of the first people to perform this modification. The oil pan had to be sectioned to fit the low silhouette and not hit the street, so Frank built one from parts of three pans. Admittedly, that's not much of a hot rod engine, but the roadster barely weighs 2,000 pounds, so the combination of meaty flathead torque and low *avoirdupois* means this baby will still scoot pretty well.

After Frank won Best Hot Rod at the first Autorama at Cobo Hall (where the event is still held), he was invited to Ford's famous Rotunda Rod & Custom Show, held in 1956, to showcase the company's involvement with young people and fast cars. Some years later, the Detroit Autorama Show producers selected Frank's car to be cast in miniature for the bronze sculpture they award each year for the best-preserved rod or custom – a fitting honor for a car that's remained constant for over half a century, and appeared at the Detroit Autorama's 50th anniversary for everyone to admire.

Mack kept the car and drove it occasionally for over 40 years. Gordie Craig, of Brighton, Michigan, told me he was after Frank for years to buy the car, but he never succeeded. "I would call him, and I went by his house near Five Mile Road in Livonia (Michigan) a few times, in the 1970s, but he wouldn't sell. Once he told me his granddaughter had just turned 16 and he was giving it to her. That car had a classic look," Gordie says, "I even thought of building a clone of it."

Frank made the unique wheel covers. They consist of brass knock-off hubs on '47 Hudson hubcaps. Wheels are 15-inch Mercury all around. Tires are 5.00 x 15 in front, G78 x 15s in back.

"I never got to ride in the Mack roadster," Gordie said, "but I recall that John Ackermann, a Ford chassis engineer (with a very appropriate name for his profession), told me he had supplied a few parts for Frank, and he made duplicates of each one."

I spoke with 84-year-old John Ackermann who confirmed much of what we know about Frank Mack. "I worked at Ford engineering full time, and in the evenings and weekends, I was a partner in the Dearborn Speed Shop, where we sold Edelbrock, Grancor, Hotton & Sullivan, Weiand, and other speed equipment. And I knew Frank very well. He made a trip out to the West Coast before he began that car. Its proportions were exceptional, and he patterned the grille after the kind they used on Indy cars."

Although Frank Mack did the lion's share of the work himself on his car, he had a little semi-professional help from his friend at Ford engineering. "I helped him with some parts for the steering system, particularly the drag link and the pitman arm," Ackermann recalls. "I made the fitting that connects the pitman arm with the steering linkage. I also went over the steering geometry with Frank. As I remember, we put in a little positive caster, and we took a few leaves out of the springs. The car rode softly and cornered very well. He moved the axle forward on the car and that gave the hood and grille the look he sought to help achieve those great proportions."

"Frank was a character," Ackermann says affectionately. "He was a Polish guy from Hamtramck; he did bodywork for a Chevy dealer located at Grand River and Livernois. And he was a great bodyman, by the way, with a terrific sense of proportion. You can see that in the car. He also had several garages filled with old cars including a 1902 Locomobile Steamer and an early brass-era Buick. After he divorced his wife, he was a bit of a womanizer. And he had a great sense of humor."

"Those brass knock-offs were a good example of his work. He cast them himself and took them to the Ford machine shops to have the threads done. Frank wasn't really a machinist, but he could do anything with a hammer and dolly, he was great with a torch, filling, and braising, and, of course, he could make more things out of a scrap pile of parts than you could ever imagine. Those E&J headlights are another example of Frank's ingenuity. He made the brackets for them, and, of course, he converted them to sealed beams."

"You know," Ackermann adds, "Frank always wanted to put an Offy in that car. During the 1960s, he looked at drop-

ping in a four-cylinder Pontiac – remember the engine that was half a V-8? The problem was, that engine would have had to have been tilted to fit in the T, and the oil pump pick-up, and probably a lot of other things, would have needed changing. In the end, he never did it."

"Unfortunately, Frank was ill at the end of his life," Ackermann recalls, "and he had to sell the T to pay his medical expenses. Gordie Craig wanted to buy it in the worst way. So did I, but neither of us had the money at that time. Frank died about three years ago; I don't know what happened to the other old cars."

Craig Smith was the lucky guy who purchased the roadster from Frank Mack. "It was in 1996 or 1997," Craig says. "I had spoken earlier with Frank, and expressed interest in the car. We had met when I was 16 at a gas station that he used to stop in with the roadster. I said 'if you ever want to sell that car, call me.' He was having health problems, and I guess that's why he decided to sell it. It was pricey, but it's a significant car, and I felt I had to get it."

When Craig went to look at it, the award-winning T had been sitting for many years in one of Frank's many garages, actually a steel shed, on a dirt floor. Mack had covered it with a thin coat of motor oil as a preservative. "We first had to get the car running. The starter was screwed up, but we fixed it. It took days to get all the oil off." In hindsight, that coating of oil is the reason the car remains in such remarkable shape.

"I never put it on the road," Smith says. "I'm too tall to fit in it, but I drove it around the field where I live. Then I started telling people it was for sale. Bob Larivee and Kirk White talked to me about it, but in the end, Bruce Meyer got the car. I took a lot of grief about selling it, but if I hadn't sold it to Bruce, it might be running around now with a small-block Chevy in it. He's taken great care of it, and the car is immortalized in history."

"This car needed to be preserved and saved," adds Bruce Meyer. "I took it to Tom Sparks and he cleaned it up and got it running. We put new tires on it, and a California vintage plate, and that's all we did. When Gray Baskerville saw it, he got so excited. It was always one of his favorite cars. He was even more excited when I let him take it to the LA Roadster Show."

"There's not a bad angle on this car," Meyer continues. "The metal work is terrific. I'm just going to keep it like it is and never restore it. Perhaps Pebble Beach should have a class for original hot rods?"

As we noted, the Frank Mack roadster is on display at the Petersen Automobile Museum, along with the Bill Niekamp '29, the 1950 Oakland winner. Thankfully, enthusiasts who never saw these two notable roadsters when they were first built can admire and appreciate them today, and for all time.

Complete instrumentation is courtesy of a '37 Ford. The steering wheel is from a 1923 T, with the spokes plated.

Frank initially put a V-8/60 in his car, but soon found it was underpowered. There was a 239-ci '48 Merc in it for a while. The present mill, a 255-ci, basically stock '50 Merc flathead, runs Edelbrock heads and was converted to 12-volt operation. Frank adapted the intake manifold to accept the single GM 2-bbl Rochester carburetor.

Extensive use of white striping, the white front axle center, white-painted grille bars, and whitewall tires mark this as a late 1950s rodding exercise. Hot Rod magazine called it "Tony's Sports Deuce," stretching the metaphor somewhat, but the low center of gravity probably meant the car cornered nicely, even with bias-plies and solid axles. When owner Tony La Masa rented it out, Ricky and David Nelson drove it on the Ozzie and Harriet TV show. (Bill Andresen)

(21)

Sporting unquestionable provenance, this lowboy '32 Ford roadster, built in the 1950s, hit a new price high for historic hot rods. If this channeled '32 looks familiar to nostalgia-prone baby boomers, it's not surprising. It's the same car that David and Ricky Nelson drove in a memorable episode on the popular *Ozzie and Harriet* TV series. Legend has it that young Ricky desperately wanted to buy the roadster with some of his show earnings. Ozzie reportedly refused, saying, "No 1932 Ford is worth $3,500."

Despite Ozzie's skepticism, knowledgeable hot rodders value cars like these. Authentically restored examples of significant early hot rods – cars with rodding magazine feature credentials, trophies, and awards from 50 years ago, real timing tags from California's dry lakes, and/or timing slips from drag strips – are bringing large sums these days, privately and at auctions. You can't create history and provenance out of thin air, in any segment of the car hobby. Hot rods are no exception. Those rods that have it, the ones Boyd Coddington likes to call, "our ancestor cars," are the ones collectors want. This neat little lowboy is a good example.

The car's well-documented history starts in 1951 with Ray De Fillipi of Los Angeles. Most West Coast roadsters of the period were highboys, but Ray channeled his. The result was a dramatically lowered silhouette. If you raced at the dry lakes, this wind-cheating modification bumped you up one racing class.

De Fillipi's deuce lowboy featured a bored and stroked 286-ci Ford flathead with an Edelbrock dual manifold, rare Harrell high-compression heads, a Winfield SU-1 cam, and Kurten dual-coil ignition. The transmission was a '40 Ford column shift, fitted with a close-ratio Lincoln Zephyr first and second gear cluster. Ray sectioned the filled grille shell to match the car's new proportions, then fabricated a new three-piece louvered hood with a bubble to clear the carbs and "lunch box" latches to open and close the top portion.

The reversed rear wheels were a pioneering feature, along

Tony La Masa's '32 Roadster

with the attractive, faired-in door hinges. A '40 Ford dash was narrowed to fit. The car's workmanship and its blazing "fire-engine red" finish were first class, earning Ray a feature in *Hop Up* magazine in April 1952. The car's proportions were nearly perfect, something that was very hard to achieve with a channeled car. The three-piece louvered hood was neatly done, and the lusty flathead was all that was needed, in that era, to provide brisk acceleration.

The ex-De Fillipi roadster reappeared in *Rod & Custom* in April 1956, now owned by Tony La Masa (whose name also appears variously as La Mesa and Le Masa). Giving no credit to Ray De Fillipi, unfortunately, this feature implied that tough, cigar-smoking Tony had built the car from scratch. On the contrary, as a starting point he bought a car that was very well done.

For his remake, La Masa installed a 277-ci John Geraghty-built flathead with a Navarro triple manifold and Navarro heads. The identical Winfield cam was specified, along with a Harman & Collins dual ignition. The car's steel wheels were changed to Mercury 15's (versus De Fillipi's Ford 16's). The roadster had been repainted lime green, a scoop was cut in the hood bubble (probably to aid cooling), and new off-white, rolled and pleated Naugahyde upholstery was crafted by Lou Penn. La Masa, a founding member of the *Roadsters* hot rod club, showed his car extensively. Famed hot rod photographer, Andy Southard, shot it in 1958 at a Long Beach show, in a photo that appears in Southard's book, *Hot Rods of the 1950s*.

In August 1960, a small shot of the La Masa roadster appeared on a composite cover of *Hot Rod* magazine. Bonhams & Butterfields' (the auction company that sold the car) description implied this roadster was *the* cover car (you have to watch auction catalogs on these details). Inside, a two-page feature (not a fold-out, as B&B described it) showed a smiling, flat-capped La Masa with his car, surrounded by show-winning trophies. The engine had been upgraded again, this time to a stock '56 265-ci Corvette V-8 with a 4-bbl carb and polished 'Vette valve covers. The roadster was extensively but not obtrusively pinstriped. A caption in the feature noted that this, "sharp roadster has been

used on TV by Ricky Nelson." It's unclear how many *Ozzie and Harriet* episodes featured this roadster, but several stills exist (and we're reproducing them) of Ricky Nelson and his brother David in the car. La Masa's roadster also appeared in several period B movies, including *Hot Rod Girl*.

Tony La Masa sold the roadster to a Bob Kazyuoshi, who in turn sold it to Bernie Sievers, who then passed it to Don Orosco in July 1997. Orosco planned to complete another vintage hot rod (the ex-Dick Flint '29 Ford) for the inaugural hot rod class at Pebble Beach that year, then he realized the Flint car restoration would take longer than he'd expected. He purchased the La Masa '32 from photographs, sight unseen. When it arrived, he called me and asked if he could change his entry to the Ricky Nelson roadster. I looked at a selection of photos he sent overnight, and agreed. When Don actually took delivery of the '32, he realized it was well preserved, but in his view, not up to Pebble Beach standards.

Orosco and his talented crew embarked on a major redo of the roadster. They only had three weeks. Despite suffering a UPS strike that held up some work, they re-plated, repainted, re-striped, reupholstered, and refurbished it in record time. Luckily, the roadster was virtually complete and still very original, so parts chasing was minimal. Don had to cross the picket line at his local UPS depot to rescue some of the

David Nelson (behind the wheel), Ricky (shotgun), and an unidentified co-star (center) get comfy in Tony La Masa's '32 roadster while Tony looks on, a bit skeptically. The roadster's column shift allowed cozy room for a trio of occupants. The car appeared in scenes on the popular Ozzie and Harriet TV show. (Ross Myers/Bill Andresen)

David (standing) and Ricky (behind wheel) Nelson, starred with their parents on the Ozzie and Harriet show, a popular 1950s-era family sitcom that began as a nationwide radio broadcast, then segued into TV. Teen idol Ricky became a rock and roll performer and enjoyed popularity with hit tunes like "Travelin' Man," and "Garden Party," until his untimely death in a private plane crash. (Ross Myers/Bill Andresen)

critical pieces, but if you know Don, whose tenacity on a racetrack is legendary, you can imagine that not only did he retrieve the critically needed parts; in the process he probably made friends with the strikers.

Fortunately, there were plenty of photos of this car for the restorers to follow, so there was no guesswork about details, from color and striping to engine and accessories. The roadster was finished and fired up, just hours before the big event. It won a creditable third place at Pebble Beach that inaugural year, behind two of the cars in this book: Bruce Meyer's ex-Doane Spencer '32 roadster and Kirk F. White's '32 Ford dry lakes racer, built in '46 by hot rod pioneer, Ray Brown.

Many hot rod restorers choose to bring a car back to the way it was first built. In this case, it was arguably more correct to redo the roadster as it had appeared when La Masa rented it out for *Ozzie and Harriet*. The car's TV appearances, with budding rock and roll star Ricky Nelson at the wheel, created a lasting impression that added immeasurably to its value today.

Orosco went on to restore the Dick Flint '29, winning the second hot rod class in 1999 at Pebble Beach. After its appearance at the Lodge, the Ricky Nelson roadster spent most of its time in Don's private museum until Orosco decided to consign it to Bonhams & Butterfields (mentioned above), a British auction firm. A few wags criticized this idea, thinking that particular sale was not the optimal venue. They forgot: it only takes one motivated buyer, although having at least two people competing is ideal.

The De Fillipi/Tony La Masa/Ricky Nelson roadster sold for a then-astonishing $192,000, including buyer's premium, at Bonhams & Butterfields' Carmel auc-

tion, August 15, 2003. (The auction company estimate for the car was $150,000-$200,000.) Historic hot rods like this are valued on the basis of their past exposure. Racing, magazine coverage, ownership, and movie history are all plusses. This roadster had all the provenance, unbroken history, and notoriety required to merit that high bid.

Although the restoration was a hasty one in terms of actual time, it was done correctly, with refurbished original and/or period pieces. The car was still extremely clean; it was detailed and well presented, and it had been driven very little since its trip over the ramp at Pebble Beach. When they fired it up for inspection, the crackle of the Corvette V-8's exhaust through the twin glasspacks was a delight to the ears.

The buyers were Pennsylvania hot rod and vintage racecar collectors, Ross Myers and his lovely and diminutive wife, Beth. "I've always loved this car," Myers said. "It's on a calendar that I have permanently displayed in my shop. And Beth is a huge Ricky Nelson fan. We thought it would be perfect for our museum. I think really good vintage hot rod roadsters – cars with lakes racing histories – are in the $150,000 to $200,000 range. There are a few of those around, but there's only one Ricky Nelson roadster. Besides," Myers says with a smile, "Beth fits in it perfectly."

As this is written, authentically restored or original condition, well-preserved historic hot rods from the 1940s-50s are enjoying a boomlet, partly fueled by their eligibility at Pebble Beach and other respected concours. They represent the real thing, in a sea of fiberglass-bodied imitators with ubiquitous 350 Chevy V-8s and TH400 transmissions. They're in big demand at top

The La Masa '32's best profile (in my opinion) is its side elevation. It's low-slung and nicely proportioned, with a level hood top, full-length hood sides, and a sectioned grille, plus steelies with early Ford caps – a fine example of how nice a channeled car can look. (Bill Andresen)

The Tony La Masa/Ricky Nelson channeled '32 roadster started life in 1951-52 when Ray De Fillipi built it in LA. A Hop Up feature car in April 1952, the roadster packed a strong stroker flathead with an Edelbrock Super intake, rare Harrell high-compression heads, Kurten ignition, twin coils, and the hot Winfield Super 1A cam. (Bill Andresen)

concours throughout the country. Even the conservative AACA permits historic rods in their events. Class 24-A allows properly documented cars, 25 years or older, if owners can validate a racing history. The ex-La Masa, "Ricky Nelson" '32 would not be eligible for AACA shows under the present rules, but an ad hoc committee is actively petitioning to create a new class, which would recognize authentically restored or preserved hot rods with period magazine and show history, even though they weren't lakes, Bonneville, or drag racers.

of this book. What we can say is that historic hot rods, in the foreseeable future, particularly while baby boomer demand is high, will remain rare, and thus quite valuable. Bottom line, the real value lies in taking one of these cars for a fast spin. Sure, bias-ply tires have their limitations, and if the frame isn't boxed and reinforced, there'll probably be noticeable flex, but the crisp bark of a well-tuned flatty, or the shriller rumble of a sharp Chevy V-8, will provide all the musical accompaniment you'll ever want.

The rear 3/4-view of the La Masa '32 accentuates the car's slight rake. The small nerf bars were a necessary adjunct for a car that apparently saw a lot of street service and movie work. Cleanly built cycle fenders, probably made from tire covers, kept LA's occasional rain at bay.
(Bill Andresen)

We know of several historic hot rods that have sold privately, and a few that have sold publicly, in the low six-figure range. In this instance, the buyer got a beautifully proportioned, great-looking hot rod with a unique history. With its light weight (about 2,000 pounds) and powerful Chevy V-8, and despite its three-speed, early Ford gearbox and Lincoln hydraulic drum brakes, Ricky's classy old roadster is eminently drivable, easy to maintain, and it will be welcomed at contemporary hot rod shows and prestigious concours for years to come.

Can we say with certainty that if you restore a significant historic hot rod, assuming you're reading this book in 2005, that it will be worth a sum approaching a quarter of a million dollars? Not really. And that's certainly not the purpose

A sectioned '40 Ford dash was in this car from its inception in 1951. Stewart-Warner gauges ensure the driver knows what's happening under the hood. The white art-deco steering wheel is a '40 Ford classic, while the rearview mirror is from a Jaguar. The tachometer is on the left-side steering column; the shifter is on the right. Ashtrays (a necessity for "smokin' Tony" La Masa) and glove compartment are all operative. The period pearl white Naugahyde interior has traditional "roadster roll" behind the floor-level seat.
(Bill Andresen)

The lovely hood scoop ensures a supply of fresh cool air to the Corvette 4-bbl. It was a bubble when the car was first built. Charter LA Roadsters member La Masa, in conjunction with John Geraghty's shop, grabbed the tin shears and nipped this neat opening. (Bill Andresen)

Cycle fender brackets bolt securely to the '48 Lincoln Bendix brake drums. The tight-fitting fenders are very attractive and provide some protection – it makes you wonder why more people don't run fenders today. In California, many rodders think the cops are too young to know there's still a fender requirement. (Bill Andresen)

Striping highlights the Ford rear end. Neat, simple nerf bars are replicated front and rear. The inverted accessory license plate light was a common touch in that era. The fuel tank was relocated to the trunk. (Bill Andresen)

La Masa roadster's stock '56 Corvette engine displaced 265 ci, developing a factory-claimed 210 hp. A 3-speed '39 Ford box with a Zephyr cluster and a '50 Mercury clutch put power to the pavement. The engine compartment was snug, but there was room for a fan. The Corvette mill was a popular swap in the mid 1950s. Flatheads were getting tired (sigh!). A stock 'Vette put out an easy 200+ ponies, with utter reliability – they were less prone to overheating than Henry's old boiler. (Bill Andresen)

Roth adroitly captured the essence of the Ford Model T's minimalist shape, raked the body, and ran a splashy set of plated headers down each side. When the "T" appeared in Car Craft, it had steel front and rear wheels, with big-and-little whitewall tires, '51 Merc hubcaps, and accessory bullets. Later Ed spiced it up with a dragster's brake-less front wire wheels, but retained the T's spindly windshield (actually he used a '22 Dodge wind-shield frame), as if he real-ized he'd gone far enough.

Traditionalists hated this slinky glass "T" when it first appeared. Years later, it's rolling proof of Ed Roth's twisted genius. The late Ed "Big Daddy" Roth created mind-altering, yet memorable rods that are still the subject of intense debate. But Ed's keen insight wasn't always apparent at first. If the editorial staff at *Car Craft* had thought that Roth's dramatically different, fiberglass-bodied T roadster was a major breakthrough when it appeared on the January 1960 cover, they certainly kept it hidden. The subhead read, "Saucy T-Styled Roadster Built From Fiberglass is Futuristic yet Traditional." In fact, it was a really radical little piece.

Ed called the new car *Excaliber*, reportedly because its shift knob had been fashioned from the handle of an old sword. No one immediately picked up on the fact that the spelling of the name was incorrect; it should have been "Excalibur," as in King Arthur. But that didn't matter for long, because the car's name was soon changed to *Outlaw*. And it was pointing the way to the future...

Pat Ganahl's book, *Ed "Big Daddy" Roth, His Life, Times, Cars, and Art*, should be required reading for everyone who wants to know more about the zany Mr. Roth and his ahead-of-the-curve ideas. According to Pat, Ed got the notion to build a fiberglass car when he was in the Air Force stationed in Africa. Apparently, Roth had seen that famous *Life* magazine photo of Henry Ford wielding an axe at a prototype plastic deck lid on a '41 Ford sedan. The elder Ford was a proponent of soybean plastic, a material used on many Ford trim and electrical items as World War II began. Although Ford's soybean plastic deck lid never found its way into production, the dramatic photo impressed a lot of people.

Fiberglass was hardly a new item in 1959. Chevrolet's Corvette had used a fiberglass body as early as 1953. By the late 1950s, fiberglass in paste (remember Bondo?) and cloth plus resin form was commonly used for bodywork by home builders and the pros. But fiberglass roadster and coupe bodies weren't yet available, so Roth was something of a pioneer here.

Ed Roth's Outlaw "T"

Ed Fuller told Ganahl that Roth had begun working on the *Outlaw* at his Maywood, California, shop on Slauson Avenue. Reportedly, he was influenced by Norm Grabowsky's TV-starring *Kookie T*, and he wanted a car that would attract attention for him and his work. Traditionalists (and I'm one of those) hated Roth's stylistic interpretation of the T form. The *Outlaw* featured an abbreviated, free-formed fiberglass body, a stingy little nose, and a '59 Chevy grille piece and turned dash knobs. It had a then-contemporary '58 Chevy steering wheel and bullet-filled '58 Chevy Biscayne tail lamps, with '56 Chevrolet lenses, and those garish '59 Rambler headlights set off by metal flake paint and scallops. It was a rolling cliché of T cues, laced with all the fads of the era – trick paint, chromed wheels with bullet caps, mini nerf bars, and then-fashionable (if a bit faddy) quad lights.

In hindsight, we can see the brilliance of Ed's design. Roth adroitly captured the essence of the T's minimalist shape, smartly raked the body, and ran a splashy set of plated headers down each side. When the "T" appeared in *Car Craft*, it had steel front and rear wheels, with big-and-little whitewall tires, '51 Merc hubcaps, and accessory bullets. Later, Ed spiced it up with a dragster's brakeless front wire wheels, but retained its progenitor's spindly style windshield (actually he used a '22 Dodge windshield frame) as if he realized he'd gone far enough. The bulb horn was an amusing conceit from a goofily funny, eerily talented man who may be best known for his creation of "Mickey Mouse's evil twin," the drooling, mother-taunting Rat Fink.

Like the powerplant in Grabowski's trendy T, the *Outlaw*'s engine was an OHV Cadillac V-8, in this case a 1949 model, according to the serial number. Four plated Stromberg 97 carbs, with SP flared tops, and green neoprene fuel hoses, sat atop a side-by-side, polished Cragar intake manifold (these were made from the Horne patterns by Roy Richter at Bell Auto Parts). The engine was fitted with finned accessory valve covers and chromed, capped, three-tube, over-the-frame headers. The jazzy neoprene fuel lines were later replaced with chromed metal lines. Fritz Voigt, who built the engine, also built the blown Olds in the *Beatnik Bandit*, and he was even better known for building the four Pontiac engines for Mickey Thompson's 400+ mph *Challenger* Bonneville streamliner. According to *Car Craft*, the engine had "a few internal goodies," but that's all we know.

A full tonneau covered the cockpit, so it's not certain whether the *Excaliber/Outlaw* was upholstered when it was first featured in *Car Craft*. Right from the beginning, Roth fabricated a unique top for the car out of wood framing, aluminum, and Naugahyde. It was hinged in the middle, so you didn't have to take it off to get in or out – you could just lift one side. The top appeared in the *Car Craft* feature. Reportedly, it blew off while the car was being transported

Ed Roth, shown here clowning around, said Norm Grabowski's TV-starring Kookie T influenced him, and he wanted a car that would attract attention for him and his work. Traditionalists (and I'm one of those) hated Roth's stylistic interpretation of the T form. But I've grown to respect this car.
(Robert Genat)

Imagine seeing this car in January 1960 – we didn't know what to think. Neither (really) did the editors at Car Craft. They called it "Futuristic Yet Traditional."
(Robert Genat)

Coming or going, the Outlaw, one of Ed Roth's first big attention-getters, was a brilliantly conceived piece. The jaunty top blew off when the car was being trailered on a Midwestern road trip and was never repaired or replaced. The top was hinged in the center, so you didn't have to take it off to get into the car. (Robert Genat)

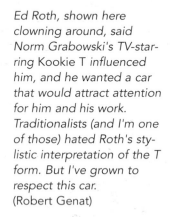

With its abbreviated, free-formed fiberglass body, stingy little nose, '59 Chevy grille piece and turned dash knobs, '58 Chevy steering wheel, bullet-filled '58 Chevy Biscayne tail lamps with '56 Chevrolet lenses, and garish '59 Rambler headlights, the Outlaw, nee Excaliber [sic] was a rolling cliché of T cues. It was laced with all the fads of the era: trick paint, chromed wheels with bullet caps, mini nerf bars, and then fashionable if a bit faddy, quad headlights.

on an open trailer to a show somewhere in the Midwest. Perhaps it's hanging on some garage wall in Des Moines?

Ed claimed he only had $800 in the whole project, and he offered copies of the body shell for $230. Supposedly, three of the bodies were sold. Ed Fuller apparently had some earlier fiberglass experience. He told Ganahl that they fabricated the basic shape of the body out of wood, covered it with screening, and then troweled plaster on top of the screen. The resulting rather crude mold was made in four pieces, held together by toolbox latches. To make the body molds, the two Eds smoothed the plaster, waxed it, and laid fiberglass cloth over it. It was a rather inexpensive way to make a totally wild car.

After the base molds were used, Roth gave them to Jim "Jake" Jacobs, who in turn gave them to Robert Williams. Pat Ganahl said that striper/sculptor Jimmy C acquired and cleaned up the molds with the intention of building a buck from the originals, then using that to make modern, bolt-together molds, and making a small run of bodies from them. As this is written, that hasn't yet happened.

Pat noted that there were photos of Ed making the plaster for the nosepiece, but no shots of its steps before completion. There's one by Colin Creitz in the *Car Craft* article that depicts Ed layering plaster on a nose buck that's positioned on the front of the unfinished car. Pat surmises that the two Eds may have laid the glass over that plaster core, and that the car's nosepiece and its abbreviated "fenders" may still have the original plaster underneath. After all, it was mainly built as a show car.

As Pat Ganahl wrote: "No one had ever built, or seen anything like it before. It looked as though Ed had brought one of his airbrushed caricature cars to life."

The *Outlaw* marked a key turning point for Ed Roth. Uninhibited and unpretentious, Roth liked the free publicity his ideas garnered, so he built that car, and all the ones that followed, with the idea that he'd receive extensive (and free) magazine coverage. Who needed an ad budget? The zany cars themselves generated a lot of publicity, even beyond the magazines, and led to a contract with Revell models. Naturally, the canny Ed received a royalty on every $2.00 Revell kit that was sold. As well, show promoters wanted Ed at their events, so he was usually given his spot gratis. That gave Roth a chance to sell the items he made, and he could spend his time painting t-shirts and trashcans and generally entertaining the crowd. Ed's "show car *du jour*" was usually an important part of his display, and he himself always drew a legion of fans. Roth soon became a counter-culture idol, and his work was seen all over the country, and soon all over the world.

Pat Ganahl extensively examined the *Outlaw* at the Petersen Automotive Museum. I'll recap a few of his comments and add some of my own. According to Pat, the frame rails

could be early Ford. They are 6-1/2 inches deep in the center, and they taper to the front and rear. The front crossmember is fabricated; the rear is Model A Ford. The front axle is a chromed tubular '37 Ford V-8/60 unit, similar to Grabowski's, and there's a chromed Panhard bar made from an abbreviated Ford tie-rod. Four-bar radius rods and a drag link were all fashioned from Ford tie-rods, and then plated.

Flared SP tops on a quartet of plated 97s look sharp. These are still being reproduced. But if you want a Roth Outlaw body like the one on this car, you'll just have to make it yourself.

The front suspension consists of coil springs, positioned in cups that are welded to the front axle. Tubular shocks are used front and rear. *Car Craft* stated that the plated front coil springs came from a '58 Chevrolet, and they're used with Airflow trailer cushions. The steering consists of a '41 Ford cross-steering box that's been turned on its side. As a result, the pitman arm points vertically. A Model A rear spring stylishly lifts the narrowed '48 Ford rear end. Brakes were '48 Ford all around, but the fronts were removed when the wire wheels were substituted later in the car's life.

Ed Fuller, one of Roth's workshop elves, had some earlier fiberglass experience. He told Roth authority Pat Ganahl that they fabricated the basic shape of the body out of wood, covered it with screening, and then troweled plaster on top of the screen. A crude mold was made on four pieces held together by toolbox latches. To make the body molds, the two Eds smoothed the plaster, waxed it, and laid fiberglass cloth over it. The result was a rather inexpensive way to make a totally wild car.

A '39 Ford 3-speed transmission was adapted to the Cad bell housing and mounted on a pair of rubber biscuits. The Ford-based torque-tube driveline and rear wishbone were retained, after severe shortening. There's a hydraulic slave cylinder for the clutch throwout arm. As befitting a show car, everything that could be plated was plated. Ed's sponsor here was Chrome Nickel Plating in Southgate, California. The sword shifter never appeared, it seems, and the present shifter is a turned plastic item that resembles an elongated dash knob.

The car was reportedly fully functional, but in a zany Roth sort of way. For example, trident-shaped connector pipes discretely run from each header, into two mufflers under the car, and then they exit with down-turned pipes just behind the classic Ford rear end. Under the car, there's a square battery box and a similarly shaped and sized square gas tank. According to Ganahl, it "...couldn't hold more than three gallons." He suspected the filler was under the seat. There was no provision for a key, but there's a strategically located toggle switch that might be the culprit. The windscreen was tinted blue, and there's even a hand-turned wiper on the driver's side. The tiny radiator was adapted from a German DKW automobile. (Ironically, DKW in German means, *Die Kleine Wunder*, the small wonder.)

Upholstery in this car appeared in several stages, beginning (probably) with next to nothing for the *Car Craft* shoot, progressing to a simple black and white seat, and finally a

major sculptured aqua and white, tuck-and-roll effort by the talented Eddie Martinez. The same sequence of changes appears to be true for the car's finish. It was painted at Barris' first. Apparently, Roth reserved painting space for the project, according to Hershel "Junior" Conway. For the *Car Craft* cover, Pat Ganahl astutely points out that the scallops appear to be green and lavender, with gold pinstriping. The green seems to be more intense in later photographs. Photos also exist of the *Outlaw* in 1968, in Rock Island, Illinois, where it was painted (by "Dirty Doug" Kinney) in "Peacock Metallic." The car was restored once again when it was in the Bill Harrah Collection (more about

this shortly), and the paint details are slightly different, as is the striping, from the way it first appeared.

The instruments are period Stewart-Warner black-faced dials. The 0-160 mph speedometer has no cable and was thus not connected, and perhaps never was. An 8,000-rpm tach balances the speedo, and there's a plethora of other gauges. There's speculation that although the car was built to run, Ed never drove it more than a mile or so. Pat Ganahl was given the opportunity to drive it, but he's very tall, and he said he simply couldn't fit behind the wheel.

Pat Ganahl's exhaustive research says that Ed Roth sold most of his cars to Jim Brucker, who put them in his Movie World: Cars of the Stars Museum. When Movie World closed, the always-astute Bill Harrah bought many of Ed's cars. The *Outlaw* and the *Beatnik Bandit* were subsequently and very accurately restored in 1980 in Harrah's superb 30-man restoration shop under the supervision of Clyde Wade. They must have looked strange alongside the elegant Duesenbergs, Bugattis, and Franklins that Bill Harrah favored.

After Bill Harrah died unexpectedly, many of the cars in his enormous collection (over 1,600 restored and unrestored vehicles) were sold. Next, the *Outlaw*, and several other Roth cars, passed to Domino's Pizza magnate, Tom Monaghan. Monaghan's company was in trouble financially in the early 1990s. In a sale of assets that included most of Monaghan's 25 or so collector cars, the *Outlaw* was sold yet again – this time to Richie Clyne and Don Williams (representing the Imperial Palace Collection) in Las Vegas. The *Beatnik Bandit* remained in what's now called the National Automotive Museum in Reno, and it can be seen on display there today.

According to Pat, "I remember being astonished to see Clyne and two friends actually drive the *Outlaw*, *Surfite*, and *Wishbone* into the LA Roadster Show in 1991 or 1992, single file, then line them up and put a big 'For Sale' sign next to them. They didn't sell that day."

That's a '58 Impala steering wheel. The instruments were conventional Stewart-Warners. Making the instruments unique would have really cost money, something Ed didn't have, and like the polished, powerful-looking Cadillac engine, they draw you back to realizing this car might look a bit zany, but it's really a hot rod. Or is it?

Wire wheels evoke a dragster theme, especially without front brakes. The Outlaw was as much about a look, or a feeling, as it was about being a functional machine. It was just the beginning for Ed Roth, who'd go on to build even wilder creations. No one, Barris included, ever caught the public's fancy in quite the same fashion.

Clyne offered the *Outlaw* again at auction in 1992, and this time there was an interested buyer. Bruce Meyer had been advising his car-crazy friends to collect historic hot rods. So Meyer's pal, Bruce Lustman, who owned several impressive Ferraris, bought the *Outlaw*, ostensibly as a gift for his then-young son. It's believed that the transaction price was something in the $40K range. Lustman then contacted Bruce Meyer saying, "I did what you suggested; I bought a hot rod."

Meyer, who at the time owned the historic, ex-Andy Southard/LeRoy Titus '32 Ford roadster and had begun restoration on the Pierson Brothers' '34 Ford coupe, gently told Lustman, that the *Outlaw* wasn't exactly what he meant by "hot rod."

In 1993, Pat Ganahl curated a Kustom Car Show at the Art Center School in Pasadena, and Bruce Lustman, who was living at that time in Florida, generously shipped the *Outlaw* west for the show. In 1994, it went to the newly opened Petersen Automotive Museum. During my tenure there as director,

The tailpiece has an impudent little kick-up. The bullet-filled '58 Chevy Biscayne tail lamps, with '56 Chevrolet lenses, are neatly framed by the nerf bar. The Model A rear spring is barely visible.

The front suspension consists of coil springs, positioned in cups that are welded to the front axle. Tubular shocks are used front and rear. Car Craft stated that the plated front coils came from a '58 Chevrolet and they're used with Airflow trailer cushions. The steering consists of a '41 Ford cross-steering box that's been turned on its side, so the pitman arm points vertically.

HOT ROD MILESTONES

Bruce Meyer convinced Lustman to donate the *Outlaw* for permanent display. As this is written, thanks to Bruce Lustman, Ed Roth's clever creation has a place of honor in the Bruce Meyer Gallery, where it can be inspected and admired.

From a styling and even a technical standpoint, with its trick front suspension, the *Outlaw* was miles ahead of most contemporaries in 1959-60. It still looks right, even if it's a bit dated today. Critics have commented that Roth's supercharged *Beatnik Bandit*, which followed, with its 1960s-space-age bubble top and central "monostick" that controlled steering, acceleration, and braking, was Ed Roth's masterpiece. I wouldn't disagree. But the *Outlaw* preceded it, and it pointed the way, in a far-out direction that only Ed Roth understood at the time.

The *Outlaw* will always be an inimitable hot rod icon. Over time, it has proven to be one of Ed's milder forays into the curious. It took me a long time to appreciate Roth's genius. I probably saw too many airbrushed "Mother's Worry" monster t-shirts back in the day, and they tend to throw you off the track. While I was at the Petersen, I took the opportunity on several occasions, to study the *Outlaw* closely. It's truly remarkable. Roth captured a look, a feeling, and a sense of motion that took hot rodding forward into its next

iteration and ensured that, for the future, there would be no limits on creativity.

In his foreword to Pat Ganahl's book, perhaps Robert Williams said it best: "Roth inadvertently altered the logical purpose of the automobile, from transportation and sport to a realm of vicarious mental adventure. That experience made Ed's bewildering hot rods 'art.'"

I didn't "get it" then, but I do now.

Hammered lid, sectioned grille, wide whites, and moon discs. Bill Couch's cream-colored coupe is the essence of 1950s cool, yet it appears oddly contemporary, too.

(23)

We'll bet you didn't think to hold on to your high school ride, but Bill Couch did. Joaquin Arnett of the San Diego *Bean Bandits* built this cool chopped, sectioned, and shortened '34 Ford coupe back in 1950-51. Andy Granatelli bought the car at Bob Petersen's third Motorama in Los Angeles in 1952, then took it to Chicago where he added a full-race, Grancor-equipped flathead and an independent front suspension and brakes from a British Allard sports car. Bill Couch purchased the car in 1953 and has owned it ever since. Just three owners in 53 years – that's quite a tale!

Bill Couch grew up on a farm in Washington, Michigan, 27 miles north of Detroit. "As a kid," he says, "I lived vicariously through the pages of hot rod magazines." Like many of us, then and now, he'd leaf through magazines on the stand at his local drug store and sometimes buy them. "It was an introduction," he recalls now, "to a neat world I didn't know."

He bought the first issue of *Honk!* (which later became *Car Craft*), dated May 1953, and was captivated by a shot of a '34 Ford coupe on the top of page 27. It was one of 15 illustrated examples, in a story called "Build For A Purpose," by managing editor John Christy (Wally Parks was the editor), showing various types of rods and customs. The brief caption read, "Classic street coupe was sectioned and chopped to reduce height; is fully equipped for road use."

There was no mention of who owned the car, although Bill later learned it was Andy Granatelli, and he also found out that the photo was taken at a Chicago show. Bill cut the photo out and pinned it on his cork bulletin board. He also had a picture of the elaborate, multi-instrumented dashboard in Joe Bailon's famed Chevy custom, *Miss Elegance*, which he pinned up as well. Then fate intervened.

One of Bill's friends' fathers owned a large dealership, Motherwell Lincoln-Mercury, in Chicago. His friend's mom had a brand new Mercury Monterey (Bill's family had Plymouths). "We went for a drive on the south side of

Bill Couch's '34 Coupe

Chicago," Couch recalls, "and I saw this cream '34 Ford, just sitting on a used car lot. The salesman even let us get in it. When I saw that dash with 10 Stewart-Warner winged gauges, it reminded me of Joe Bailon's car. Then I realized this was my dream car – the actual coupe from Honk!"

"Remember," Bill Couch says, "I was 16 years old, and I had no money." Summoning up his courage, Bill called his dad for help, fully expecting a flat, "no." Overhearing the conversation, Mr. Motherwell said, "Let *me* talk to your dad." To Bill's surprise, his father agreed that Mr. Motherwell could bring the car to his dealership and have a mechanic check it out. Bill waited a week, then asked his dad for a loan, still believing the answer would be "no."

"Then my father said, 'oh, by the way, Mr. Motherwell says the price is a little high. But I've decided to front you the money.'" Couch can't remember the exact price, but he thinks it was $1,100. That was a lot of money at the time. But soon the coupe was his.

It was the fall of 1953, and the Chicago area weather soon went to hell. "The car sat in the dealership until Easter vacation in March," says Couch. "My roommate Dave Anderson and I went to get the car. I was a naïve 17; the battery was near dead. We pushed the car to start it, fired it up, and drove it over 200 miles back to Three Rivers, Michigan. We didn't dare shut it off, and we got it home. At one point not long afterward, I told my dad I wanted him to ride in my car. He got in; we went about 1/8 of a mile. He said, 'That's enough,' and that was the only time he ever rode in it."

Bill Couch said his father's willingness to buy the car for him was "totally out of context. I know he loved me, but he was a quiet guy who didn't say much. He said he'd loan me the money, but I never paid him back. The subject somehow never came up. We still went hunting together. My mother thought the car was cute. Dad didn't mention it. "Looking back," Couch reflects, "my father did very few things out of character, but this was one of them – just a mystery of life."

What did he do with the car? "We drag raced on Woodward Avenue. There were more hot rods in Detroit then and chopped Mercs, some even with overheads. I didn't know how to do an engine, but I learned how to rebuild transmissions." The powerful Granatelli-modified 276-ci flathead chewed up transmission gears, and Couch, on a limited budget, soon got creative about rebuilds.

"My mother had a two-door Ford station wagon. I took a blown transmission from the coupe over to the Ford dealership and the parts manager showed me how to rebuild it. I must have done 10 to 12 transmissions. I only busted a rear end once." Living on a farm, Couch was no stranger to a chain hoist. "We rebuilt those '39 boxes with whatever they had at the dealership. Now the car has Lincoln Zephyr gears."

Bill Couch spent his summers doing "…the worst possible jobs." He worked on industrial washing machines, toiled at a heat-treating plant, and labored as a millwright's assistant – up to his elbows in soot and smokestacks. There was more money on the night shifts, so Bill's playtime was limited, and many days whatever sleep he got was when he could curl up beside a piece of machinery for a few quick winks.

He raced on Woodward, usually from stoplight to stoplight. "You'd follow a guy, then line up against him. I only lost if something broke." Popular cruise destinations included Danny's Big Town on 13 Mile Road and Woodward, the Totem Pole, about 11 miles north of Detroit, and Ted's at

Here's the car the way Joaquin Arnett finished it. The coupe is shown at the drags, where it ran in the B/Altered Coupe class. It later caught second owner Andy Granatelli's eye at the Robert E. Petersen's Second Annual LA Motorama. That's where Andy offered to buy it from Joaquin Arnett. (Greg Sharp Collection)

Bill Couch's '34, a friend's deuce coupe, and the famed Tommy Foster channeled deuce roadster (See Chapter 24) get together in the Detroit area. Bill insists he'd like to recreate this picture today. We know where the Foster car is! (Bill Couch)

The Couch coupe braves a Michigan winter. Bill Couch held on to his coupe for decades. It helped to have a barn to store the car, and he kept thinking he'd "get around to restoring it." And at last, he did. (Bill Couch)

Low, lower, lowest! Here's a front shot of that famous gathering. Note that Couch's chopped and sectioned '34 is nearly as low as Foster's chopped and channeled '32. (Bill Couch)

Here's a young Joaquin Arnett working on the coupe, half a century ago. "I took four inches out of the windshield," he recalls, "and reattached the top to the front 'poles.' I welded it real straight. The coupe door was longer than the sedan's so I used a sedan door and cut that down (and obviously reshaped the lower edge) to match the top and the sectioned body." I asked if he'd jigged the frame and body to keep everything aligned. "No, I just used jacks to support the frame when I cut it to shorten the car," he replied. (Joaquin Arnett via Steve Coonan)

Restoration time. Fortunately, Bill Couch was able to store his worn-out '34 coupe for decades in a barn on his property. So when it was time for restoration, most of the key parts were all there, although they were not in the best of shape. Couch held onto the '34 because he loved the car, and he had the space. (Bill Couch)

Square Lake and Woodward. Bill says he and his friends would drive from one to another, looking for action. At night, with its luminescent cream paint, you could see that car from blocks away. It must have been like a magnet.

He'd read about hot rod clubs in *Hot Rod* magazine, and once, while stopped at a light, he was invited to join the *Camblers* (that's cam, as in camshaft, not gamblers) of Royal Oak. "I started meeting like-minded guys. We had gold jackets…there were about 25 of us, and that got me into a bigger pond. The quickest car around was a '36 Ford five-window coupe that was always missing one of its rear fenders. He had a 3-3/8 x 4-1/8 (296-ci) engine, but I could beat him."

"One of the wildest-looking cars was a chopped '47 or '48 Ford coupe." says Bill, "I didn't realize how radical my car really was…I just drove it everywhere, even to work. I didn't show it." The suicide doors were a problem. The passenger-side door would fly open and the handle would crease the bodywork. "I got so I could dive across the seat and catch it before it did any damage," Couch says with a laugh. "Finally I started tying it."

At the time, there were no drag strips in the Detroit area. So Bill attended the Half-Day Drags in Illinois, but he didn't bring his car. Interestingly, that's where Andy Granatelli, as a promoter, had run his coupe somewhat earlier. Bill did run his car near the GM plant in Livonia where there was a clear quarter mile of road. "GM actually let us use it, with a flag man, as a drag strip." On one occasion, a guy running a channeled deuce roadster with fenders beat Bill's car on their final run. Couch recalls, "I remember thinking, where did this car come from?"

Bill remembers the '55 Chevy V-8 as, "the car that killed hot rodding. My car went into the barn in 1955 and stayed there." Couch went off to college at the University of Arizona. His car sat "and went to hell a little bit more each year." The wheels were appropriated for a hay wagon; the car got moved around; the hood was taken off, water got into the engine and it froze up. He took it out once when his kids were little, but through the late 1980s, the car was virtually abandoned. He considered having it restored around 1985, but the attempt was unsuccessful. He'd lost money on that first effort so he let the car sit for another eight years. The coupe "got moved a few times, but it was always under my control. I'd just look at it from time to time and dream about it."

In his second year of college, Couch bought a '56 Plymouth Fury for $2,600. He soon began attending races at Phoenix Dragway, where he saw the famed Speed Sport Roadster and met driver Lyle Fisher. He raced the wheels off the Fury and actually had it striped, during a weekend trip to Los Angeles, by none other than Von Dutch.

"I first went to visit Barris' shop," Couch says, "and then went to see Von Dutch. He was sitting cross-legged in the back of his panel truck playing a flute. I thought, 'what have I gotten into?'"

Bill arrived at Dutch's shop on a Saturday morning and asked the price of the striping work. The answer was "$25 bucks and a case of beer." "The place was a dump," Couch remembers. "He told me to come back at 5:00 P.M. When I returned, he was smoked…and drinking beer and wine. He drew a caveman in a diaper on the glove compartment holding a headless cat dripping blood." You can draw your own conclusions as to the symbolism. Suffice it to say, Bill used to cover the glove compartment door with tape when he went out on a date. "Dutch worked on the car off and on, all night long. I finally went to sleep. That was my big trip to California."

Over the years, far away from home, why didn't he simply sell the coupe that was languishing away back home in the barn? "That car was so personal to me," Couch says, "that I could never sell it." Someone actually tried to swindle him out of it, but thankfully that failed. Many people tried to buy it.

"Indefinitely, in the back of my mind," Bill Couch says, he always thought about restoring the coupe. "I kept asking myself, am I ever going to do this?" Asked if he ever considered getting another, newer car, Bill responded. "I'd had a deuce roadster since 1955 (which he still owns), but as far as the coupe went, I never wanted another car. Why bother? I already had the world's best."

Down to bare metal, Couch's coupe awaits the body man. If you look closely, you can see the lines where Arnett chopped and sectioned the body. Note the split wishbone. (Bill Couch)

Joaquin Arnett's clever carving essentially reduced this '34 coupe to about 7/8 scale, while basically retaining its inherently nice proportions.

Viewed from the side, the Arnett/Granatelli/Couch coupe looks channeled, but it's not. It was chopped and sectioned. Arnett, who'd had plenty of practice building bodies for hearses, did his metal magic on this car without ever taking the body completely off the frame.

Just like the full-sized grille only smaller. Nothing tricky here, but great skill was obviously required. Arnett cleverly re-proportioned the '34's handsome grille and, to my eyes, he lost nothing in the process.

Bill Couch became a part of the informal breakfast club of about 80 people that meet on weekends in Rochester, Michigan. "We have hot rod and custom guys, and classic car owners. We'd meet at 8:30 and it was a first class car show, with no formal planning. I wanted to get my car done and didn't know where to go. Someone took me to Paul Reitter, a talented metal crafter in Mt. Clemens, Michigan." Bill had a bad experience previously with restorers, but Paul "seemed like a nice guy. I thought, 'what the hell. I'm gonna do it.'" That was May of 1996.

Bill's friend Al Maynard put him in touch with Mark Kirby, owner of Motor City Flathead, in Dundee, Michigan. Mark Magnafluxed the engine and the old block was still good. Kirby had Couch's flathead two years and eight months. "He rebuilt it, checked every last nut and bolt, and made it run real good," says Couch.

Bill Couch wanted to have the car ready for the Detroit Autorama in 1998, since it was eligible to win the Preservation Award. It helped to have a deadline to work towards, but it was a fight to the finish.

Scott "Willie" Peart did the tuck-and-roll upholstery in Port Huron, Michigan. He reupholstered the seats and side panels in avocado and parchment vinyl, neatly matching what was there. Couch says Willie told him he would lock his shop door on Friday and on the following Sunday, the car would be done. Come Monday, there was also a new headliner, and the car was ready. "We never talked about price," Bill admitted. "The final bill was $2,800, I think that was fair."

Paint – custom-mixed mint white – was done at Bob Watters' Watters Works, also in Port Huron. Greg Bock did the pinstriping. The coupe looks almost exactly the way it did when Bill bought it – wide whites, chromed caps, green accented wheels, full fenders and bumpers – a time warp.

February 1998, Bill's freshly redone coupe made it to the Autorama at six o'clock on Wednesday night. There was just time to fire it up and check everything. Bill and his wife Ellen rented an ice cream counter, stocked it, and built a 1950s style display. "I wanted to honor Ellen," he says. "I met her when I owned it. She learned to drive in that car and I taught her how to speed shift in it, too."

The Couches had a great time at the Detroit Autorama. The car won its class, and the display won an award too. Ed Reavie featured the car the following year at his St. Ignace show, and at Eyes on Classic Design, a prestigious Detroit event, the coupe won its class and beat out Gene Winfield's *Maybelline* Cadillac custom. Since then, the car has won awards at Meadow Brook and Bay Harbor.

Graciously accepting my last-minute invitation, Bill rounded out the coupe class at Pebble Beach in 2001. Bill says since he finished the car, he's met people he hasn't seen in years, and he gets a kick out of watching people photographing and enjoying his coupe.

Aside from the single photo published in *Honk!*, the Arnett/Granatelli/Couch coupe was never featured in a magazine, *per se*, but it appears, negotiating a slalom course, on page 39 of the February 1952 issue of *Hot Rod* magazine in an article about the *San Diego Knuckle Busters*' first annual Reliability Run, where it was driven by *Bean Bandit* luminary, Joaquin Arnett. The black and white photos show the car in a dark color; we now know it was black. By popular acclaim, Joaquin won People's Choice at the event. Arnett was a low-key, jack-of-all-trades who could build a motor, work a torch, or expertly pilot one of the *Bean Bandits*' many competition cars and dragsters.

I spoke with Joaquin Arnett about the '34, complimenting him on the work he'd done so long ago, and I asked him where he'd developed the skills to build so radical a coupe. "I worked for a company called Burner's (in the San Diego area)," he said, "building bodies for funeral cars on Packards and panel deliveries; I also worked for North Park Iron Works. I built my first Model T in 1951 – it was a full-fendered pickup with a flathead engine that could run 117 in the quarter. Soon afterward, a guy asked me to cut a '32 coupe. They said they didn't think I could do it without cutting the (side) window glass. When I finished (and the glass was intact), they flipped."

Arnett did extensive custom bodywork at that time, for other owners on cars that included a '37 Ford Club cabriolet, a '40 Mercury, and a '40 Ford Tudor. He obviously had the welding skills and access to the best equipment. Moving up in scope, he also chopped and sectioned a '34 Tudor. "That was easier to do than the '34 coupe," he recalls. "You just cut the body apart and push the back section up." How easy he makes it sound.

I asked him how he modified his '34 coupe and he remembered every step. "I took four inches out of the windshield," he says, "and reattached the top to the front poles. I welded it real straight. The coupe door was longer than the sedans' so I used a sedan door and cut that down (and obviously reshaped it on the lower edge) to match the top and the sectioned body." I asked if he'd jigged the frame and body to keep everything aligned. "No, I just used jacks to support the frame when I cut it to shorten the car," he replied, with the confidence of a man who knew a straight line when he saw one, "and I cut a little off the front fenders. I made a lot of my own metalworking tools." Arnett inferred that he'd done very little pie cutting and reshaping – he also left the top insert in originally. The top was subsequently filled.

To really appreciate this remarkable car, look closely at the pictures – Joaquin Arnett truly performed a metal miracle. He chopped the top, sectioned the body (no small effort

there), and then, perfectly preserving the proportions, he cut 11 full inches out of the frame (and body) length, and expertly stitched it all back together. The result looks for all the world like a 7/8ths-scale Ford three-window – but it's beautifully done, and it's low. Although the car looks channeled, it's not.

You can't see the scale change too well in the photos – that's how beautifully the car is done. But standing alongside it, you appreciate how low it really is. The tall tires are a clue, but the rescaled proportions really work thanks to the sectioned grille, high-mounted small headlights, and slightly clipped taillights. The stock '34 bumpers look right at home. The only other bodywork (aside from the chopping and sectioning), includes the filled roof, the removal of the top door hinges on each side, and the solid hood sides.

Inside, a big 160-mph Jaeger speedometer dominates the panel, along with eight Stewart-Warner convex-lensed, winged gauges, a tachometer, and an 8-day Jaeger clock. The handsome steering wheel is from a '50 Chevy, finished in the same shade of green as the dash. The shortened and re-contoured '39 floor shifter is topped with a swirled glass shift knob that's period perfect. Ford pedals and a '32 teaspoon throttle are evident. In keeping with the car's 1950s origin, the rear and side window surrounds are plated. The cozy cockpit, with its tuck-and-roll split bench, is devoid of a heater (although Granatelli was a distributor for South Wind heaters), and a single wiper on the driver's side tends to raindrops in inclement weather.

Joaquin Arnett built this car with the intention of selling it – and he did so, right off the show floor at the 1951 Petersen Motorama in Los Angeles – to Andy Granatelli.

But the story of how it got there is interesting, too. "The show was mostly for new cars," Arnett told me. But I own a mint original copy of the program for the November 1951 2nd Annual Motorama held at the Pan Pacific Auditorium on the 7th through the 11th, and in it are pictured antiques, new cars, concept cars, customs, and hot rods. Producers Robert E. Petersen and Robert R. Lindsay were the co-founders of *Hot Rod* magazine and *Motor Trend*, of course, so their show included nearly everything on wheels.

Walt Woron wrote some of the program notes. Looking back, he could have written this section specifically about Arnett's coupe. "What makes up a hot rod? One thing sure," Woron wrote, "it doesn't have to be a roadster sans fenders. If the car is built for faster acceleration, higher speed (and even greater economy), if the engine glistens with mechanical improvements, if it looks as if it's meant to 'go' and 'go' safely, then it is a hot rod…regardless if it is a sedan, coupe, roadster, convertible, pickup, belly tank, or streamliner."

Arnett's coupe caused quite a sensation at the show, and apparently it fooled several people who thought it had actually been built by Ford Motor Company because Joaquin had cleverly figured out a way to retain the original glass in the door sides, complete with Ford factory lettering. Joaquin also cut down the hood sides and painstakingly retained the original louvers. "I was able to cut through those louvers, then work the metal straight with no warpage," he says proudly today.

At that time, Granatelli owned a speed shop in Chicago with his brothers, Joe and Vince. He was listed in the first issue of *Hot Rod* magazine as the magazine's Midwest correspondent. Bob Petersen told me he knew Andy Granatelli from the beginning, and that it looked good for *Hot Rod* magazine to have geographic representation. The Granatelli brothers had been shipping California-built speed equipment back to Chi-town since the early 1940s. They opened Grancor (for Granatelli Corporation), in 1944 and sold their own Grancor brand flathead intakes and heads. The Grancor dual manifold closely resembled the famed

A narrow windscreen and thin seat squab are the price you pay for lowness. The steering wheel is the popular art-deco 1940 unit; the floor shifter tops a '39 Ford 3-speed.

during the 500 race a few years later. "His (Granatelli's) brother would drive it to the track and they'd drive it in the pits." Arnett, who went on to considerable fame driving the *Bean Bandits*' dragsters, did several more radical chopped and sectioned cars after the coupe, including a '34 Ford Tudor for a wealthy Mexican woman from Tijuana. None of the others survive, except in photographs.

I spoke with Andy Granatelli recently about his old '34. Of course, he needed no reminding. "I fell in love with that car the first time I saw it," he says, and you can hear the enthusiasm in his voice. "I'd like to have it today."

Granatelli confirmed he bought the coupe right off the floor of the Los Angeles Motorama in 1952. "It had a soft top (roof insert) then and it was black. I paid Joaquin Arnett $1,500 for it. (Arnett insists it was $3,000). He wouldn't take a check, so I hadda get cash for him. Then he took the train back to San Diego."

Of course, Bill Couch wanted to connect with Arnett and Granatelli, and now he's done that too. In California with his old friend John Vernon, "who'd been around since the beginning," Couch visited with Joaquin Arnett, in San Diego, who showed him photos of the car under construction and gave him a trophy that the coupe won in its hot rod infancy.

And he made a pilgrimage further north to see the car's second owner. "Andy Granatelli lives well," says Bill Couch. "He's got a beautiful house in San Clemente, overlooking the ocean."

The decision to go to California was made at the famed Mackinaw Hotel near St. Ignace, Michigan. Bill's wife Ellen recalls, "I wanted him to go. I said, 'if you don't do it, something will happen. You've got to do it.'"

What do you say about a car you've had for nearly half a century? "This car has always been around me," says Bill. "I've had it forever and I guess I'm car crazy. After all these years, I realize that if I hadn't lived on a farm, I might not have kept it. Having a place to keep it made a big difference. And, no, I'm never going to sell it. It's always been lurking in the background as a part of my life."

Does Bill Couch have any more goals for his coupe? "I'd like to recreate the period photo I have of my car with the Tommy Foster '32 roadster. It's great when you can relive your dreams."

Perhaps you're wondering, why did Andy Granatelli sell the coupe? "I've owned hundreds of cars," he says, reflecting. "I loved that car, but you can't keep 'em all."

Don't tell that to Bill Couch.

Edelbrock Super, but Grancor's triple manifold was unique. It featured 97 three-bolt carbs at either end and a GM four-bolt Rochester carburetor in the middle, for better economy and low-speed performance.

Joaquin told me Andy said, "I'm buying that car." Arnett insists he turned down Andy's offers until the $3,000 mark was reached. He'd been making $3.00 a day, "So that was a couple of year's wages," he said.

"Granatelli wrote me a check," Joaquin remembers, "but I told him there was no way a guy like me could get a check like that cashed. He said he'd get the money and he did, a few days later. He even gave me a money belt (remember those?) and bought me a ticket back to San Diego."

It appears Andy bought Joaquin's coupe for promotional reasons, as he probably couldn't have found a more attention-grabbing car in the Midwest at that time. Of course, Granatelli soon added his own touches. He confirms he installed a split front swing axle from a British Allard sports car, along with Allard brakes and hubs, adapted to Ford wheels. Interestingly, Fat Man Fabrications is currently selling a kit to split a tubular front axle. Allard and Granatelli thought of that idea a half-century ago.

Andy added then-fashionable solid hood sides (to Arnett's chagrin today – he thinks that was a mistake) and had the car painted a cool, light shade of custom white with a hint of mint. He also installed the current 276-ci Grancor-equipped flathead. The brothers dealt in Winfield cams, so it's reasonable to suspect the coupe's Granatelli-installed motor had one of Ed Winfield's popular flathead grinds, perhaps an SU-1A. At one time, the car was fitted with a Lucas distributor, like those in the flatheads Sydney Allard installed in his sporty Allards years ago.

Joaquin Arnett said he saw his old car one more time at Indy

This roadster is baby blue with a big **Caddy, too.** Half a century ago, a few East Coast hot rods set high standards that had California guys shaking their heads. Tommy Foster's '32 roadster was one of them. A Detroit area native, Foster learned about hot rodding from them, not from weekend trips up to the dry lakes. There was nothing like El Mirage in the state of Michigan, and in that era, drag strips there were thin on the ground.

No matter. Foster created a smooth, sexy roadster that was resplendent in cool, ice-blue lacquer. His car quickly became a frequent show winner, virtually from its first appearance. An early feature in *Hot Rod* (August 1952) certainly helped spread its notoriety. Tommy's '32 could stand smartly on its own wide whitewalls, against any street roadster from the West Coast.

Foster began his effort in 1949, after purchasing a deuce roadster body that another rodder had channeled the depth of its Z-ed frame rails. Tommy smoothed off the body and

24

filled the cowl vent. The door and deck handles were shaved and the gas tank was relocated inside. Smooth was the operative word for this car – Tommy fabricated an inset rear license setup, neatly rolled the rear pan, and finished things off with '48 Pontiac taillights. Tommy was a GM engineer, and he hailed from Pontiac, Michigan.

Over the ensuing 15 months, he dropped in a bored-out, relieved '39 Ford flathead with an Edelbrock dual intake manifold, finned 8:1 high-compression heads, and an Iskenderian 3/4 cam. Neat chromed Porter headers ran to steelpack mufflers under the car, and exited in "baloney-sliced" chromed exhaust extensions that were faired into the rolled pan. Foster must have run up quite a plating bill – the regulator, horn, and generator cover all received the shiny dip, as did the ignition looms, acorn nut covers, radiator hoses, fuel and oil filters, and a myriad of other small pieces. There never was a hood for this car; so all that brightwork was part of its much-admired signature. The transmission was a '39 Ford toploader, and yes, the shortened shift lever was plated.

Tommy Foster's '32 Roadster

In front, the frame horns were clipped, and their edges were rounded to match a plated straight spreader bar. Foster also fabricated a unique front plate with his name on it in chromed letters. It was flanked by NHRA and SCCA (Sports Car Club of America) badges. Further lowering was accomplished via a plated, dropped, and filled front axle – purchased via mail from Ray Brown – along with a spring with reversed eyes. Tall tubular shocks from a '48 Pontiac were attached to plated homemade brackets. The rear shocks were adapted from a Henry J compact. Smooth accessory items later replaced Cadillac Sombrero hubcaps.

Rounding off the frontal aspect, the '32 grille shell was filled, but not sectioned – a popular East Coast practice. Foster made his own headlight stands, chromed them, and ran the wires through them for a clean appearance. That's typical of the attention to detail that is prevalent throughout this milestone roadster. The windshield was not chopped. Its stanchions and posts were plated and new glass, without the top frame edge fitted, further enhanced the car's streamlined look. The cowl was filled and, curiously, the radio antenna was center-mounted on the top edge, just behind the firewall. That setup was removed some time later, but you can see it in early photos of the car.

Inside, in keeping with the practice of the day, ivory and blue tuck-and-roll Naugahyde was highlighted by a big ivory Ford Crestliner steering wheel. The satin-finish dash panel was a slick Stewart-Warner eight-gauge accessory item as sold by Bell Auto Parts and So-Cal Speed Shop for a then-pricey $89.65. Tommy originally ordered his from So-Cal's founder, Alex Xydias. They are highly coveted today.

In 1952, Foster procured a new 331-ci Cadillac V-8 from Jerome Cadillac that pre-dated today's crate motor practice, but you'd have to consider it the same thing. He also purchased a Detroit Racing dual quad intake, and topped it with a brand new set of Carter 4-bbls he purchased for $92.50 (he still has the invoice)!

Tommy fabricated his own transmission adapter from sheet steel and kept the doughty '39 Ford box. He ground off the Cad's exhaust manifolds and porcelainized them for a

smooth, finished appearance. Again, the Cad's valve covers, wire looms, fuel lines, and many other items received the chrome treatment. That practice was very popular 50 years ago. Hot rodders were proud of their engines, and a "sanitary" engine bay was proof positive a guy knew his stuff.

About this time, Tommy fabricated a pair of front fenders from a Mercury station wagon tire cover. Buick wheels were reversed with Ford centers for the rear – and they were fitted with popular 8.20 x 15 wide whites. The current rear tires are from Coker in Nashville, Tennessee. The fronts are 5.50 x 16s on Ford steel wheels – the same vintage double whitewall motorcycle tires that Tommy installed back in the 1950s. Those hydraulic brakes, with chromed backing plates, came from a '41 Mercury. Despite the rubber difference, this car always sat comparatively level. Foster eschewed the "California rake, down in front," attitude that was more popular on the West Coast.

Tommy Foster retired from the Pontiac Division of General Motors, after 39 years of service, in 1978. He sold his old roadster. That buyer kept the car a short time and then sold it to another man who disassembled the car and let it sit for nearly 10 years.

Fortunately, Pat Sleven found the car and carefully restored and refurbished it, preserving as much as he could of Foster's efforts. Sleven sought out Tommy, who was delighted to help

With its door open, you can see the Foster deuce's deep channel. The frame rails were painted gloss black. That array of trophies attests to this car's show success. Tommy didn't plan to have that flathead in the engine bay much longer. (Tommy Foster/Richard Munz)

Here's an early shot of Tommy's deuce, taken in 1952 at an indoor show. Many of the car's signature elements are in place: deep channel, hot flathead, Pontiac taillights, molded exhausts, Cad Sombrero caps, and the '32 windshield with no frame at the top. (Tommy Foster/Richard Munz)

A close-up of Tommy's flat-head shows its fine level of finish. It was a bored-out, relieved '39 Ford 24-stud block with an Edelbrock dual intake manifold, finned 8:1 Edelbrock high-compression heads, and an Iskenderian 3/4 cam. Chromed Porter headers ran to steelpack mufflers under the car, and exited in "baloney-sliced" chromed exhaust extensions that were faired into the rolled pan. There never was a hood for this car; the under-hood brightwork was part of its much-admired signature. (Tommy Foster/Richard Munz)

with the project. Miraculously, although much of the car was in pieces – literally stored in cardboard boxes – all that was missing was the key drive for the tachometer.

After keeping the car a few years, Pat Sleven sold the roadster to Kirk F. White, who had it on display at the Hershey AACA National Fall Meet in 1995. When I saw it there in Kirk's display tent, I really felt as though I was seeing an old friend. The Tommy Foster '32 roadster had been one of my favorite magazine feature cars when I was a kid – and there it was, replete with well-worn chrome, old but carefully polished paint, and the same perky attitude I'd remembered from a clip of the car that I'd displayed on my bulletin board. The special details had all been neatly preserved. I recall the asking price was in the $50K range – it was a good deal then, and it's a bargain now.

Here's Tommy Foster at an early car show. His distinctive "Tommy" plate and NHRA badge were memorable cues. Foster's deuce made the show rounds from Detroit to Chicago to New York, and even down to Florida, taking trophies nearly every time. Tommy Foster created a smooth, sexy roadster, resplendent in cool, ice-blue lacquer. His Detroit area deuce became a frequent show winner, dating virtually from its first appearance. An early feature in Hot Rod (August 1952) certainly helped spread its notoriety. The bottom line was: Tommy's '32 could stand smartly on its own wide whitewalls, against any street roadster from the West Coast. (Tommy Foster/Richard Munz)

Kirk soon sold the ex-Foster '32 roadster to Harry Levy of Pennsylvania, who kept the car a short time and then passed it on to Richard Munz of Madison, Wisconsin, in 1996. Munz has a large collection of cars, which includes the Neal East '32, some beautiful fat-fendered cars, and several modern, Roy Brizio-built rods.

"I was familiar with the Foster car, going way back," Munz told me. "I saw the car when Kirk displayed it at Hershey. I'd had classics and exotics, but I'd decided that wasn't where it was at for me. At the time, I was just starting to get re-interested in the cars I'd lusted after when I was a kid: Fords of the 1930s, particularly '32s and '36s."

"The first car I ever wanted was a '32 Ford three-window coupe that was out behind a Shell station when I was a kid. The guy wouldn't sell it, so I bought a '40 Ford, then a '40 Merc, and then a '50 Mercury. I never did get that '32 Ford, and I couldn't get it out of my mind. It was etched there forever."

"About that time, I met Roy Brizio, one of the finest human beings I know. At Americruise, through mutual friends, I met Harvey Levy, who had a place in Boca Raton, Florida. He'd just acquired the 'Tommy' car. Not long afterward, he bought another car, and the Foster '32 returned to Kirk, and that's when I had the chance to buy it. The head gaskets needed replacing, and the Carter carburetors, which were originally set up for a Pontiac, were too much for that Cadillac. After some work, we re-jetted the carbs and dialed them back. It runs really well now."

Wasting no time, Richard proudly displayed the roadster in 1997 at the first Pebble Beach Hot Rod Class. He'd completed the carb rebuilds, and he had the soft baby-blue finish meticulously rubbed out again. Although the car did not win an award (against very tough competition), it was a crowd favorite. The distinctive soft blue finish, which stands out whenever the car is displayed, glowed like an azure billiard ball on Pebble Beach's immaculately prepared lawn.

Richard Munz brought Tommy's old roadster to Meadow Brook Hall in 2000 and later displayed it in 2002 at the 50th

It's 1953, and GM loyalist Foster finally has a Cadillac V-8 in his Ford. The frame is still gloss black, and the show queen obviously approves. Foster pioneered the crate motor concept in a way. He ordered the big Cad mill from a local dealer, Jerome Cadillac, took it home, fabricated his own transmission adapter, and dropped it in. (Tommy Foster/Richard Munz)

Tommy Foster's dropped deuce sits alongside his full-fendered, unchopped, '32 three-window coupe. The Cadillac's in place; so's the radio antenna in the cowl. Although the baby-blue finish looks dark, that may be because the photograph has aged. The Cad valve covers aren't plated – yet. Note the small front fenders made from a tire cover. This is the only photo we've ever seen of Tommy's car with a top installed. It looks neat, doesn't it? (Tommy Foster/Richard Munz)

Although it's not even credited inside the magazine, that's Tommy Foster's channeled deuce on the cover of Rodding and Re-styling, for April 1955. Earlier, Tommy's car had been featured in Hot Rod (August 1952). His smoothed-off, super-low roadster was a sensation in Michigan. It was rolling proof that Midwest and East Coast guys could build serious feature cars.

Fifty years after his '32 Ford won the Michigan Hot Rod Association's "Most Outstanding Car" award at the 1953 Detroit Autorama, Tommy Foster stands proudly with his old car, now owned by Richard Munz, at the 50th Annual Detroit Autorama. The Frank Mack Roadster (winner of "Best Hot Rod" at the first Autorama) is in the foreground. Crowds swirled around both cars for the entire 200 show at Cobo Hall. (Richard Munz)

In 1952, Foster procured a brand new 331-ci Cadillac V-8 from Jerome Cadillac that pre-dated today's crate motor practice, but you'd have to consider it the same thing. He also purchased a Detroit Racing dual-quad intake and topped it with a brand new set of Carter 4-bbls he purchased for $92.50 (he still has the invoice)! When this roadster was built, real rodders rarely considered automatic transmissions – they were for sissys. Foster also ground off the Cad's exhaust manifolds and porcelainized them for a smooth, finished appearance. (Thomas Glatch)

Foster first purchased his deuce roadster body in 1949. Another rodder had already channeled it the full depth of its Z-ed frame rails. Tommy then smoothed off the body, filled the cowl, shaved the door and deck handles, and relocated the gas tank inside the trunk. (Thomas Glatch)

Detroit Autorama. Both times, Tommy was along to take a few well-deserved bows and answer questions from people who recognized him and admired his powder-blue baby. Many people had him autograph their programs. I chatted with Tommy briefly and could see how proud he was of his car, and how pleased and gracious he was as he acknowledged accolades from people (and I was one of them) who fondly recalled his car from their youth.

Tommy Foster's '32 is one of those distinctive vintage hot rods that most old timers know the minute they see it. "I have no plans to ever sell the car," Richard Munz says. "When Tommy realized that, he packaged up all his own trophies and sent them to me. I especially like the one from the 1953 (Detroit) Autorama."

The Foster '32 is a perfect period piece that's unlikely to be duplicated today, although many of its more distinctive elements may find their way into vintage-style cars. Fashions have evolved, and the look of a strictly show, hoodless and channeled '32, with a massive, heavily plated, big-displacement OHV engine, is one that's stayed pretty much rooted in the 1950s. That's a shame, because Foster's fabulous Ford deserves to be copied and cloned. Perhaps some young gun in the highly creative rat rod community will take the plunge?

Inside, in keeping with the practice of the day, ivory and blue Naugahyde was highlighted by a big ivory Ford Crestliner steering wheel. Notice that the '39 Ford shifter sports a knob that matches the wheel. (Thomas Glatch)

The plated, dropped, and filled front axle was purchased via mail order from Ray Brown Automotive. Tommy reversed the front spring eyes for that extra drop. Tall tubular shocks from a '48 Pontiac were attached to hefty home-made plated brackets. The rear shocks were adapted from a Henry J compact. Smooth accessory items later replaced the Cadillac "Sombrero" hubcaps. (Thomas Glatch)

Smooth was the operative word for this car. Tommy fabricated an inset rear license setup, neatly rolled the rear pan, and finished it with '48 Pontiac taillights. Foster was a GM engineer, and he hailed from Pontiac, Michigan, so his use of those soon-to-be-popular round Poncho rear lights were just the beginning of his concessions of loyalty to his employer where this '32 was concerned. (Thomas Glatch)

Although Tommy had a convertible top for the car in the early 1950s, there's no canvas lid now. Discrete snaps around the seatback show where it once fastened. (Thomas Glatch)

Beautifully restored today, looking substantially the way it did it its heyday, the Aztec Gold Woodard/East/Moeller/Mc Manus/Sievers, and now Munz, deuce roadster lives happily in Madison, Wisconsin. The filled and peaked grille shell is perfect. (Thomas Glatch)

This is arguably the finest full-fendered '32 – ever. Full-fendered '32 Ford roadsters aren't usually celebrated, but this one is an exception. It's been a hot rod for over half a century. And it's a respected icon whenever anyone mentions full-fendered deuces.

Bill Woodard, of Eagle Rock, California, first saw this roadster back in 1954 in the San Fernando Valley. Already extensively modified, it packed what Woodard described as a full house flathead with "all the goodies." It was slightly raked, with a dropped axle. The top was chopped three inches, and its bright white canvas set off the roadster's fire-engine red finish. Woodard, a high school senior at that time, had to raise $500 (not an inconsequential sum in that era) to buy it. Reportedly, the seller had to help Bill finance the purchase.

Three years later, Woodard dropped in a low-mileage, stock-dimensioned, 265-ci '56 Chevrolet V-8 with a 4-bbl carb and a Stellings & Hellings air cleaner. He had to perform the swap virtually overnight, as the '32 was his sole

(25)

means of transportation. So he bought the requisite quantity of beer, and he and several friends did the dirty work, retaining the '39 gearbox (with its 25-tooth Lincoln cluster) and the early Ford driveline. The next day, the newly energized deuce was towed to a nearby muffler shop for a new exhaust system. Bill and his buddies apparently didn't have any welding equipment.

In those days, you could purchase a complete engine swap kit from vendors like Honest Charlie or Bell Auto Parts. It was comprised of bolt-on engine mounts, a transmission adaptor plate (in this case manufactured by Hildebrandt), and a throw-out bearing adaptor. After you plugged two of the '32s four radiator outlets, and converted the charging and starting circuits (and often the whole car) to 12-volt electrics, you were in business, and could be ready-to-rumble in a day. Bill's neat OHV Chevy V-8 installation had room for a cooling fan, but he chose to omit it.

Woodard wasn't quite through. He had the door hinges

The Woodward/East/Moeller
'32 Roadster

frenched and the roadster repainted an iridescent shade of Bahama Blue. We're not sure if the '39 teardrop taillights were already in the rear fenders, but when this roadster appeared for the first time in Hot Rod in February 1958, they were in place, along with a dropped headlight bar and small accessory headlights. The overall look was not unlike the Chuck Price '32 roadster, photographed on the first custom of *Rod & Customs*, in May 1953. (The title became *Rod & Custom* in its second issue.)

For that first Hot Rod feature on the Woodard '32, simply titled, "Deuce-Chev," the grille shell still bore the stock cap. Sometime later it was expertly filled and peaked. Bill's '32 retained a stock, ribbed front bumper in 1958, raised to better suit its function. Curiously, the rear bumper was taken from a Mercury station wagon, and a trailer hitch had been installed. The license plate light was a cut-down '46-'48 Ford unit, sans deck-lid handle. Additional bodywork included a filled trunk lid that was electrically actuated. Bill also removed and filled the door handles. Hot Rod reported the body-color steel wheels were 15s in front, 16s in the rear, for that "just-right rake." The small hubcaps came from a '47-'48 Ford.

Inside, white Naugahyde with black piping was used for the attractive tuck-and-roll seating. The carpeting was black, and so was the '40 Ford steering wheel. Lou Penn, of Eagle Rock, was the trimmer. His name crisscrosses through vintage hot rod articles, and he must have been a talented man. The '32 dash panel was filled, and eight Stewart-Warner instruments were installed. A crossed checkered flag badge was centered between the tachometer and the speedometer, and a small radio was fitted beneath the flags. The '39 shifter was plated and topped with a modest chromed knob. The running boards were covered with white rubber, and short, chromed "Bellflower stacks" protruded just in front of the rear wheels.

We'd have called this car a custom rod in its day. It was a handsome, functional street cruiser that was quick and classy – in short, a great everyday driver. Chevrolet V-8s in early Fords were becoming increasingly popular by 1958. That was the year Bill decided to blow the car apart and redo it for local show competition. Interestingly, rather than do more extensive new bodywork, he focused on details like

the undersides and the running gear. Virtually every driveline piece, right down to lock washers, received the chrome plating treatment. The oil pan, transmission, front wishbone, drag link, driveshaft, and rear end (to name just a few parts), all received the shiny dip. The firewall and the undersides of the fenders were painted gloss black.

Bill did the exterior himself. He apparently purchased a spray gun and shot the car in Chevrolet Sierra (possibly Aztec?) Gold in his backyard! This was probably the time

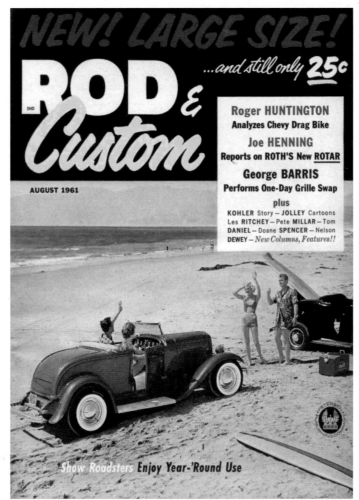

The '32, then owned by Bill Moeller, shows its stuff. Note that the hand hood side has been completely removed to show off the plated and polished Chevy V-8. It looked quite stock, until you started adding up the plating bill, and with its full complement of road equipment, including fenders and a windshield wiper, it appeared to be a practical ride. Dropped headlight bar and small lights look great; so do the stock bumpers. (Neal East)

Neal East's classy gold roadster starred on the August 1961 R&C cover when the magazine changed from a "little book" to full sized. In a feature called "Everyday Deuces," the East '32 was paired with Murphy Tiffany's more traditional, flathead-powered car. Richard Munz owns the Woodard/East/Moeller '32 now. Does anyone know where Murphy Tiffany's car is? (Ken Gross Archives)

The roadster's interior was perfect for the time – the stock dash is filled wall-to-wall with Stewart-Warner gauges and a Firestone accessory AM radio. The steering wheel is from a '58 Chevy Impala, done in black and white to match the upholstery. Neatly arrayed seat belts are typical of hot rod photography of the time. (J. Neal East)

The '56 Chevy small-block was neatly turned out with Offy valve covers and an Offy 3-carb intake topped with Stromberg 97s. The level of detail on this engine is outstanding, even by today's standards – one of the reasons it counts as a milestone car. Note the Hedman Hedders especially – they presage today's mass-produced block-hugger headers. (J. Neal East)

This is a look we're still aiming for, more than 40 years later. The dropped axle, rubber rake, and chopped windshield enhance the roadster's lines, and the dropped headlight bar and King Bee-type headlights visually lower the car further. The car was as functional as it was beautiful though – East drove the car to work at Rod & Custom daily.

when the grille shell was filled and peaked. The roadster also received a new, black and white '58 Impala steering wheel. Woodard's choices were subtle, vis-à-vis more radical bodywork, but the effect, especially in the "mild" modifications class, was a guaranteed crowd pleaser.

The Woodard roadster subsequently appeared in several hot rod and teen-oriented films, thanks to George Barris' recommendation. Bill told Jerry Weesner (in a November 2002 *Street Rodder* magazine article) that he was paid the princely sum of $35/day for the use of his car by the film company rental departments. Woodard and his soon-to-be wife Joyce had their first date in the roadster, a trip that included driving home from San Diego in the rain without a top. The glittering gold/bronze deuce subsequently served as transportation to bring the Woodards' first child home from the hospital. Although it con-

tinually won its share of trophies, it was also the family car.

By 1959, Woodard's priorities had changed. Needing capital to buy a new home, he sold the '32 to his friend, Neal East. At that time, Neal owned a clean '32 five-window, and he and Woodard frequently cruised and showed their cars together. Once he had the roadster, Neal (then the associate editor of Rod & Custom), frequently drove it on the street, as well as to car shows, where it represented the magazine. Improvements at this time included chromed Hedman Hedders, Corvette ignition, a polished three-carb Offenhauser intake manifold, and finned Offy valve covers. When *R&C* went from "little book" to full sized in 1961, the Woodard/East deuce shared cover honors with another full-fendered '32, a flathead-powered, wire-wheeled version, then-owned by Murphy Tiffany.

Just after the *R&C* cover story was completed, Neal East had the opportunity to acquire the Doane Spencer '32, and he jumped at the chance. He'd already placed an ad for his car in that same issue of *R&C* where it was the cover feature (for $2,075!). It wasn't long before he received a call from the Washington, D.C. area. Bill Moeller was a 20-year-old hot rod enthusiast with a relatively new Corvette, but when he saw the gold '32, he flipped. "I kept looking at the pictures," Moeller said, "and I thought, 'Wow!'"

"I didn't know Neal yet, but I called him and said 'I love your car.'" Moeller asked if the '32 had been sold. When the answer was "not yet," he immediately put his 'Vette up for sale. Fortunately, neither car sold quickly. Undaunted, Moeller called East again to see if the car had been sold (the answer was still, "not yet"), and wondered if Neal thought his roadster could be driven cross-country? Neal's answer was "sure, I've taken it on a lot of trips."

Moeller found a buddy who was planning to attend school on the West Coast. To get some extra cash, he pulled the 'Vette's 4-speed gearbox, sold it, and replaced it with a cheaper 3-speed. Not unlike Route 66 a few years later, the two youngsters headed to California via a circuitous route that took them as far north as Boise, Idaho, and Yakima, Washington, and as far south as Yellowstone National Park. They headed

straight south from Klamath Falls, Oregon, cruising through the high desert with the top down. "When we got to Pismo Beach," Bill says, "I knew I was finally in California."

When they arrived in LA, Bill wholesaled his Corvette to a dealer on Washington Boulevard for $2,000 (who told him "if you've got any more of those, I'll take all I can get."). Then he talked a patient Neal East into taking $1,975 (!) for the roadster, so he'd have $25 gas money for the return trip. You have to remember that gasoline was only 25 to 30 cents per gallon, so 25 bucks would buy as much as 80 to 100 gallons of gas. That was all Bill needed.

"Before I left California," Moeller says, "I really made the rounds. I drove it to San Mateo; I went to Harvey's Broiler, and I saw A. J. Watson there with his scalloped Cadillac. I visited the NHRA offices, then I went out to Ed Roth's and met Dirty Doug and checked out their little shop, too."

Before he left for his return coast-to-coast drive, Moeller wisely taped towels over the front fenders and the front bumper to protect the '32s dazzling finish. "You know," he says today, "the paint was a lot brighter when I had the car. They must have toned it down a little when they restored it. When I owned it, it just popped. It was lower in the front, too. And it never had the side pipes after it was painted bronze."

But again, we're getting ahead of our story. Now driving by himself, Moeller headed east, first to Las Vegas and the Grand Canyon, then he set a course for Indianapolis. "I left in a typical beach fog," Moeller remembers. "I had no top or side curtains. I hit a rainsquall between San Bernardino and Vegas. So I turned on the windshield wiper and it pitched the blade off in the desert. That's the only thing that went wrong the whole trip."

"Whenever I'd stop in a town, hordes of people would come out to look at the car. Usually it would start with the one guy in a town who had a cool car, and he'd tell everybody else. Meanwhile, I couldn't wait to see the Grand Canyon. Then I headed east on Route 66. I remember crossing the Mississippi as the sun came out, having lived for a few days on a diet of coffee and coke."

Conveniently, the NHRA Nationals and an accompanying car show were going on when Bill arrived at Indy. He went to a nearby muffler shop, put the '32 on a lift, and cleaned all the chrome under the car. I wiped it off and applied Vista wax," he remembers. Attesting to the appeal of the roadster, Bill's new purchase took second place in its class, behind a '36 Ford convertible that was a trailered show car. "We probably shouldn't have been in the same class," says the ever-competitive Moeller. "Some guys from my club came out to that show," Moeller recalls. "Really, I was excited just to be there."

Bill says, wherever he drove the '32, it stopped traffic. By 1961, road-driven hot rods of this caliber were becoming rare. You could buy a stock 409 Chevy that would hammer most street roadsters. So many cars were mothballed, and nobody thought street rods like Bill's roadster had much of a future. Incredibly, Moeller continued to drive the '32 as his street car, to and from college, and he took it to more shows, as well.

Is it any wonder the rest of us wanted to be California hot rodders? East photographed the roadster in 1961 on the beach at Santa Monica. The simple rear view includes '39 Ford taillights, a simple license frame mounted to the spreader bar, and an overall clean, uncluttered look. Note that stock '32 bumpers have replaced the chromed nerf bars seen in the car-show photo. All that's missing is the surfboard. (J. Neal East)

White diamond-pattern running board covers aren't common today, but when this car was built, the color white was all the rage, for interiors, carpets, trunks, tops, you name it. (Tom Glatch)

With its gentle rake, plated wheels, baby moons, side pipes, and mild de-chroming (door and deck handles), this '32 spans the late 1950s/early 1960s custom rod era. The side pipes were an earlier touch, removed when East owned the car, then added back on. We like 'em. In earlier times, the rear bumper was from a Mercury station wagon; the stock '32 is a better-looking replacement. (Tom Glatch)

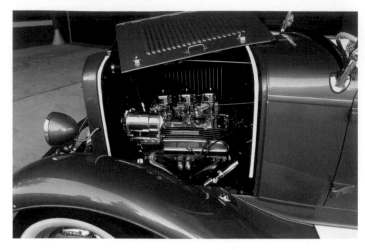

One of the first street-driven, full-fendered deuces to receive a Chevy transplant, the so-called "Deuce-Chev," was featured in Hot Rod in February 1958, when owned by Bill Woodard. Retaining the vintage-style Delco generator today is a nice period touch. (Tom Glatch)

Virtually every part of the running gear that could be removed, and most of the small hardware, was plated. Even the transmission case got the dip. LA's Okie Adams did the dropped and filled front axle. Neal East still drove the car nearly every day in Los Angeles, and it appeared in many shows representing R&C under his auspices. (Tom Glatch)

When you talk about the definitive full-fendered deuce, you need look no further. We'd have called this car a "custom rod" in its day. It was a handsome, functional street cruiser that was quick and classy – in short, a great everyday driver. Chevrolet V-8s in early Fords were becoming increasingly popular by 1957-58 when this car was built. (Tom Glatch)

"When I had the '32, it was known as 'The Californian,'" he says. "I entered it in ISCA shows one season, driving to Philadelphia and Norfolk. Then I rented an open U-Haul trailer and towed it to shows with a '51 Ford business coupe." Moeller made it to a lot of events. "I finished fourth in the ISCA Championships in 1962," he notes proudly.

"When I started working for ISCA," said Bill, "we used the car in the display booth." Moeller remembers driving the '32 to Cobo Hall for the Detroit Motorama one chilly February. "It was sooooooooo cold, driving without a top," he says with a laugh, "I froze the tips of my ears."

His ISCA job required a great deal of travel, so Moeller rented winter storage space in a garage in Detroit near where Bob Larivee lived. The space was owned by a hot rodder. That was the good news. The bad news was that he moonlighted in stolen cars. He supplied his illicit gains to another man who trucked the cars to other parts of the US, and offered them for sale. You've probably guessed the rest. One day Bill Moeller went to retrieve his '32 and it was gone. The garage owner's alibi? He said he thought Bill had already taken the car.

Apparently, the local cops were on to this thief, but the FBI wanted the crook's partner, the guy who transported the stolen vehicles by the truckload across state lines. Bill Moeller is nothing if not determined. He put an ad in Hot Rod magazine, along with a photo and the car's description. Gold '32 roadsters weren't exactly plentiful, even then – especially ones with plated undercarriages. Soon he began receiving calls from people all over the country who thought they'd sighted the missing deuce.

Several of the calls came from the Louisville, Kentucky, area, and one tip sounded promising. Bill eagerly headed for Louisville, with the FBI on his heels. The roadster was located, parked on a dock near the Ohio River. Unfortunately, it had been badly abused in the three months it had been away. The undercarriage was filthy, there were a number of dents, and numerous parts were missing. Bill admits he was discouraged with the scope of work that had to be done, so the car sat for a while.

In 1968, Bill Moeller decided to sell the roadster, as it was, because he was much too busy to rebuild it. There were two interested buyers, so Moeller asked them each to submit a bid. Pete McManus's $2032.32 bid was the higher of the two. McManus was from Indianapolis. A member of the Indy Idlers car club, he also became an out-of-area, associate member of the LA Roadster club in 1969, and the gold roadster is pictured in the LA Roadsters' anniversary book. After he bought the '32, McManus touched up the paint and plating, got the car running again, and drove it to the first Street Rod Nationals in Peoria, Illinois. The year was 1972. There, Bernie, Paul, and Joe Sievers spotted the car. Bernie Sievers told McManus that if he ever wanted to sell the roadster, he'd be a customer.

Two years later, the plot took a strange twist. With deuce roadster prices accelerating upward, McManus decided to reverse directions and make a stocker (!) out of the Woodard/East/Moeller roadster. Jerry Moon had obtained a

stock '32 Ford Tudor sedan for a project, so McManus traded him the modified parts, like the filled grille shell, the firewall, the front suspension, and, of course, the Chevy engine. Later, Jerry sold the modified parts, along with what was left of the sedan, to Don Ennis.

In 1975, McManus had several pending projects and needed some funds, so he called Bernie Sievers to see if he wanted to buy the now stock, but not yet completely restored, '32. The roadster was soon on its way to Vincennes, Indiana, less a few key parts, but Pete kindly told Bernie where to find them. Funny thing is, at the time, Bernie wasn't interested. His plan, as well, was to finish making a stocker out of the once-modified deuce. And that's what he did. He painted it in black lacquer with apple-green wheels, reinstalled cowl lamps, and even put a period '32 flatty under the hood. The born-again '32 was finished in 1978. No trace of the hot gold deuce remained.

Fast forward to 1992. Under Pat Ganahl's inspired leadership, *Rod & Custom* presented a special "60th Anniversary Deuce" issue, with a six-page section on significant '32s – including the Woodard/East/Moeller car as it had appeared in gold. That got Paul Sievers to thinking. Hot rodders had begun to restore historic hot rods by then. Bernie Sievers decided that since he had most of the original '32 that comprised the show car, he'd simply rebuild it back to its ISCA show-winning configuration. Bernie knew how to find Don Ennis, fortunately, and Don still owned the plated suspension and the other pieces he'd bought. The interior, chopped windshield, and folding top were owned by another Ohioan.

Luckily, Sievers had saved some other modified parts that he had removed, including the doors with the faired-in hinges. So Bernie and his brother Joe re-restored the '32 once more, converting it back to its hot-rodded form. The plating bill was over $10K, so it's clear they didn't spare the key details. With the preserved old interior as a guide, Ed Thralls, of Mitchell, Indiana, duplicated it in white Naugahyde with black piping. The running boards were recovered with white rubber. Paul Sievers even re-popped the original yellow '56 California license plate.

Bernie kept the car for three years and then decided to advertise it for sale in *Hemmings Motor News*. Richard Munz, who owns the ex-Tommy Foster channeled '32 that's featured in this book, was very interested. He knew the gold roadster from years back and saw it again, because it was featured a second time on the cover of *R&C* in November 1995, just after its restoration was completed. It was featured along with a roadster that it inspired – a contemporary, Brizio-built, full-fendered, blue/violet, white-trimmed, SVO Ford-powered '32 roadster. (Richard Munz later owned Roy's dazzling purple deuce for a time, and then traded it back to Brizio.)

Richard Munz told me he was always interested in the Sievers-owned now-restored ex-Woodard/East/Moeller deuce, and he offered Paul Sievers a price "…that I thought was more than adequate," but at first, they couldn't agree.

After attending the 2000 Oakland Roadster Show in the Cow Palace and seeing the restored Joe Nitti '32 (also in this book), Munz said he reluctantly acknowledged that the prices for historic cars were "…getting up there." He got together again with Bernie Sievers and this time, they reached a deal. Richard Munz really likes his freshly restored old roadster. "It's spectacular," he says.

Richard Munz is pleased to own two significant historic deuces: one channeled, without fenders, the other a highboy with fenders. Munz also owns a more modern Brookville-bodied, Brizio-built, full-fendered deuce roadster that's finished in a variation of the old car's Aztec Gold hue – so he's got all the bases covered. This car's a keeper, at last. Don't look for the Woodard/East/Moeller/McManus/Sievers/Munz '32 highboy to become a stocker ever again.

A vintage R&C decal is the perfect touch for the lower windshield corner. The original chop was three inches, and the windshield was raked rearward a few degrees for a racier appearance. (Tom Glatch)

The '58 Impala wheel looks a bit over the top today, but back in the day, it was considered just right for a show and street roadster. The plaque on the dash is for the first Street Rod Nats in Peoria, Illinois. (Tom Glatch)

A dropped California plate, Ford license plate light, low-mounted '39 teardrops, plated stock bumper…what's not to like? (Tom Glatch)

Index

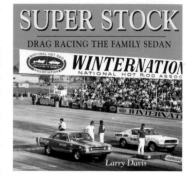

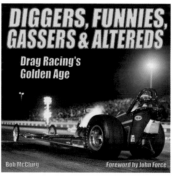